*Aly*

*Aly*

A Biography

by Leonard Slater

Random House     New York

First Printing

© *Copyright, 1964, 1965, by Leonard Slater*

*Library of Congress catalog card number: 64-11989*

DESIGNED BY JEANETTE YOUNG

*To*
*BETTY*
*with love*

# PROLOGUE

I last saw Aly Khan as he climbed into the cabin of an Air France jet at Idlewild Airport in New York. He was late, as usual. His United Nations adviser, Jack Ross, and I stood at the foot of the ramp, simultaneously waving good-bye and motioning him into the plane.

By any ordinary man's calculations, we had been late when we left Pakistan House on East Sixty-fifth Street, Aly's headquarters as Pakistan's ambassador to the United Nations. The airport was a good forty-five minutes away on Long Island. But Aly was not ready to go. He ordered the chauffeur to stop at a fashionable apartment house in the East Seventies. "Just to say good-bye," he explained. Ross and I waited in the car, chatting desultorily, glancing at our watches. Twenty minutes passed. Aly dashed out, murmuring apologies. In the car he resumed a conversation with Ross about United Nations affairs; he was polite, attentive, quick to grasp the points Ross was making and to add a few of his own. Moving out along East River Drive, we passed a red convertible, its top unseasonably down, a pretty redhead at the wheel, alone.

Aly signaled the chauffeur to slow down. He peered out,

waved until he had caught the young woman's eye, then swung entirely around for a last look through the rear window. "If only I had more time," he muttered, shifting his attention back to Ross. Now he told the chauffeur to hurry. Emboldened by desperation, the driver leaned on the Rolls's accelerator—and on the sanctity of its diplomatic license plates. No other passengers were in sight when we reached the Air France terminal.

From the moment Aly walked in, he baffled the Air France people. Nothing in their training manuals covered Aly Khan. He distributed smiles all around, gave orders on how the baggage was to be weighed, lost his bulging briefcase, found it, gave it to his chauffeur to hold and then decided he should carry it himself. He asked so many questions, looked so busily at each bag as it was lifted onto the scales, that he gave the impression of moving very quickly. And yet, anyone with an orderly mind realized immediately that he was gumming up the works. Snobbery— after all, it *was* Aly Khan—collided with schedule and sent Air France's morale flying in all directions.

Everyone consulted the clock and his neighbor, everyone except Aly. I noticed that he was covertly watching the door. Suddenly a black Cadillac limousine drew up outside and, in a few moments, a pale, orange-haired young woman came through the door with a chauffeur and a tall, harried-looking young man. The trio walked past Aly without a glance, the young man handed over her ticket at the counter, the chauffeur helped with her baggage, and then, as if by sleight of hand, she vanished in the direction of the plane. Aly returned to his own baggage and now things went smoothly. Somewhat desperately, a tall brunette in an Air France uniform asked us to follow her. Aly looked her up and down, grinned, jiggled his eyebrows, and fell into step beside her. We all marched out with several escorts from Air France to fill out our ranks. Everyone talked about how late we were, even Aly. Finally he shook hands all around and darted up the steps, two at a time. The orange-haired young woman had boarded the plane several minutes ahead of him. Only a few of us knew that she and Aly were traveling together. The man who had brought her was one of Aly's secretaries. I had recognized her as the woman I'd seen Aly with at the theatre a few nights before.

Sixteen days after I said good-bye to Aly, he was dead.

His friends were shocked and unbelieving. Several of them expressed their feeling to me in almost the same words: "He was too alive to die."

I had not known Aly very long but I had spent a lot of time with him in the last months of his life, visiting him at his Chateau de l'Horizon on the French Riviera; traveling with him to his stud farms in Ireland, the heart of his enormous horse-racing operations; chatting with him after United Nations sessions in New York. I had liked him from the start. It was impossible not to.

His undeniable charm, however, would not account entirely for the emotion Aly continued to arouse in people after his death. Recounting their fading episodic memories, some of his friends would lapse unconsciously into the present tense as if he were still alive. Newspapers, magazines, and books still referred to him as a phenomenon, a paragon of a very particular type. A legend was developing before our eyes. How much was fact and how much would be fancy?

*Had he actually lived so fast, so furious, so frolicking a life? What manner of man was he, really, to have lived that way? Did he fall into it or was he pushed? What about his serious side? What about the women in his life? Were there really so many? Was his prowess really so extraordinary? Was he happy? Surfeited? Where did all his money come from? As a matter of fact, where did Aly come from?*

When I decided to undertake this book, two years after Aly's death, his obituaries were neatly filed in newspaper morgues; his will had been opened and read, disbursements made, bills and taxes paid, possessions scattered. Unlike his eighteenth-century counterpart, Jacques Casanova, Aly had left no memoirs. Casanova's had been published in twenty-five languages since 1822; a scholarly annual review still is devoted to him.

No single person, not even Aly, had known his whole story. No library held all the documents and mementos of his life. He had moved too fast, traveled too far. In the end it took me two years, the help of several of my former colleagues in journalism, and thousands of miles of travel. My wife gave up her own writing to help me full time.

Our research extended from the primitive upcountry of Pakistan to the locked and guarded erotica collection of the British Museum, from Hollywood choreographers to Islamic scholars. We interviewed more than one hundred persons, corresponded with many more. Some doors were slammed in our faces, but scores more were opened wide and we were asked to stay awhile. Some interviews rambled on for hours, while our long-playing tape recorders caught every nuance and clue, and there were some persons we came back to again and again. Often the tape ran out while the reminiscences ran on . . .

L. S.

*May, 1964*
*Beaulieu-sur-Mer, France*

# Illustrations

*Aly's friends: Juliette Greco . . .*
KEYSTONE PHOTO

*Lise Bourdin . . .*
COURTESY TOUR D'ARGENT

*Bettina.*
UPI PHOTO

*As painted by Sybilla Szczeniowska: "Aly was a serious person, really, and a little sad; that's what I tried to catch in the portrait."*
COURTESY SYBILLA SORONDO

*Aly*

# Chapter I

For every man who collects stamps, first editions, nonobjective paintings, or antique automobiles, there are thousands who dream of collecting women. Most go on dreaming. Under the confused standards of our society, the great lover is regarded as a scoundrel—who has everything. He is pictured as attractive to women, virile, aggressive, and yet unworthy of a decent man's emulation. He is a shining portrait of unfettered masculinity, and therefore dangerous. He is dismissed as dissolute, cynical, bored—none of which described Aly Salomone Khan— and yet all of us, men and women alike, wish he would write a book on what every young man should know.

Even our language provides no explicit place for him. "Great lover"—unfortunately, there is no better word in English—contains more than a trace of a sneer. And French, that most precise of Western languages, compromises on *"coureur"*—which is just more of the same old run-around.

Yet he survives—the underground folk hero of our times—

in the movie star, the crooner, the hero of much of our fiction, and the playboy of the night clubs and the gossip columns. Young men try to emulate him; women see in him their romantic ideal. Even big business acknowledges his existence in the design of sports cars, the advertising of cigarettes, the necklines of women's clothes. The great lover typifies our hypocrisy about sex, the clash of our instinctive sexual drives with our Puritan traditions. Publicly we condemn him; secretly we exalt him.

This is the career in which Aly Khan cut the same broad swath through the twentieth century that Casanova had sliced through the eighteenth. Each epitomized the great lover of his time. In doing so, each defied convention, scorned censure, and unmasked hypocrisy.

In his lifetime, Aly Khan appeared in many guises. To the Ismailis, the Moslem sect which considered his family divine descendants of the Prophet, he was a godhead who could do no wrong and an agent of their security in a hostile world. To Pakistan, his adopted country, he was a capable diplomat, its representative to the United Nations. He was an able soldier when he chose to be, and a sportsman who rode, raced, and traded horses all over the world. He was a millionaire in his own right and the son of a millionaire. Yet the career in which he made his mark was neither racing nor religion, diplomacy nor business, but as a lover of women.

How much Aly's choice was a conscious one, no one, not even he, ever knew. Nor was he much interested in the hidden forces which pushed him on. No man likes to examine his motives in an endeavor in which, for all its cloak of tenderness, instinct roams nakedly and a man flaunts his masculinity like a brigand's banner. Like the warrior who points to his patriotism and the boxer who does it for the wife and kids, the great lover pleads a nobler purpose. "I think only of the woman's pleasure when I'm in love," Aly liked to say.

He was singularly well-equipped for this career. He had the time and the money. He possessed more than a normal man's share of physical fortitude and grace, a knack of stubborn con-centration on his own goals, and an intuition as sensitive as radar.

He had a gambler's daring, a racer's reactions, and the nomad's ability to travel lightly and, if the need arose, depart without a trace. He had taste and gentleness and a manner that knew when to knock softly and when to crash through the door, when to relax and when to stimulate. He had the Moslem man's attitude toward women as a shield and his father's reputation as a great lover as a goad.

Any man whose ego requires it and who has the money can pose as a great lover. He can hire a pride of press agents or a covey of call girls and establish a reputation almost overnight. He can resort to simple-minded lures like mumbled marriage proposals and mortgaged mink coats. The Hollywood actor can promise a career; the Latin American diplomat, his country; the Texas tycoon, shares in a natural-gas field. But their credentials will not bear examination; they are no more Aly's equals than a man who buys lithographs in wholesale lots is an art collector. It is a measure of Aly's qualifications that he didn't promise marriage, he had no careers to offer—unless the lady wanted to be a jockey—and his gifts were more apt to run to roses than to mink. He gave few costly gifts and those only to the half dozen more important women in his life. While a lesser lover would have felt impelled to offer a packaged holiday-in-the-sun with all expenses paid, Aly simply invited the girl home. It was more or less the same thing. His favorite homes were at resorts.

A woman took potluck with Aly. There are women whose memories of him are of hasty dinners in hotel suites, fast trips, sleepless nights, and endless comings and goings. More than one made her own reservations and paid her own way. The kind of women Aly favored were not particularly impressed by holidays, luxury, or plane rides, or, in many cases, by the possibility of marriage. Quite often they were married and, as far as the world knew, happily.

What Aly gave every woman was the memory of a great, if fleeting, love affair.

Casanova is thus described by one of his biographers, William Bolitho: "His love for every one of the thousand was as real as any that led to holy matrimony; only it did not last. . . . But his women were not cheated out of their sacred due, for he gave them everything he possessed and his whole self, in one single payment." And so with Aly. As Elsa Maxwell put it: "When he fell in love with a woman, it was madly and deeply. The only thing, it might last only one night."

There was not much to single Aly out physically from other men. He wasn't tall, only five feet eight inches, although he liked to refer to himself as six feet in height. His complexion was sallow and his face had a tendency to puff up when he was fatigued. After the war, he began putting on weight; he kept his paunch under control by intensive spurts of exercise, principally tennis, but a good deal of the time he made it his tailor's job to hide it. He started losing hair in his early twenties and was self-conscious about his encroaching baldness. He often wore a hat, usually a battered slouch hat pulled down over his forehead and cocked at a rakish angle. He was not a brilliant conversationalist; his wit was limited to the retelling of jokes, to trick gadgets of the kind sold in joke shops, and to schoolboyish pranks. Yet above all these limitations towered his intense interest in women, and above that his desire to please them.

He communicated his interest to women of all social classes, backgrounds and nationalities. He was best known for his friendships with actresses because they were the ones who got the publicity. Hundreds of others did not: the unknowns whose names would have meant nothing to newspaper readers, and those others whose names, linked with Aly's, might have harmed a husband, a family, or an empire.

The number of women in Aly's life is not known; he kept no records, diaries, notebooks, or memoirs; even in conversation, he was considerably more discreet than most men. But the euphemistic figure given by the legendary Don Juan of "a thousand and three" can serve as a conservative statistic for Don Juan Khan.

To attempt a classification of his tastes in women is difficult but not impossible, and offers other clues to his success. He preferred slim women with fair complexions and long hair, and with some irregularity in their features that departed from the conventional notion of beauty. Like any collector, he looked for oddities—the tilt of a nose, the strength of cheekbones, or, particularly, the shape of the eyes. He loved almond-shaped eyes. His women tended to have long legs and straight postures; he thought more about the way a woman walked than what she carried with her. Most of his favorites had smaller busts and narrower hips than the pin-up ideal, but there were some noteworthy exceptions. Some of the women in his life were Orientals, lush and sensuous. At least one was an Englishwoman who dwarfed him in size and weight. Like many Continental men, he found the rear view of a woman more provocative than the front.

He tended to prefer European women to Americans—whom he found too aggressive—and Orientals—whom he found too passive. But Aly never thought of women in terms of stereotypes. He had learned as a child that men made the rules and women chafed under them. Growing up, he had found that, if the rules were changed, more women would play. He threw away the rule book and played the game by instinct.

What he looked for in every woman was a stirring, a faint tremor of interest no more noticeable than the fluttering of a leaf on a warm day. Call it restlessness, dissatisfaction, or frustration. It signalled a glimmering spark that he might fan into flame. One Englishwoman felt that "Aly capitalized on women's dissatisfaction with their busy husbands." Another explained how it worked: "An extramarital affair was so safe with Aly. He would show up anywhere, or send his plane. He had houses everywhere to make meetings convenient. The houses were always full of people who made everything look respectable. He would treat all the women in his party so gallantly that it took a close watch to learn which one was his current favorite." A woman could feel easier about her husband, too. An affair with Aly was, well, not so unique that a husband need feel betrayed. So many other men were in the same boat. After a while, fashion played a part in it. One old friend explained: "It was considered the chic thing to do. You weren't in the swim, and you were really déclassé, démodé, nothing, you hardly counted, if you'd not been to bed with Aly."

Aly's campaigns often began in circumstances that brought groups of women together. Perhaps because his appetite was so great. Or perhaps because he had made the same discovery that Casanova recorded in his memoirs: "In my long and profligate career in which I have turned the heads of some hundreds of women, I have become familiar with all the methods of seduction; but my guiding principle has never been to direct my attack against novices or those whose prejudices were likely to prove an obstacle except in the presence of another woman. I soon found out that timidity makes a girl averse to being seduced, while in company of another girl she is easily conquered; the weakness of the one brings on the fall of the other."

Many of Aly's encounters began at parties, race tracks, in some crowded place, but when he spoke afterward of his first meeting with a particular woman, he always recalled the circumstances as if he and she had been alone. This was not oversight, but the illumination of a technique so successful that it might go into the handbooks, if any existed. Over and over again, women told me of meeting Aly amidst a crowd and of being singled out by him for attention. An American woman who met him in Deauville recalled: "He sought you out with that eyes-across-the-crowded-room bit. He made you feel like the only woman in the room." A knowing Frenchwoman on the Riviera told me: "Aly knew that all women believe in the *coup de foudre*—the thunder clap."

There was first his steady, hypnotic, murmuring flow of talk. It was gay and frothy most of the time, but it could plunge into seeming seriousness and then out again without losing a beat. Above all it was solicitous. "When Aly spoke to you, you felt he really was interested in you, cared about you, felt for you," one woman said.

Aly was not a particularly skilfull dancer, but he loved to dance. He liked to hold a woman in his arms and he held her closely. When he took her on to the dance floor, it was cheek-to-cheek from the first step, a daring assault that skipped all the preliminaries and relieved her of the necessity of coyly resisting more tentative advances. She knew from the first moment that

he was interested; it was an electric, intensely physical com-
munion. "Aly could tell," said one friend, "as soon as he danced
with a woman what was going to happen." His right hand traced
languorous circles on her back while he fixed her with his attention. What would she like to do? Where would she like to dine?
What was she doing tomorrow? "They were just little things,
but Aly always had ideas," one woman said. "He would say to
a woman at two o'clock in the morning, 'Would you like to
take a boat ride?' Just to do something that was different for
her, you see. Just so the woman was kept interested."

To be tracked down in a lonely hotel room and shown
Paris. To be plucked out of a draughty English country house
and flown to the Riviera. To leave the city behind and drink in
the tranquil, unspoiled loveliness of the Irish countryside. It was
unreal, disoriented, like a flight aboard a magic carpet. No
wonder a woman's gyroscope went out of whack. Only Aly
seemed real and certain, sure of himself, at the controls, cajoling,
murmuring, dancing attendance. Inhibitions fell away like retreating landmarks. Somehow with Aly they dared.

It was so easy to be borne along.

And there was no rough landing. He was not the type of
man whose voice and manner bespoke censure afterward. He
carefully avoided recriminations and remorse.

"Aly never stopped a love affair like THAT," said a lovely
blonde, snapping long, flame-tipped fingers. "He used to find
a new one and go back to the first and find a third one and then
go back to the second. He would rarely break with anybody.
Sometimes the women would make the break. He was so charming, but wicked. They were so furious they had to leave."

But often a woman who had departed angrily would be
won all over again when Aly cabled from six thousand miles
away and invited her to meet him in Deauville or London or
Cairo. Her phone would ring and it would be his private message
center at the London Ritz bringing in Aly's voice from Bombay
or Hollywood or Rio de Janeiro to ask her how she was, what
she was doing, to tell her how much he hoped to see her soon
again. Roses would follow. To remain angry would be ungener-

ous. It would be gauche and unsophisticated. If some of the women suffered, they suffered in silence. Afterward they were never angry or bitter. Their memories were of charm and generosity. And, of course, for some, there was more to remember.

# Chapter II

> "*My sister was a pure young girl when she met the Aga. She knew nothing of life and men. Naturally, she had idealized everything. It was to be a story from* A Thousand and One Nights."
>
> —Aimée Passet-Magliano

Everyone who knew Aly wondered about him and tried at one time or another to figure him out. Often their speculations ranged no further back than the previous night. But a great lover is not made in a night, any more than Rome was built in a day. The story of Aly Khan began in the last glittering years of La Belle Epoque at the turn of the century, and, appropriately enough, in the place that later became his favorite playground—the French Riviera.

If you were very rich, La Belle Epoque was a wonderful time to be alive. And there was no better place to enjoy that good life than on the stretch of green coastline descending to golden beaches and blue-green water along the southern coast of France. The climate, the sea, the green hills flecked with olive groves and the ruins of ancient towns were indigenous; the fisherfolk and peasants, give or take the blood strains of centuries of invaders, more or less so.

Everything else came from somewhere else. Even the name, Côte d'Azur, came from the title of a book by an obscure poet, Stephen Liegeard. Once the rich had discovered the Riviera, the fishing boats gave way to yachts; the fishermen's rock-hewn huts to ornate villas, and, in and around the towns, olive groves and vineyards were cleared for hotels and casinos. The fishermen, who had their own idea of what was quaint, donned powdered wigs and knee breeches and became the flunkies of the rich. Their sons yearned for the pocketless dinner jackets of the casino croupiers. And more than one of their daughters learned that there was more to life than mending fishing nets.

Everyone who could afford it came in the winter, fleeing the northern chill; it was not until after World War I that the virtues of summer swimming in the Mediterranean were discovered. But the climate was not everything; in fact, tunnels were constructed in Monte Carlo between the Hotel de Paris and the Casino, a walk of a hundred yards, so that ladies could avoid the imminent threat of sunstroke. There was another reason for the popularity of the Côte d'Azur, whispered then, spoken softly even now, for there are still the prudish who prefer not to think of it as one of a resort's attractions, like sun and surf. It was sex. France was the most understanding country in Europe; nowhere else could one enjoy that most delicious, and licentious, of pastimes so openly, with so much encouragement, and so much company. At home, the British upper classes took sex with a stiff upper lip, as another of man's burdens if he were destined to propagate an empire. The Germans treated it as a military action, like Uhlans leveling their lances. The Russian aristocracy, unhappy with their own, had adopted French morals, culture, and language, but felt the need to refresh themselves regularly at the source; their special trains took weeks to reach the Riviera. When the brother of Czar Nicolas II came from St. Petersburg to Cannes, railway traffic all over Europe slowed down, for the Grand Duke Michael had a weak heart and insisted that his private train go no faster than thirty miles per hour. He and his fellow dukes brought along serfs to sleep outside their doors and every conceivable portable luxury to soften the rigors of the trip. In the big hotels, they took over whole floors, establishing enormous households. When the hotels bored them, they built villas. Prince Tcherkasky used to have the flowers in his garden changed every night by a noctivigating crew of forty-eight gardeners so that a new vista of beauty would greet his eye each morning. Almost the same could be said of the way that the Grand Duke Michael's son, the notorious Duke Michael, changed his women. Not to forget some Russian women. The Grand Duchess Anastasia Michaelowna, whose daughter had married the German Kaiser's son, occupied a villa in the tiny hilltop town of Eze from which she sailed out periodically in search of young men. When she saw a man she liked, she invited him home. He would emerge three or four days later, exhausted and wan. One survivor of the Grand Duchess's ministrations, meeting another, said: "She is like the measles. Everyone must experience it once." "Yes," the other man winced. *"C'est la Route Nationale."*

Naturally, so sensual an atmosphere attracted the best of the demimonde. The greatest courtesans of La Belle Epoque also wintered on the Côte, where their particular services were greatly in demand. They advertised their creamy presences by parading along the seaside promenades in Cannes or Nice, or outside the Casino in Monte Carlo, while gentlemen leered and proper ladies blanched at the sight of *"les dames qui matelassent"* (literally, the ladies who mattress). Caroline Otéro, the Spanish Gypsy, counted Edward VII of England and Kaiser Wilhelm II of Germany among her conquests, and supposedly inspired the mammary shapes of the twin cupolas of the Carlton Hotel in Cannes. Liane de Pougy was one of several mistresses of Leopold II, King of Belgium, a man of enormous wealth—he was sole proprietor of the Belgian Congo—and of such meticulous tastes that he had the creases ironed out of his newspaper every morning. For eighteen-year-old Caroline Dubois, a waitress who had caught his fancy, King Leopold not only created a baronetcy, making her Baroness Vaughan, but built the sumptuous Villa Leopolda above Beaulieu-sur-Mer which later became the property of Gianni Agnelli, the scion of the Fiat motor empire and a good friend of Aly Khan. Another leading cocotte was La Juniory, who carried out the seaside motif of the Mediterranean in a bed made in the shape of an enormous conch shell. A man's mettle along the Riviera of those days was measured by the depth of his acquaintance with these skilled practitioners in the arts of love, as well as his reputation as a seducer of more innocent doves.

With competition so keen, a French financier was bragging to his friends about his conquests one day in the sidewalk café of the Hotel de Paris. Just then a large and handsome woman walked out the door and entered a luxurious carriage. "I slept with her the day before yesterday," boasted the financier. "But," exclaimed his friend, "she is the Queen of Rumania." "You don't say," the imperturbable financier replied. "She never told me."

For years, La Belle Epoque's choicest gossip revolved around Albert Edward, Prince of Wales, who during the long reign of his forbidding mother, Queen Victoria, used the Riviera as his bedding ground. It was there that he began his celebrated affair with Lily Langtry, and it was to the Côte d'Azur that he returned after his coronation as Edward VII, calling himself Baron Renfrew, as incognito as Big Ben, to rekindle old flames. Naturally, these liaisons, short and long, sincere love and passing fancy, sometimes led to healthy, squalling accidents. There was more than one by-blow of a Riviera winter. An apocryphal story tells of two women meeting in a narrow corridor of the Hotel de Paris. Neither would turn aside to let the other pass. "Excuse me" said one, shoving forward, "but I am a princess." The other stood her ground. "And I, madame, would be one too if my father had married my mother."

The Riviera was that kind of place during La Belle Epoque, that intermission between wars and revolutions, when everything seemed to have been invented, written, sung, decided, discarded, and parceled out and the balance of power swayed as gently and as deceptively as a hammock. (Sometimes hammocks fall, as this

one did in 1914.) Nowhere else was the setting so perfect—
the golden sunlight, the golden mimosa, the golden coins glinting
beneath the casino chandeliers. And so the very rich came. So
did the very powerful who were, more often than not, the very
same people. The very talented who could amuse the very rich
came, and so did the new rich seeking their place in the sun.
And so also came young men seeking wealth or power, or both,
and young women seeking romance.

2

Sooner or later, everyone met on the promenade before the
Casino in Monte Carlo. Twice a day, in the morning between
eleven and twelve, in the afternoon between five and seven, they
all paraded through the gardens, past the Hotel de Paris and the
Café de Paris with its sidewalk café, past the Casino, the copper-
domed architectural monstrosity that was their shrine.

On a January day in 1908, a saffron-complexioned, stocky
young man was staring hard at all the passing young women on
the promenade. He did this not by divine right—although he
could have made a good case for it in India, his homeland, where
he was considered a living god—but because, even with eyeglasses, he was frightfully near-sighted.

Although a latecomer to the excitement of La Belle Epoque,
he came with the best of introductions. He had plenty of money
and Edward VII of England for a friend. He also knew the
Grand Duke Michael and some of the other freewheeling Russians. The Riviera was used to an occasional bejeweled sultan and
maharajah among its visitors, like a peacock among hawks, but
a living god who spoke faultless English, wore the finest London
tailoring, ordered like a gourmet and ate like a gourmand, was
something new. The Aga Khan III, Imam—or divine ruler—of a
Moslem sect called the Ismailis, had made his first trip to Europe
at the age of eighteen, seen Paris and London, dined with
Queen Victoria and done the town with Edward, then Prince
of Wales, and he had never been the same since. Europe, and
especially the Riviera's attractions, drew him like a golden mag-

net, although he didn't swim, drink, or smoke, and had plenty of sunshine back where he came from.

When he returned to India from this first trip abroad, he found that his mother, a shrewd and strong-minded woman behind her discreet white veil of purdah, had arranged a marriage for him with a cousin, Shahzadi, a strange and ill-starred union which would haunt his later life and Aly's. The wedding festivities lasted sixteen days; twenty-five thousand guests came from all over the Ismaili world by ship, rail, bullock cart, horse, and even camel. Unfortunately, the ceremony was the high point of the marriage. It soon slumped into unhappiness for reasons at which we can only guess. In his autobiography, the Aga says: "We were both ignorant and innocent; our ignorance and innocence set a gulf between us . . . inevitably we drifted apart."

In the light of subsequent events, it seems unlikely that the Aga's needs in women could have been satisfied by any one woman, especially a shy and untutored young Ismaili. Begum Shahzadi was the last Oriental woman with whom he had any permanent liaison. In Europe, where he began to travel extensively, he found the women that intrigued him most. In 1908 he sailed for the Continent, ostensibly on another visit, but actually to live.

Sniffing the delicious scent of the Riviera, its perfume, its beauty, its freedom, he hurried across the garden in Monte Carlo to the kiosk near the Café de Paris. He scanned the newspapers on the kiosk walls, glanced at his watch and looked impatiently about him. A group of graceful young women were crossing the gardens toward the Casino. They were dancers in the Casino's corps de ballet on their way to morning rehearsal. The young man recognized them and watched intently. One of them left the group and walked hesitantly toward him. He smiled and gave her a courtly bow. As she came close, he reached out and kissed her hand. This was what he had been waiting for. The young lady was Teresa Magliano, a nineteen-year-old Italian dancer, who also had come to Monte Carlo that year, but under somewhat different circumstances.

Teresa, or Ginetta, as she was familiarly known (all of her family had a penchant for changing their names), had arrived from Turin, quietly and inauspiciously, to take a job as *première danseuse* with the Casino ballet, her first professional dancing engagement. She was slender, pale, and romantic, the eldest child of a tiny, attractive, tough-minded woman who felt she had married below her station and never let anyone forget it. The orphaned daughter of a family of vaudeville entertainers, she had eloped when only fifteen with Giovanni Magliano, a thirty-three-year-old ironworker, artistic but poor.

The love match of Giovanni, or Michel, as his children later were to call him, and Teresa Lomello, better known as Rosa, was fruitful. Their first child was Teresa, or Ginetta; then came Attilio, who called himself Antonio; next came Emmy, who became Aimée, and finally Mario, who never changed his name. Giovanni changed occupations as well as his name and began to inch up the economic ladder. He became a varnisher of furniture and moved his family to the center of Turin, near the railway station, on the Via Nizza—the road to the Riviera, which Ginetta first and then, one by one, all the other members of the family, except him, were to take. In the courtyard of the big stone tenement house, he opened a small shop employing several apprentices. He taught himself to paint and later became a restorer of church frescoes, which gave him steady employment with the municipality of Turin, but, his daughter Aimée recalls: "He was never rich enough. You know what it's like to have three ladies in the house. My mother had extravagant habits. She loved luxury and display. She had gotten from her grandmother a chinchilla coat—imagine, chinchilla! And she cut it up into little coats for my sister and myself. She wanted us to be fine ladies."

Rosa made sure that her daughters took ballet lessons and when Ginetta was eight, sent her off to Milan to live with an aunt, another Teresa Magliano, a retired dancer who had made a good marriage to a manufacturer of printing equipment. Aunt Teresa had danced at La Scala, Milan's famous opera house, and arranged for young Ginetta to take lessons there, closely supervising her training until she felt she was ready to start a professional career.

When Ginetta left for Monte Carlo she had a contract for

one season, a suitcase of clothing and, perhaps most important, a certain sense of destiny. "She was never really ambitious," recalls her sister Aimée, "but she was romantic about herself." And she was going, after all, to Monte Carlo, where anything could happen.

In Monaco, Ginetta found a room at a pension in the marshy Condamine section of the tiny principality. For five francs a day ($1) she got three hearty Italian meals and a sunny bedroom all to herself. Her fellow roomers were two other young ballet dancers, both, like her, Italian-born; a middle-aged woman pianist, and a young French violinist, the lone male of the quintet. They took their meals together, helped carry up the large pitchers of warm water with which they made their toilets—there was no inside plumbing—and gossiped and joked about their fellow artists and the *haut monde* they entertained.

This was before the great days when the tempestuous Russian impresario, Diaghilev, brought his ballet to Monte Carlo. Ginetta was part of a troupe of dancers, hired and hastily rehearsed to perform in the new Opera House in the west wing of the Casino, before audiences less interested in their pirouettes than in their legs.

The Aga was always in the front row. He was a familiar figure to the dancers, some of whom also had interests that went beyond their *tours jetés*. He had flirted with several of them but the bisque-doll appearance of Ginetta electrified him. It still brought a wondering shake of the head to one of the other dancers, Gina Lamy, recalling the event fifty years later in Paris, where she now lives in retirement, a birdlike little grey-haired woman.

"In those days, Monte Carlo was small," she recalled nostalgically. "We little dancers, when we had finished dancing, we would go and sit on the benches in the Casino garden. One evening, after our performance, the Aga asked an English journalist to present him to Ginetta. So this journalist, he came to Ginetta in the garden and said, 'I know a gentleman who is very much in love with you. He is very rich. He can give you everything. Tomorrow morning, if you are by the kiosk outside the Casino, he will make himself known to you.' It was very romantic but that is how things were done in those days."

Within a month, the Aga left on a trip to India, but before going, he gave Ginetta an evening bag made of gold links and a long gold chain to wear round her neck. He said it was to "enchain her" until he got back. When he returned in April he was more infatuated than ever and immediately moved Ginetta out of her modest hillside pension into a suite at the Hotel de Paris. She finished the season at the Casino but she never danced again. The following year, her first son by the Aga was born, and, with an impartial nod to the nationality of each of his parents, named Giuseppe Mahdi. The Aga installed them in a comfortable villa. He kept his own suite at the Hotel de Paris. It was not an unusual arrangement in the Monte Carlo of La Belle Epoque but it nettled Ginetta. Her beginnings had been humble but her aspirations were bourgeois. She was mortified by the notation on Mahdi's birth certificate that she, Teresa Magliano, was *"nubile"*—unmarried—and unimpressed by the Aga's argument that he still was married to a wife in India and that, in any event, a Moslem religious leader could not casually marry a young Italian dancer.

When Mahdi was eighteen-months-old, he suddenly contracted meningitis and died. Heartbroken and already pregnant again, Ginetta returned to her home in Turin. Her doctor, Professor Alfredo Pozzi, prescribed mountain air, so while Rosa looked for a suitable apartment for the accouchement, Ginetta and her brother Mario took the train north to the fashionable resort of Courmayeur in the Valley of Aosta. They lingered in this lovely valley, leaving by train at the last possible moment. When they reached Turin after a three-hour ride, Ginetta had to be carried from the station to the new fourteen-room apartment her mother had taken for her at 17 Corso Oporto, in the heart of Turin's upper-class residential district; a measure of its grandeur—the Agnellis, owners of the Fiat motor works, were neighbors. Ginetta was already in labor when the carriage of Dr. Pozzi drove up. It was early in the morning. As the day wore on, it became obvious that the delivery would be a difficult one.

Aimée and Mario were sent out of the room; only Rosa remained with the doctor and the midwife. But Aimée recalls hearing later: "My sister was delivered with forceps. She was all torn. It was very painful." The baby boy, barely breathing, was handed to Rosa, who laid him down on a blanket-covered table. She counted his tiny fingers and toes, and then realized, to her horror, that he had stopped breathing. Quickly and surely she picked up the baby, pressed her mouth close to his tiny lips, and breathed deeply and slowly, forcing air into his lungs.

Nineteen infants were born in Turin on June 13, 1911, eight males, eleven females. There was no notice in the city's newspapers that one of them was the son of the Aga Khan. Four days later, as required by law, Dr. Pozzi arranged for an officer of the Turin city government to come to the house on Corso Oporto to prepare the birth certificate. The Aga Khan, who had not come to Turin for the birth, had authorized Dr. Pozzi to represent him in the registration process.

The certificate, still on file in the archives of the Turin town hall, says:

> In the year 1911, 17th of June, 5 P.M. before me, Piere Carossa, acting vice-secretary of the delegation (Dec. 31 1909), officer of the civil government of the city of Turin, has come Dr. Alfredo Pozzi, 39 years old, obstetrician, living in Turin, who declared that at 2 p.m. of the 13th of June, same year, in this house, 17 Corso Oporto, from the union of Teresa Magliano, unmarried, 22 years old, living on independent means, here in person, as a co-declarant with His Highness The Aga Khan, son of the late Aga Ali Shah, 34 years old, born at Karachi (British India), living at Monte Carlo, was born a male baby who is not present and to whom are given the names of Aly Salomone. To this are present as witnesses Francesca Crescio, 28, living on independent means, and Rosa Magliano, 39, living on independent means, both residents of Turin. The child has not been shown owing to hygienic reasons.

Again that humiliating word—"unmarried."

There was some mistake in spelling the baby's name. First it had been written "Ali," then a "y" had been drawn over the "i." It was a confusion that would continue throughout Aly's life; French newspapers, particularly, would often give his name as Ali, like that of his ancestor and namesake, the son-in-law of Mohammed. He himself always spelled it Aly.

The day after Aly's birth, a wet nurse, Maria, arrived. She was a pleasant, broad-beamed country girl with breasts like turrets and enough milk for her own newborn child and the infant she had been hired to suckle. Aly settled down contentedly at her bulging brown breasts. The family tiptoed into the big high-ceilinged bedroom to see Ginetta, who lay paler than ever, and the new baby with his ruddy skin and shock of black hair.

Several weeks later, the Aga arrived. Mario met him with a hired carriage. The Aga wore an elegant black suit. He twitched his mustachios nervously as the sights and smells of Turin's hectic railway station greeted him and hurriedly got into the carriage. Mario sat stiffly beside him. It was a warm summer day. As they neared the apartment house, Mario realized that the two white horses that pulled the hired hack were shedding. He brushed off a few hairs and jumped down to lead the way for the Aga. The Aga was glowering. With both hands he brushed off his black suit which looked as though he had come through a light snowfall. "Never, never," he sputtered, glaring at Mario. "Never white horses in summertime." Still picking away at the white hairs and his mutilated dignity, he made his way upstairs to see his infant son.

# Chapter III

> *"My father was a very definite person, had a character very much his own, and I think I had also. So our characters may not have been alike but there was . . . tremendous love and affection. He . . . was a wonderful father. Most kind and generous. Used to use his temper now and again. Not very often, but when he did, he used to get pretty angry."*
>
> —ALY KHAN

Fussed with and chuckled over, his bottom pinched, his masculinity admired, Aly began life in the warm and billowy lap of his Italian family. The Maglianos accepted their change of fortune with the equanimity of people who had always felt superior to their station in life. Rosa helped with the baby, the servants, and the luxuries the Aga's long-distance patronage had suddenly put within reach. The Aga seldom came to Turin. Old friends clucked sympathetically as Rosa held court in the big apartment, hinting at secret East-West diplomatic missions which kept the baby's father busy. This was 1912 and the newspapers more or less backed her up. The Aga was occasionally in the news as Britain's unofficial emissary to the Moslem world; his effectiveness in this role is still hard to assess but by the end of World War I it had earned him a reputation in Britain as the leading Moslem of India and given to his Ismailis political leverage far out of proportion to their numbers. While Rosa expounded on world affairs, Giovanni, wheeling Aly's pram beneath the chestnut trees on the Corso Oporto's broad esplanade, fretted over his daughter's vague status, and his own.

Shortly before Aly's second birthday, the Aga requested Teresa to return to Monte Carlo with their son. He installed them first in the Villa Ginetta on rue Bel Respiro above the Monte Carlo Casino and later in the Villa Terpsichore, a red-tiled Florentine mansion which he built for them on the flank of a hill in Cimiez, a suburb of Nice, which had been made fashionable by Queen Victoria.

Eventually the Aga bought Ginetta three more houses: a four-story town house on the rue de Prony in Paris, a country house outside Paris at Maisons-Lafitte, and a handsome three-story Norman-style villa facing the Atlantic Ocean on the beachfront at Deauville which Ginetta patriotically renamed the Villa Gorizia for a fought-over town which Italy hoped to win from the Austrians during World War I.

The Aga made Ginetta a gift of all of these houses and she owned them under her own name: Mademoiselle Cleope Teresa Catrina Gabrielle Magliano. She and Aly migrated seasonally among the houses while the Aga continued to travel widely on political and religious missions, to visit the fashionable European watering spots—he especially favored the French spa, Aix-les-Bains—to live in hotel suites and go his own way, visiting Aly and Ginetta when it pleased him. He spent only three weeks out of the year under the same roof with them. That was in Deauville, where they went every summer, doctors having recommended its bracing air for Aly's health. Ginetta, remembering Mahdi, fussed endlessly over Aly although he always seemed strong enough. The Aga, sending his cook ahead, would arrive at the Villa Gorizia on July 25. Dressed in white flannels and blue blazer in deference to the resort's English influence, he would parade on "Les Planches" (the boardwalk) where he might run into Maurice Chevalier, the young singer, or Georges Carpentier, the boxer, or the Dolly sisters or Mistinguett, her daring dress displaying her lovely legs, or even the doleful figure of François André, the former undertaker's assistant who ran Deauville as shrewdly as he would later run Cannes and other French resorts. Clutching his umbrella, rain or shine, André would say: "Nothing is good that isn't expensive. I don't want anyone to sneeze without it costing at least a hundred sous."

To Aly, Deauville was a small boy's dream come true. It was a place of great white sand beaches and lots of children, where one could roam for hours away from a governess's eye, play hide-and-seek all day among the tents of striped canvas, or be a Peeping Tom while bathers changed clothes or carried on a romance.

He learned to ride at Deauville and had the first of a life-long series of sporting accidents when his horse threw him as he galloped along the beach. He also learned to play tennis. His teacher was Tommy Burke, a wiry, good-natured Irishman who gave the Aga lessons too. Aly never became a first-rate player. "He never took tennis seriously," recalls Burke. "It was a game with him. But not with the Aga. The Aga took everything seriously." Burke remembers Aly as an engaging youngster who showed up at the courts in Deauville with his gear in a cardboard carton tied with a string. "Not a beautiful leather bag like some of the youngsters. He was never a boy to show off."

During most of the year Aly led a lonely life. He grew up very much by himself, subject to his mother's and the Aga's sudden summonses. His parents, his English governesses, Mario, Aimée, Rosa, the servants—these people bounded his world. He spent hours watching Alfredo, the Italian chauffeur, polish and repair his mother's handsome automobiles. His aunt Aimée taught him to dance, and afternoons at Villa Terpsichore sometimes rang with music and the laughter of Aly, his aunt, his mother and his grandmother, all whirling around the high-ceilinged salon.

Ginetta kept him away from other children, behind the spiked fence of Villa Terpsichore. His one close friend was Henri Macchieraldo, son of the gardener, who lived on the grounds. In later years Aly often proudly recalled how Henri grew up to become a schoolteacher, then went into the French army, became an officer, and was killed in action in Indo-China.

No explanations were ever given to Aly as to why he traveled so much, why he was kept so cloistered in Cimiez, not even who he was. Race, religion, ancestors, the exotic visitors who occasionally came with his father, the servants' gossip, his mother's spells of moodiness—all were mysteries.

He adored his mother and clung to her. She was the center of his universe. He was in awe of his father. The Aga would arrive loaded down with expensive gifts—jewels for Ginetta and toys for Aly. All Aly had to say when he spotted something he liked was, "Papa, I want that," and the Aga would buy it. "Sometimes Aly did not even open the package when he got home; it no longer interested him," an old family friend recalls. He also remembers one day when Aly, out driving with the Aga, spotted some ragged children playing in the street, burst into tears and insisted they stop the car and give the children the toys the Aga had just bought for him.

The Aga's visits would start in great joy, but they often dissolved into anger and tears. "Aly had a stubborn character," his uncle Mario recalls. "He was proud and he didn't always obey." The Aga had little patience for a young boy's caprices and he would slap him angrily. Even language was a problem: Aly spoke French and Italian with his mother; with his father, he was required to speak English. With the Italian servants, brought from Turin, he spoke an Italian patois. Gianni Agnelli, the Fiat scion, recalls that years later, when Aly visited him in Turin, he always would pay a visit to the kitchen and speak the local dialect with the cook.

There was never any genuine intimacy between father and son. Mario recalls that the Aga was "a very grand personage. He had a high sense of his authority. And when he saw Aly, it was with the governess, a warm but constrained meeting, you understand. More than this could not exist. The Aga kept at a distance from people, even his own son. So there was a restraint and a suspicion. They would never show their feelings. Aly, even if he hurt himself, would never say, 'That hurts me.' And he remained like this always. If he had a cold or a fever, he would not admit it. In the bottom of himself, he always carried that view—that one should not, before others, abase oneself by showing weakness."

During the Aga's long absences Ginetta spent most of her time with old friends, like Gina Lamy, who came to visit her every year, and the members of her family, whom she had gathered about her and helped out with the ample funds the Aga gave her. Aimée became a ballet dancer, Antonio an orchestra leader at the Casino in Cannes, and Mario bred horses for the Aga in Normandy. Rosa was something of a problem. She lived in Monte Carlo, and had taken to wearing heavy make-up, flirting with young men and running up gambling debts which often had to be settled by the Aga. Only father Giovanni remained in Turin.

Ginetta rarely accompanied the Aga when he went out in society. A friend recalls seeing her at the Deauville Casino, resplendent in glittering jewels. "People followed her through the lobby to look at the jewelry," the friend says. "The Aga liked that, he liked to show her off. But it made Ginetta uncomfortable." At home, she dressed and lived simply.

Her temper, always short, snapped whenever she was reminded of her ambiguous position. A woman recalls being briefed before meeting her: "Call her madame, not princess. She is with the prince but she is not his princess." To the Aga's servants she was known as "Madame Ginetta," and old-timers recall that there was lively speculation about her among them. Asked once whether the Aga and Ginetta were married, the Aga's valet replied: "Nobody knows." Ginetta grew pretentious with servants and tradespeople. She often took to her bed. She was gaining weight and that worried her.

Bored and lonely, she looked for other things to do. She and brother Mario studied with the famous French sculptor Antoine Bourdelle. She built a studio in the garden of her

house at Cimiez and exhibited her work under the name "Yla"—
an anagram of Aly. "To amuse herself, she sang a little," Aimée
recalls. "She did a revue at Monte Carlo. And then, another
time, she danced a little in a performance of Cleopatra. She
suffered very much from not being able to dance any more."

She became even moodier when the Aga was about. His
presence—bulky yet evasive, demanding yet uninvolved—un-
nerved her and made her more sensitive than usual. She took
it out on Aly in scolding and slaps. "It was her temperament:
she was nervous," Aimée says. "My sister was very severe. She
wanted Aly to have good manners, to learn his lessons. But his
father would arrive suddenly and give him all the money he
wanted and fuss over him and then disappear."

And so Aly learned he could get attention by being
"charming"—by being what other people expected him to be.

Or he could get what he wanted by mischief and frenetic
behavior that scarcely veiled the resentments he felt against
adults.

One day, he and his mother and Mario went to St. Tropez
for a swim and a picnic. Mario recalls: "Aly and I began to play,
to run and wrestle. Aly played far too hard, kicking at me. I
said to him, 'Now listen, enough of that.' Aly continued; he
liked to tease people. And so I said to him, 'If you continue, I
shall push your head under water.' He continued, so I picked
him up and threw him into the water. Ginetta shrieked terribly.
The water hardly came to his waist. He stood up, weeping and
furious. All his life he reproached me with that, whenever we
had the slightest dispute. 'You always hated me,' he would say.
'When I was a child, you tried to drown me.' "

Sometimes Aly ran away, from his mother or his governess.
He would climb an old tree in the garden of Terpsichore and
sit in a crotch for hours—catlike, seemingly daydreaming, silent
—until Ginetta would discover him there and scream that he
might fall. Then he would climb down, grinning and satisfied.
There were certainly times when he felt nobody really cared
about him, that his family wanted to get rid of him, perhaps even
have him die as had Mahdi. And over all his anxieties loomed

the shadow of that corpulent gentleman in the white suit and the glittering eyeglasses. His father.

2

Aly never went to school. The Aga preferred to have him instructed by a series of young Swiss tutors. His education was sketchy, frequently interrupted by travel, and lacking in any direction. The Aga once told a tutor that he thought Aly might be a businessman when he grew up. He never had him instructed in the Moslem religion nor in any Eastern language. Once he told a friend: "There is no use stuffing Aly's head when he is so young; he will learn everything he needs to know when he is bigger." By then, of course, it was too late; Aly's character had been formed in another mold.

Edmond Grin, who was hired by the Aga to tutor Aly when he was nine years old, remembers his first encounter with him: "The Aga took me in and said, 'Monsieur Aly'—he always called him that, never Prince Aly or just Aly—'I present your new professor. I hope that all will go well. He is very kind: you must be very kind. Now I will leave you together.' Aly and I began to work."

Grin found Aly "very intelligent, but not very persevering. One had to change subjects every five or ten minutes. He understood well the explanations that were given him, but as soon as an effort was required of him, to do a mathematical problem or take dictation in French, he would lie down and say, 'Oh, Professor, I am tired.' "

He disliked reading, but loved to be read to, particularly fairy tales and legends. Grin found him dreamy and imaginative. "If I did not tell him, 'Monsieur Aly, you have to work,' he would have remained for hours on a divan, sitting and dreaming, saying nothing."

He loved to go to the movies and spent most of his small weekly allowance on them.

The Aga, when he took the time, puzzled about his capricious and dreamy, distant yet painfully affectionate, son. When Grin, whom Aly adored, informed the Aga that he wanted to resign in order to finish his studies and get married, the Aga offered to buy him the books he would need to pursue his studies on his own, to double his salary so he could marry, and to take him and his bride on a trip to India. When even these inducements could not persuade Grin to stay, the Aga begged him not to tell Aly until a successor had been found. "That way," the Aga said, "the break will not be too painful." But in spite of the Aga's concern, Aly burst into tears when he heard the news, threw himself into Grin's arms, and cried: "Professor, I never thought you would abandon me."

Thirty-five years later, when Grin was appointed rector of the University of Lausanne, Aly telephoned from Paris to congratulate him and later came to Lausanne to see him. "One would have thought that we had never been separated," Grin said.

The Aga tried to encourage Aly's interest in sports. He counseled the boy to follow his own example and take regular exercise. The Aga loved sports and methodically learned one after another—tennis, boxing, golf. He usually arrived at the Riviera or Deauville trailed by professional trainers and athletic equipment. He was an early riser, no matter how late he'd been up the night before, and fretted about his digestive system and those of his friends, insisting they eat figs as laxatives.

The Aga had other strong beliefs about physical culture. He felt, as did many Moslems, that frequent sex relations were necessary for health and stamina. He was a student of the sexual lore of India and would amuse friends, male and female, discoursing about it. He was fascinated by the mating techniques he watched at his stables. But talk was not his only strong point. In his own life, he imported the sensual sexual customs of the East to colder climes, where women had not known such consideration. He insisted there could be no pleasure for the man if the woman was not first helped to achieve her pleasure; only in the woman's heightened pleasure could the man feel truly satisfied. A theory like that could not help but win him admiration and attention. It might also have served to advertise his special gifts for self-control. He practiced patience and fortitude in sex as well as in sports. Sometime later he passed this knowledge along to his son, but at this point in our narrative, something else about Aly's sexual potential worried the Aga. He saw a boy given to temperamental outbursts, to long spells of daydreaming, and to exuberant displays of affection toward Grin. Once, the Aga was horrified to see Aly jump on Grin's lap and kiss him, exclaiming: "Professor, I love you so much." He accused Ginetta of making a sissy out of Aly, and he bore down on the boy all the harder. Ginetta worried about it too, but she, the daughter of an earthy Italian family, proposed a simple solution. "When Aly is fourteen years old," she confided to a friend, "we'll get him a mistress."

# Chapter IV

> *"Aly seemed driven by the feeling, 'I must impress the world that I am Prince Aly Khan.'"*
>
> —THE EARL OF CARNARVON

Aly was eleven years old, going on twelve, when his mother and father were married in a Moslem ceremony in Bombay. The effect on him of this belated event can only be surmised. He never spoke of it as an adult. Nor did any other members of the family. For by then, the Aga's youthful romance had been sanctified by time—and rewritten by biographers. With prudent hindsight, the date of the wedding had been put back to 1908, three years before Aly's birth, and the Aga's *"petite amie,"* as Ginetta is still remembered in Deauville, had been elevated, as of the year of her meeting with the Aga, to the status of Begum, the title given his wife.

Only in the course of a careful search of documents and ransacking of memories relating to Aly's childhood, did it become evident that the official family version of these crucial early years fell somewhere on the far side of candor. There were Aly's birth certificate which proclaimed his mother to be *"nubile"*—unmarried; the documents in various municipal archives relating to Ginetta's houses—in Monte Carlo, for instance, the record of the *Services Fiscaux* on the sale of the Villa Ginetta in 1919, states: "Mademoiselle Magliano has declared: that she was single and of adult age . . ."; the 1921 census report for Nice which lists the *"chef de ménage"*—head of household—of the Villa Terpsichore, as "Magliano, Ginetta." Finally, there was the Aga's will which, of course, came to light only after his death, its contents known to only a limited circle. This testament makes the fascinating assertion that the Aga married Ginetta not once, but twice. The 1908 ceremony, the only one hitherto mentioned by biographers and interviewers, was revealed to be a *muta* marriage—a strange form of temporary Moslem marriage which requires no ceremony, no witnesses and can be contracted for an hour, a night or a hundred years. The only requirements are consent of both parties and fair payment— *muta* means pittance.

An ancient practice, *muta* dates back to pre-Islamic times in Arabia when a special class of woman was kept for the purpose. The prophet Mohammed at first forbade his followers to take women in *muta* marriages but during the nomadic years when his warriors were conquering the Arabian peninsula in the name of Allah, leaving their wives at home for long periods, they came to him and asked "whether we should emasculate ourselves." Mohammed relented and permitted them to resort to *muta*—but only for awhile. With their final victory at Mecca, he forbade the custom once more.

The vast majority of Moslems today regard *muta* as adulterous, "the sister of harlotry." Only a few sects still condone its practice. "Its chief object," explains an Islamic authority, Dr. U. M. Daudpota, in the Journal of the Bombay Branch of the Royal Asiatic Society, is "not so much the establishment of a household or the begetting of children as the providing of a man with a wife when he is away from home." *Muta* is common during military service, business trips and long pilgrimages to the holy Moslem cities.

In a way, the circumstances fitted the Aga. He was a long way from home and he was still married to Shahzadi, who lived obscurely in purdah in Bombay. She had grown grotesquely

stout; old-timers recall that a reinforced chair had to be carried
about for her to sit on. The Aga says in his autobiography that
he never saw her after leaving India in 1907, but he did not
divorce her.

It is easy for a Moslem to divorce a wife; he need only
repeat "I divorce you" three times in front of witnesses. For a
living god who could do no wrong, it should have been superbly
simple. But the Aga did not divorce Shahzadi. The explanation
probably lies in the violently bizarre circumstances that surrounded that marriage—another bit of family history which has
been forgotten or glossed over but which gives a tantalizing
glimpse of the tempestuous Oriental clan into which Ginetta
Magliano unwittingly had borne her infant son.

In 1896, a year before the Aga's marriage to Shahzadi, her
father and brother were killed while on a pilgrimage to Mecca.
The assassins were said to be fanatical followers of the Aga Khan
who bore some religious grudge against the pair. The Ismaili
community was rocked by the tragedy. The assassins were quickly
arrested by the British, but before they could be brought to public
trial, they were found poisoned in their prison cells, supposed
suicides. The whole affair was hushed up and quickly followed
by the announcement of the Aga's betrothal to his cousin. In his
autobiography, the Aga described the murders as "dastardly
religious fanaticism"; the true circumstances are still a mystery.
But in 1908—the year the Aga met Ginetta in Monte Carlo—a
suit was heard in Bombay, brought against the Aga Khan and his
mother by a group of relatives, including members of Shahzadi's
immediate family, who charged, among other things, that the Aga
and Lady Ali Shah had instigated the murders of Shahzadi's father
and brother.

Justice Louis Pitman Russell, the English judge who heard
the case, rejected all of the charges; the innocence of mother
and son was officially affirmed. But the community remained
unsettled. It was obviously no time for a divorce.

Shahzadi notwithstanding, there was nothing to prevent
the Aga marrying Ginetta in full Moslem rites if he had so desired.
As a Moslem, he was permitted four wives. His Ismaili followers would not have objected. Western religions might expect

their prophets to be ascetics with flashing angry eyes; Islam does not. Mohammed's eye was a roving one. The prophet took fifteen wives. His favorite, Ayesha, in whose arms he died (of a concubine's poison) when he was sixty-two and she eighteen, once reminisced: "The Prophet liked three things most: women, scent and eating, but mostly women." And French law, which accepts all bona-fide religious marriages, including plural marriages, would have recognized the Moslem union. But the Aga, apparently, was not prepared for the twain to meet, at least not yet. Instead, he had, as usual, the best of both worlds: a "Captain's Paradise" of his own devising.

Finally, in 1923, although he was still married to Shahzadi, the Aga took his European family with him to India. Perhaps it was at the urging of his mother, Lady Ali Shah, who reminded him that he was no longer a youth, but forty-six years old— time to be thinking about an heir to succeed him as Imam. Perhaps it was because La Belle Epoque with its easygoing ways had vanished, along with his youth. Perhaps it was because he could no longer equivocate about the future of Aly, who was approaching adolescence.

On January 23, 1923, in Bombay, he and Ginetta, according to his will, went through "the permanent form of marriage—observing the ceremonials which are customary among Shiah Moslems." Even this ceremony is shrouded in mystery. Attempts to find out about it in Bombay were repeatedly turned aside by secretive and suspicious Ismaili leaders. There were two English witnesses. One of them, Sir Stanley Reed, the former editor of *The Times of India*, and a lifelong friend of the Aga's, is still alive, at ninety-one, living quietly in London, his memory brimming with anecdotes about the Aga, whom he recalls as an influential political leader. He, too, is reluctant to discuss the marriage ceremony.

"It was a private matter between the Aga and myself," he explains. Only three or four people, including a *mullah* [priest] were present. They went through a certain ceremony. You must remember, the Aga was a law unto himself. If he said, 'I marry this woman,' he was married."

One must go back to the Riviera, to the municipal archives

of Nice, stored in an old building just a stone's throw from the Villa Terpsichore in the hills of Cimiez, for concrete evidence that something significant for Ginetta and Aly took place on that January afternoon in Bombay. The quinquennial census for 1926 again listed the residents of the Villa Terpsichore. This time the name of the *chef de ménage* was: "Khan, Teresa."

## 2

In India young Aly was introduced to a world out of one of his storybooks. Land's End, his grandmother's beautiful house at Malabar Hill, was a far cry from the homey, bourgeois Villa Terpsichore. Lady Ali Shah, a commanding, alert woman with a round, bright-eyed face framed by a white veil, was surrounded by ladies-in-waiting draped in jewel-toned saris. With all the pomp and panoply of a royal court, she kept the reins of Ismaili leadership in her own two capable hands during her son's long absences in Europe. Ismaili dignitaries wearing their traditional gold turbans came to ask her advice and receive her judgments.

For this rare visit of the Aga, the Ismailis of Bombay turned out by the thousands. Aly must have watched, dumbfounded, as his father doffed his Western clothes, took a perfumed bath in a huge silver basin, put on a robe of embroidered brocade over white muslin trousers, slipped on golden slippers and a high astrakhan fur cap to mount a golden throne in the garden of Aga Hall, the Ismaili headquarters in Bombay. Imaginative and romantic, he could not but have been dazzled by the parade of the faithful, come to pay homage to their Imam, to deliver to him their offerings of gold, and to seek his *didar* (glimpse) or the laying on of his hands, both of which they devoutly believed would bring them good fortune in this world and the next. It was probably the first time Aly got an inkling of who he himself was—the son of a living deity, the end product of a strange religious sect with a turbulent and exotic history. It was a history which he had never been taught and which he would have to piece together for himself.

## Chapter V

*"I am leaving behind me two things: the
Book of God and my descendants. They are
tied with a long rope and cannot be separated
till the Day of Judgement. Verily if you cling
to them, you will never go astray."*

—MOHAMMED

In later years, visitors to Aly's French Riviera home,
the Chateau de l'Horizon, were often shocked as they entered
the elegant dining room of their dapper, cosmopolitan host to
find themselves face-to-face with a somber portrait of a black-
bearded, fierce-eyed Persian cavalryman staring down at them
with icy disdain. Mohammed Hassan Husseini, the first of the
Aga Khans, was not the kind of skeleton who hangs peaceably
in any descendant's closet—especially Aly's.

In 1845 he had clattered into Bombay at the head of a troop
of cavalrymen that looked remarkably like him—perhaps because, as the legend has it, eight hundred of his best men were
his sons. In those days, when rulers enjoyed *le droit de seigneur*,
recruiting an army was a personal mission. Word of his coming

had sped ahead to the Ismaili community of Bombay: its men, women, and children had flocked out to meet him, prostrating themselves in the dust close to the prancing hoofs of his horse; only a few among them had ever seen their Imam, whom they regarded not only as a descendant of the Prophet, but as the living incarnation of God. He had lived in Persia, receiving tribute and pilgrims from Ismaili communities all over the East, and was regarded as an important and powerful chieftain by the Persian Shah, who had given him the title of Aga Khan (Lord Chief) and the hand of one of his daughters in marriage. But the Aga, in 1838, had become embroiled in a dispute with the Shah's Prime Minister and had been forced to flee. With as many horsemen as he could muster, he had first made his way to the Sind province of India, where he found an Ismaili community waiting to welcome him. Arriving a penniless refugee, he had reminded them of his divine status and blessed them from a portable throne carried on one of the horses. The community promptly handed over one tenth of all its possessions, an extraordinary levy which tested its faith down to its last cup of curry, and set the Aga up in business in an entirely new location. Re-equipped and revivified, he moved on to larger things. He offered the use of his cavalry to the British, who were engaged in pacifying the tribes of Afghanistan—a stroke of genius which was to bring him under the most powerful protector in the Middle East and assure the future social standing of his descendants in such far-off places as Buckingham Palace, Gstaad and the 21 Club. With the British to pave the way, the road to power, fortune and the French Riviera lay open.

He settled down in Bombay where his new British friends were overseeing the establishment of a great mercantile city, and notified his flock, scattered from Syria to China, that all payments and pilgrims should be addressed to his new *durkhana* (headquarters).

He led a dual life as a divinity and a sportsman. Once a week, he allowed the local Ismailis and patient pilgrims to enjoy his *didar*, to kiss his hand, and to solicit his advice. On special occasions, he led prayers in the *jamat-khana* (the

Ismaili equivalent of a mosque) and distributed water mixed with dust from their holy city of Kerbela (in present-day Iraq).

The rest of his time he spent at the horse races. Limping slightly, dressed in a green tunic and tall black sheepskin hat, he soon became a familiar figure, "the most assiduous frequenter of the race track in the island," according to a Bombay newspaper account of the time. The British paid him a pension for his military services which, added to his other income, started him off with about fifty thousand dollars a year. He steadily built up his fortune with contributions from his prospering followers. It led to considerable grumbling among a portion of them who resented what *The Bombay Times and Standard* of May 4, 1861, called "the mercenary efforts of the old man to appropriate for his own use all the property of the caste and, if report speaks truly, his attempting the same thing with their women."

In 1866 a group of wealthy Ismailis, tired of paying tribute to the Aga, tried a new field of battle. This time, to the Aga's horror, it was a British law court. Ismailism is a sect schooled in secrecy, its history thick with mystery. Now its adherents met in a stifling plaster-walled courtroom in Bombay, before a be-wigged judge and bewigged attorneys, while, in a strange language, all their secrets were revealed. The plaintiffs claimed that they were not Ismailis at all, that they owed the present Aga nothing and, in fact, wanted everything they had given him in the past returned. The Aga Khan and his codefendants displayed a remarkable talent for bookkeeping and an unexpected Anglo-Saxon bent for documentary evidence as for twenty-five days they retraced the turbulent history of the Ismailis.

2

They were a tiny subsect of one of the two main branches of Islam: the Shiahs (the other, larger sect called themselves Sunnis). For a brief time in the tenth and eleventh centuries, they had ruled Egypt and established an empire—the Fatimite Caliphate—which stretched across North Africa and, according to the historian Edward Gibbon, rivaled in riches, elegance and learning anything of which contemporary Europe could boast. After two hundred years of glory, the empire crumbled and the sect sank into obscurity. In many countries its followers were forced to practice *takia* (hiding or adapting one's true beliefs) to survive. Persecuted and dispersed, Ismailis wandered into the highlands of Syria, Lebanon and Persia, drifted into southern Egypt, Yemen, Iraq and Afghanistan, and later into central Asia and the mountains on the southern boundary of Russia.

Oddly enough, even under these circumstances, they managed to win converts. In India, during the fifteenth century, an Ismaili missionary named Pir Sadruddin converted thousands of Hindus of a pariah trading caste, by convincing them that his Imam was their god. He did this, in the best tradition of *takia*, by borrowing a familiar bit of Hindu theology—the belief that God appears from time to time as an incarnation in human form, an *avatar*. The Hindu god, Vishnu, declared Pir Sadruddin, had appeared on earth ten times—the last time as none other than Mohammed's son-in-law Ali, whom the Ismailis, in common with all Shiah Moslems, revered as the Prophet's only true successor.

The ignorant and credulous Hindus whom Pir Sadruddin called Khojas, or disciples—eagerly accepted this new *avatar* along with Pir Sadruddin's explanation that the Imam of the Ismailis was a direct lineal descendant of Ali and thereby the bearer of all his godly attributes.

A book, *Das Avatar*, which Pir Sadruddin wrote to explain the whole thing, is still read by Khojas and a great deal of other Hindu lore and law have been preserved as part and parcel of their doctrine, making them something of a despised anomaly in the Moslem world.

Ironically, it was descendants of these Khoja converts, rather than of the original Ismailis, who welcomed Aga Khan I when he galloped out of the Persian hills heading for India. And it was some of them who were sitting now in the Bombay courtroom, challenging his divine right to rule them—and to exact tribute.

The decision handed down by Sir Joseph Arnould in 1866 gave the Aga a complete victory. Justice Arnould pronounced the Khojas "a sect of people whose ancestors were Hindu in origin; which were converted to, and had throughout abided in, the faith of the Shiah Imam Ismailis." He ruled that the Bombay community's payments to the Aga were traditional and unconditional. They were his to do with as he pleased; he was not even obliged to account for them. The judge also ordered the plaintiffs to pay the costs of the trial.

No living god could have asked for more.

## 3

Aga Khan I lived to be eighty-one and was succeeded by his son Aga Khan II, who was Imam for only four years before dying of pneumonia. His only surviving son—two older sons had died—became Imam in 1885 at the age of seven, a small boy with bad eyesight and a weak heart. A shadowy photograph remains of his coronation: a tiny figure in an oversized turban sitting cross-legged on the *gadi*, a low ceremonial throne, almost obscured by the long beards and voluminously ornate robes of his *wazirs*. These advisers quickly found themselves shorn of everything but their beards and robes by the young Imam's mother, Bibi Shamul, Lady Ali Shah, the granddaughter of a Persian Shah. She had tremendous strength of will, experience in ruling learned in her own family's court, and the tiny ear of the boy Imam. She brought up the young Aga so sternly that a courtier once complained that one of the frequent beatings she had ordered might permanently impair her son's health. Her reply, heard over the boy's screams, was: "Better his health than his mind."

The young Imam was tutored in English, French, Arabic, and Persian. He studied Ismaili tradition for hour after weary hour. At night he practiced Persian calligraphy, a particularly onerous task since he could not see well. It was not until he was fifteen that, at the insistence of a British tutor, and over the objections of religious advisers, he was fitted with glasses. On Saturdays and religious holidays, he received his followers in long stately ceremonies which he was forced to master by heart.

While the young boy prepared himself for his future responsibilities, Lady Ali Shah kept a firm grip on Ismaili affairs, and, by shrewd investment, particularly in real estate, multiplied the family's personal fortune. She was a feminist in a discreetly veiled way. She never came out of purdah herself, but she persuaded the Aga to abolish purdah for Ismaili women and to give them status in the community, with the result that women became her son's most devout and faithful subjects.

She also saw to it that her son kept up the warm relations with the British that Aga Khan I had established as a mercenary military commander. The boy took tea with the British governor-general, who was impressed by his English, his wealth, his exquisite manners, his classical references to Shakespeare, Macaulay and the Persian poets, and by his willingness to co-operate in Britain's vast task of governing India.

By the time the young Aga was twenty he had taken on sponsorship of the Moslem University of Aligarh, helped lay the foundations for the All-India Moslem League, had himself publicly innoculated at the height of a bubonic plague to provide an example to his followers, and made his first visits to Europe, where he had been received by the monarchs of England, Germany and Russia. It was a formidable record. As young Aly learned about it, he must have looked at his father in a new light; as someone at the same time less mysterious and more ominous; a powerful being who was going to be as difficult to cope with as to emulate.

The Aga looked at his son differently too. The die had been cast; Aly was acknowledged as his heir. Steps must now be taken to prepare him for his future role.

# Chapter VI

*"There was a very intriguing atmosphere of mystery about Aly. But he was charming to everybody. He was very brave out hunting. Hunters are stuffy, but if you can pass muster in the Warwickshire Hunt, you can pass muster anywhere."*

—LADY BETTY DENT

Once the Aga resolved to do something about Aly, he went at it with his customary zeal. He decided to send his boy to England to be educated. A public school was briefly considered and even more quickly put aside. Aly was not prepared for it academically and furthermore the Aga had heard things about English public schools that he was particularly anxious to avoid.

He wanted his son turned into the kind of Englishman on whom the sun set only at its own risk, the imperturbable Anglo-Saxon the Aga had so admired as a youth in India, who might not do as well as a Latin at some things, seducing a woman for example, but who made up for it in brute courage, thick skin, and iron bowels. Only in "the counties," the countryside of big houses, big estates, and long pasts, did this old-world England of landed wealth, ancestor worship, horses, and hunting still go on, as if the currents of change which had been sweeping the island since World War I did not exist. The Aga asked the advice of the India Office and was directed to a man who could not only effect Aly's transformation precisely as the Aga wished, but do it with sympathy, understanding, and patience, if it could be done.

He was Charles Willoughby Waddington, Oxford classics scholar, expert horseman and hunter, who had spent his life— as had his father and grandfather—in India, first as an Army officer and later as principal of Mayo College, a "Chiefs College," which educated the sons of princes and maharajahs for their future tasks as leaders of a British India.

Waddington had retired to England to a picturesque old country house beside a water mill where he wrote poetry, painted a little, read every scrap of news about India, and rode when the weather permitted—a pleasant life—when the Aga came to see him and made him a handsome proposal.

The Aga asked Waddington to become Aly's guardian, responsible for his upbringing until he was ready to enter Cambridge University. The Aga would pay all the bills, provide everything that was necessary for Aly's preparation as a model Englishman, a credit to the Aga and to the Empire.

One can only guess at Ginetta's and Aly's reaction to this plan. Apparently to mollify them, the Aga made another proposal: that Waddington and his family bring Aly to spend part of each winter in Cimiez. That way, Aly would remain under Waddington's supervision but would not be entirely separated from his mother.

With that agreed upon, Aly was packed off to England.

Thomas Waddington, one of Waddington's sons, who was then sixteen and is today a London investment executive, recalls Aly's arrival: "He clearly had been brought up on the Continent rather than in England. He spoke English almost perfectly but with an accent. However, he fitted in very well, mostly because he was keen on sports—riding and so on. He was jolly good fun, very generous, and he had a wonderful sense of humor. He was good at things that mattered among boys, and he was tough. We always liked him. We called him 'Al.' "

Although Aly didn't show it to the Waddingtons, he was miserably lonely at first. From a household ruled by tempestuous Latin affection, where meals were bounteous, delicious, and highly spiced and life went along on no particular routine, he had been transplanted to the austere restraint of an English country house. There were no more slaps, but no more afternoons of dancing with Aunt Aimée either.

Waddington's two sons and a daughter were at boarding school, home only during vacations; the Waddingtons were gracious and welcomed Aly warmly—but they were English. His days ran on a regular schedule. Colonel Waddington hired a succession of tutors, but it was still hard to interest Aly in lessons. Sitting in the Waddingtons' library on rainy days, days broken only by a tasteless English lunch, watching his tutor's morning brightness turn to exasperation, Aly was not easily bent to the system. He could outwait, if not outwit, the best of tutors. In time, the system bent to him. Thomas Waddington recalls: "Father was extremely fond of Aly; he found that he was extremely intelligent and had a very quick and very able brain, but he was not a scholar. He wasn't interested in things of the mind. His tutors found him difficult to reach. Obviously he was by no means stupid; the trouble was lack of attention and lack of a real willingness to concentrate. I don't think there was any question of whether he could concentrate; when he was interested he could concentrate very hard. He was extremely quick, had a very retentive memory, but was easily bored and wanted to get on with something else. He was restless, both mentally and physically."

Aly's second year with the Waddingtons was better. Both Waddington boys, Thomas and Nesbitt, had become his good friends. During school vacations there was plenty of riding and play. Aly looked forward to a visit from his father, that winter, and maybe even his mother. Certainly there would be another stay on the Riviera.

Throughout the cold winter of 1926 he was anxious to get to Cimiez but the trip had to be postponed. His mother had taken ill and was in a hospital in Paris. She seemed to be recovering when, on the eve of her release after a minor operation, a blood clot suddenly formed.

Only her old friend, Gina Lamy, had been with her. They were chatting in her hospital room after lunch when suddenly Ginetta cried out: "I'm choking, I'm choking." Before a nurse could be summoned, she was dead.

With horror and disbelief, fifteen-year-old Aly learned that his mother had died.

White-faced and shaken, he rushed to Paris. Moslem funeral ceremonies were held at the newly-opened Paris Mosque. Then Ginetta's body was taken back to Monte Carlo to be buried beside her dead baby, Giuseppe Mahdi, in the Magliano family plot in Monte Carlo's hillside cemetery overlooking the Mediterranean. The romance of the Oriental prince and the Italian ballerina had lasted no longer than La Belle Epoque which spawned it. Everything else, even their marriage, had been an aftermath. Discussing it recently, Ginetta's sister Aimée said: "My sister could never understand why the Aga lived the life he did and what her life accordingly was to be like. In time she might have begun to understand, but she died and so she never did."

One week after Ginetta's death, the Aga finally divorced Shahzadi.

Aly was inconsolable. Feeling more alone than ever, he resumed the schedule that Waddington had established for him,— the restless tussle with lessons under the eye of a patient tutor, afternoons of play or of riding. He never talked of his mother— or of his father.

The Aga was busy with his own activities and rarely had time for Aly, whom he considered well placed with the Waddingtons and well taken care of. Besides, he felt the boy should learn to be more independent. In the absence of his father, Aly found other intimates. The Aga had a large stable of race horses in England. One of his jockeys, a dapper little man named Michael Beary, became Aly's closest companion—his riding instructor, confidant, mentor and guide to society. With Beary, Aly haunted the Aga's stables, begging the trainer, Dick Dawson, for a chance to ride the Aga's horses in amateur races.

All of the concentration Aly failed to show in the Waddington's library, he poured into his study of horseflesh. He was a natural rider, he had "good hands" and handled a horse with daring and authority; he became an excellent judge of horses— a quality which would stand him in good stead in later years when he became one of the world's leading horse dealers; he absorbed the folklore and know-how, the statistics, records, and pedigrees of horses the way American boys learn baseball scores.

In the world of the British landed gentry in which Aly was growing up, horses were not a casual hobby—they were a way of life; the calendar was set by the hunting seasons, the racing seasons, the horse sales, and the hunt balls.

It was at least as important to sit well on a saddle as to win an honors in classics at Oxford. A good rider, the owner of winning race horses, had a ready-made entrée into society. "There was no better way of advertising yourself," one English peer explained to me. "That's why all the *nouveaux riches* buy race horses. They don't become champion rose-growers or go in for archeology."

One of the Aga's purposes in sending Aly to the English counties for his education was to make him proficient in these important equestrian arts. At his suggestion, the Waddingtons took houses in Sussex so that Aly could hunt with the Southdown Hunt, and in Warwickshire, to be near the Warwickshire Hunt.

The foxhunting set regarded Aly with sceptical curiosity. They studied his dress. "Hunting people are very critical about such things," a friend who remembers Aly from his early hunting days recalled recently. "They notice it if you have your pin a quarter of an inch too high. Aly's coat was often open, his collar a bit askew; he was always a careless dresser, quite unvain. But his clothes were from the best tailor. He also had excellent mounts; the Aga saw to that. And he was a fearless rider."

His courage and his charm soon won over the young people.

Their elders were more reserved, and Aly soon rudely discovered another aspect of his heritage. To these upper class

Britons he was not merely a foreigner, but also colored. The cosmopolites of London might accept the Aga Khan as one of their own—London after all, was the capital of an empire of many races and peoples—but the counties were much less tolerant. "English aristocrats, the English gentle class," explained one leading member of that group, "don't like the idea of cohabitating with Indians or Asians or Chinese or anyone of color. They are very conscious of it."

The members of the hunt showed none of the outright rudeness one might find, for example, in an American country club. Good breeding and good manners held sway. "But out of earshot," recalls a long-time friend of Aly's, himself a titled British aristocrat, "they were always saying to me, 'Your greasy green friend, Aly, that old bugger, the bloody nigger, won another race'; and so on and so on—nonstop."

Only once, to this friend's knowledge, was Aly insulted to his face. It was during a horse race. Aly was in second place, pressing forward. "Give me room, give me room," he called to a rider blocking his way. The man turned around furiously and shouted: "Shut your bloody mouth, you God-damned nigger!"

2

Aly soon learned that there was more to the hunts than the hunting. There were also gay, often hilarious, hunt balls and house parties when members and their guests, many of them debutantes invited down from London for the week end, gathered in one of the larger houses for an evening that began as sedately as a Royal garden party. How it would end was anybody's guess. One of Aly's acquaintances remembers a hunt ball where an otherwise distinguished matron used an empty champagne bottle as a phallic instrument to climax a drunken dance, while titled aristocrats urged her on to greater frenzies.

Having won his way at the hunts by his riding and daring, Aly found he could thaw another segment of British society— its women—with his warm Mediterranean charm, which broke through like sunshine on the wintry English countryside.

Daphne Fielding, who was then Lady Weymouth, remembers

meeting Aly for the first time with a group of friends: "We all went to a fair near Newbury. Aly must have been about sixteen, but he pretended he was older. He took me on all the merry-go-rounds and was beside me all the time providing me with darts, shots for the rifle range, and coconuts."

Aly still saw little of his father. The Aga came to London occasionally, making his headquarters at the Ritz Hotel, attending the important horse races, escorting several aristocratic English women, one of them the possessor of an impressive title. But he never stayed for long because he did not want to be subject to British income taxes.

In the summer of 1929, he suddenly announced that he was going to marry again. The bride would be none of the highborn Englishwomen he had been courting, but a Frenchwoman, Mlle. Andrée Carron, of Aix-les-Bains. The reason for the Aga's frequent visits to Aix-les-Bains over the years now became clear. As he delicately disclosed in his autobiography, he had known Mlle. Carron "for twelve or fourteen years, indeed, since she was quite a young girl."

Mlle. Carron's father ran a restaurant and one of the Aga's biographers contends that what first attracted the Aga, and then drew him back again and again, was the way M. Carron prepared fish. This may have been the case, although the Aga was never a man without other fish to fry. The newspapers fell with cries of delight upon the love affair between the portly Aga and the little girl from Aix-les-Bains. They told how they had met when Andrée, at eighteen, sold the Aga caramels, pralines, and nougat in an Aix-les-Bains candy store. The Aga, for some reason, was outraged by this sugary anecdote and took pains to deny it several times.

In any case, by the time she married her family's old friend, Andrée was thirty-two and, with her sister, operating an expensive dress shop on the fashionable Boulevard Haussmann in Paris, a *métier* much more appropriate and more conveniently located for a good friend of the Aga Khan. She wore green and chocolate, the Aga's racing colors, at the wedding. But Aly did not attend. He was furious and flabbergasted; to him, the marriage meant that the Aga had quickly forgotten Ginetta—and him too.

Several months later Aly sulkily met his new stepmother. "He was polite, nothing more," she recalls. "It was a bit difficult for me but I understood how he felt. I had been through the same thing when I was about twelve; my mother had died and my father remarried. I tried my best to be nice." Princess Andrée even proposed to the Aga that Aly come to live with them. "A child without a mother suffers," she explained. The Aga dismissed the idea and she seldom saw Aly after that. In 1933 Andrée gave birth to a son at the American Hospital in Neuilly who was named Sadruddin. Aly refused to see him at first too. Not until years later, when Princess Andrée and the Aga were divorced and she and Aly were neighbors in the South of France, did they become close friends. They found then that they had as much in common as any two members of that widely-assorted family. "He was always so gay, so charming," Princess Andrée recalls. "His interior life? Who knows if he was happy or not. He was all mixed up but I never knew what was bothering him."

With the Waddingtons, Aly continued his training as the perfect English country gentleman. He was in full revolt now against his father, a revolt that was to power his life. He continued to fear the Aga, to respect him, often to long for his approval, but there was always an undercurrent of defiance which kept them at odds. Aly never again took his father completely seriously—nor himself.

## 3

By the time Aly was eighteen, school and studies had been left behind—the idea of going to Cambridge had been quietly dropped. Instead, Aly moved to London. Although he always thought of himself, at least in retrospect, as timid, he gave others quite another impression. One friend who met him about this time recalls him as being a youngster "with the savoir-faire of a man several years older." He had a cocky athlete's walk, sleek black hair, soft brown eyes, and a ready smile.

He also had plenty of money. His mother had left him the considerable fortune the Aga had given her, including the houses in Paris, Deauville, Cimiez and Maisons-Lafitte. The Aga continued to provide him with an allowance, until a five-million-dollar trust fund he had established would become operative on Aly's twenty-first birthday.

Aly was a first-class horseman, looking forward to riding and racing his own horses. He already had had affairs with at least three women. Henceforth, his ruling passions would be women and horses, in that order. On the racetrack he would find the recognition he never bothered to seek in more serious spheres. In bed he would make the social conquests begrudged him in the drawing room because of his race.

As he told one friend:

"They called me a bloody nigger and I paid them out by winning all their women."

## Chapter VII

> *"It is said abroad that the English have the finest women in Europe and least know how to use them."*
>
> —Sir Richard Burton, in his Terminal Essay to *The Book of a Thousand Nights and a Night*

The London to which Aly moved in 1929 was in the throes of a social revolution that wiggled its hips, stayed out all night, and ridiculed Victorian concepts of virginity and fidelity. The young upper-class Englishwoman was in revolt, seeking satisfaction and adventure on the emotional barricades that suddenly stretched from darkest Soho to a man's flat in Mayfair. The war had cast off the corsets of the Victorian era in favor of "one last fling." Postwar uncertainties threw off everything else. Economic crises, Bolshevism, restless natives in the Empire—they made the future seem not worth waiting for. Everybody was doing it, doing it, as if there were no tomorrow. The flapper wore skirts that slithered around her knees, shingled her hair in an Eton bob, and knew all there was to know, then, about birth control.

Ready and willing, she came bang-up against an obstacle: the Englishman. By and large, he was not interested in being a good lover. A hunter, yes. A trencherman, perhaps. A sportsman, of course. Those were the traditional pursuits of the Briton. But sex? That was a game for foreigners. Where so wide an opportunity existed, Aly, the English country gentleman who was not really English, finally fitted in.

It was not what the Aga had had in mind when he sent his son to live with the Waddingtons in England. But at least it was not what he had feared.

2

As Evelyn Waugh wrote in *Vile Bodies*, it was a time for parties. "There were Masked Parties, Savage Parties, Victorian Parties, Greek Parties, Wild West Parties, Circus Parties, almost naked Parties in St. John's Wood, Parties in flats and studios and houses and ships and hotels and nightclubs, in windmills and swimming baths."

Aly got to all kinds. A Wild West party he gave with seventeen other young bloods in a borrowed house in Lancaster Gate was such a rip-roaring whingding that the police had to straighten out the stampede of Rolls-Royces, Daimlers, and Bentleys and help the hosts keep out uninvited rustlers. Thirty years later, the man whose house it was still remembered what a shambles it had been when dawn came up.

With Michael Beary, Aly gave parties at the Cavendish Hotel, presided over by Rosa Lewis, the Cockney cook who had been a favorite of King Edward VII and who now, drinking vast quantities of champagne, loved to tell the young people about the backstairs escapades of their fathers and grandfathers. She still knew how to arrange a discreet liaison in the Cavendish's rooms if the situation called for one. Later, bowdlerized almost beyond recognition, Rosa became the inspiration for Eliza, the flower girl, in George Bernard Shaw's *Pygmalion* and, later still, *My Fair Lady*.

Beary introduced Aly to Edgar Wallace, the mystery writer,

a flamboyant personality of the day. A party at Wallace's London flat might include actresses, jockeys, detectives, thieves, aristocrats, and literary figures, a mixture which must have fascinated Aly and which he would one day emulate to a certain extent at his own parties. Wallace, the illegitimate son of a small-time actress, had been a soldier and journalist before he became a one-man writing factory who wrote 150 books in 27 years. He also found time to write a racing column for the *Daily Mail* and gave Aly a certain fame by mentioning his first wins as a gentleman jockey.

Aly and Beary made the rounds of all the race meetings. Aly loved the breakneck drives to the track, the tense consultations among owners, trainers, and jockeys in the paddock, the gossip with the bookmakers, the rising swell of excitement in the grandstand. As soon as he could, he bought a horse and registered his own racing colors, green and red, the Ismaili colors. When his father years before had tried to register the same colors, they had been unavailable, and the Aga had had to settle for green and chocolate. Trivial as the triumph was, Aly always grinned at the memory of it.

He made the pilgrimages to Newmarket, the Mecca of British horse racing, where horses have the right of way over cars at crossings, and everyone and his daughter turns out for the sales. Mornings found him on Newmarket Heath, watching the morning gallops with the owners, trainers, and jockeys from the hundred-odd stables and stud farms in the vicinity. He began hoping for membership in the Jockey Club, the secretive, dictatorial organization which rules British racing and has its headquarters in Newmarket. Its only known requirement is to be "a proper fellow" but it takes longer to be screened for membership than to become Prime Minister. Winston Churchill didn't make it until 1950. The Aga never became a full member, attaining only honorary status. Aly never made it at all and saw the Jockey Club interior only as a guest or as a witness before its stewards.

In 1930 the Aga entered two horses in the Derby. Rustom Pasha with Beary in the saddle was his favorite. But it was Blenheim, at eighteen to one, that won. His first Derby victory, an upset, gave the Aga the thrill of leading in the winner as other top-hatted, morning-coated gentlemen rushed up to shake hands. Behind him, elated, shouting greetings, completely in his element, strode Aly. The picture was to become familiar as the Aga's stables turned out winner after winner—Aly dogging the Aga's footsteps, both grinning. Nothing bridged the gap between father and son like a winning afternoon at the track. Racing was one thing they enjoyed in common and could always talk about.

Still, the Aga felt that Aly needed something more serious to do. Although a university education was out, he could read for the bar. His plans racing ahead, the Aga saw Aly as a barrister, standing for the House of Commons from a safe Conservative constituency, giving the Ismaili community a voice in the Parliament that governed the Empire.

Through his solicitor, the Aga met a brilliant young barrister, Charles Romer, who agreed to take Aly into his chambers in Lincoln's Inn, one of the four Inns of Court which, since medieval times, have controlled admittance to the bar in England.

Aly began studying in Romer's office. He also was required to "keep his terms"—to attend a number of dinners at the Inn, at which fine points of the law were discussed. When one of the Masters of the Inn deemed Aly ready to be called to the bar, he would formally present the candidate to the other Masters.

Aly fell in with the perquisites of the plan. He rented a house in Carlton House Terrace, close by the House of Commons, his ultimate destination, so he could "study in comfort." Then, to provide surcease from his studies, he took a week-end place in Warwickshire for the hunting. To get himself to Romer's office on time, he bought a blue Alfa Romeo which attracted a crowd of admiring law clerks and office boys whenever it was parked in the New Square of Lincoln's Inn. It wasn't parked there very often.

Romer found that "Aly was very intelligent but didn't like to work. It was not for lack of good intention but for want of application." Romer, who during his distinguished career became a High Court Justice and a Lord Justice of Appeal and who was knighted in 1944, is now retired and living in Kent. He remembers

Aly as "a charming eighteen-year-old who was not all that interested in law. He had a wide circle of friends and it was more
tempting to go around with them than to read uninteresting law
books. He read in my chambers for about a year and passed only
one preliminary examination in criminal law."

Once again, Aly hadn't chosen to take a step that was well
within his abilities. The only triumph of his legal career was won,
typically enough, on horseback. For two years he won the Bar
Steeplechase of the Pegasus Club, an organization of lawyers and
law students interested in riding.

For some time Aly kept up a pretense of reading for the bar.
It gave him a reason to be in London. And it provided an excel-
lent excuse for leaving one young woman's company in order to
see what another was doing. One of them still recalls angrily how
Aly used to disappear on the pretext that he had to dine at
Lincoln's Inn. Romer isn't sure he ever attended a dinner.

Soon Aly gave up the house he had rented near Parliament
and bought a maisonette on Aldford Street in Mayfair, the gayest
part of London. It was a narrow house, two stories high, with
bedrooms on the second floor for Aly and his Ismaili valet.
The downstairs Aly transformed into a scaled-down replica
of an old English castle, its drawing room paneled in oak and
dominated by a medieval stone mantelpiece. The dining room
reproduced a castle's banqueting hall in miniature. Aly explained
that his love of antiques had inspired this Arthurian decor, which
conjured up fantasies of bold knights and buxom wenches strain-
ing at one another through a melee of chain mail and thrusting
bosoms. As befitted the teetotaling son of a Moslem dignitary, the
bar was concealed behind a secret panel.


## 3

When Cyril Hankinson, editor of *Debrett's*, the social register of Britain, retired not long ago, he permitted himself a
discreet sigh for the vanished glories of the British aristocracy.
He said he was sorry to think "that London is never likely again
to see the cars of debutantes on their way to Buckingham Palace,

with the crowds peering through the windows admiring the women in their exquisite dresses and the men in their gorgeous uniforms."

A Court presentation was the show window of the British Empire. It was a great tourist attraction, similar in some ways to Mme. Tussaud's Wax Museum as the Best People sat rigidly in their motorized display cases. On such playing fields was the unshakeable composure of the British upper classes won. It helped, of course, to have undergone first the torments of a British public school, for by then embarrassment passed for poise.

Debutantes were presented in May, blossom time in the temperate zone.

For the Court presentation of May, 1930, the limousines began to come down The Mall in late afternoon. In one of them sat the Aga, his new wife, Princess Andrée, and Aly. Cockney fingers picked them out. The Aga was well known for his racing victories: it was hard not to recognize his rotund figure, thick eyeglasses, and fixed smile. "Good old Aga!" the cry went up.

There were cheers, too, for the season's most popular debutante, Miss Margaret Whigham, a striking girl with large deep-set eyes that dominated her face. If she had any flaw, it was her strong chin, but even that helped the overall effect by thrusting out her lower lip in an attractive pout. Born in Scotland, she had been raised in the United States, where her father, George Hay Whigham, was an executive of the Celanese Corporation of America. In her memoirs, she has said that because the homework at the fashionable Brearley School in New York "was not only impossible for me but often too difficult even for my father," he and some friends had assisted an English governess to start what subsequently became one of New York's most elegant schools for girls, Miss Hewitt's Classes. Margaret had a stammer, which made her appear shy, but this was belied by a taste for publicity that few debutantes shared in that period in England. Publicity was still considered notoriety, and faintly scandalous, like marrying a Spaniard. Not until Brenda Frazier in the United States just before World War II would a debutante so capture a country's imagination. Margaret brought color and excitement to a London made drab by depression. She was "Sunset" at the Thousand and One Nights Ball; she was "Turquoise" at the Jewel Ball. Other debutantes might have sheepdogs named Sport; Margaret had a tan poodle named Gaby Deslys.

As she was leaving the Throne Room after her presentation to the Queen, Margaret saw Aly, resplendent in a white knee-length Indian tunic with a high military collar and a white turban glittering with an emerald the size of a bird's egg. He had designed the outfit himself.

"I noticed him at once," Margaret recalled years later, "and I wondered who he could possibly be. Almost the next night I met him at a ball given by the Mountbattens at Brook House. We fell very much in love and we became engaged, unofficially."

Friends still recall how shocked they were to see them dancing cheek-to-cheek at the formal balls that year. Aly still was new on the London social scene and people asked one another about the dark young man of whom Margaret Whigham seemed so enamored.

Aly and Margaret moved in London's fastest young set. Its headquarters was the Embassy Club on Bond Street, then the smartest restaurant in London, with banquettes upholstered in red velvet and walls lined with mirrors. The table to the right of the entrance was reserved for the Prince of Wales. He often occupied it with another regular patron of the establishment, Lady Thelma Furness. Their romance was the talk of London although the press, in self-imposed censorship, acted as if it didn't exist. Another place everybody went to was the Café de Paris, to see British stars like Beatrice Lillie and American entertainers like the Yacht Club Boys. It was entered by a long, curved staircase that made every woman's arrival a spectacle. When Margaret Whigham came down those stairs, the orchestra would swing into "I've Got a Crush on You." That was her song that year.

When England went off the gold standard, the Embassy Club cut its prices and Margaret announced that "as an example to the girlhood of Britain," she would have her hair set only once a fortnight and give up wearing stockings.

Stockingless, presumably, she turned out for the reopening of the Embassy Club that September. Aly was there, too, but he sat alone. Margaret's father had rejected him coldly when he had asked for her hand. They were too young, Mr. Whigham explained. "He forbade me seeing so much of Aly, and dancing only with him at every party." Margaret recalls. "I was utterly miserable. We used to meet when we could in secret. This went on for about six months, then he went out to the East and that ended it. I would love to have married Aly. He never forgave my father." Aly was convinced that race prejudice lay at the bottom of Mr. Whigham's rejection and, today, the former Margaret Whigham does not deny it.

In February 1933, Margaret married Charles Sweeny, an Oxford-educated American and champion golfer, and was immortalized by Cole Porter in the hit song of his musical comedy of 1934, *Anything Goes*:

> You're the nimble tread of the feet of Fred Astaire,
> You're Mussolini,
> You're Mrs. Sweeny,
> You're Camembert.

She divorced Sweeny in 1946, after two children, and in 1951 became the third wife of the eleventh Duke of Argyll, Ian Campbell. Twelve years later, in the most sensational divorce suit in British jurisprudence, a Scottish judge took four and a half hours and sixty-four thousand words to grant the Duke a divorce and excoriate the Duchess as "a highly sexed woman who had ceased to be satisfied with normal relations." The decision came at a time when Britain was experiencing another sharp moral change, dramatized by the disclosure that Secretary of State for War John Profumo had been involved with call girls and procurors, notably Christine Keeler and her Svengali—Dr. Stephen Ward. A government inquiry into the scandal dismissed a rumor that a Cabinet member had figured in a group of obscene photographs which had been seized from the Duchess's desk and used against her in the divorce trial.

Still a beautiful woman, her charm and perceptiveness intact, the Duchess is understandably nostalgic for the days when London lay at her feet. About Aly: "We had a great romance. He always treated me with great consideration and great sentiment. I am pleased I first knew him then. Later he became spoilt and a playboy. Women chased him and he could get away with anything. To me he was so terribly sweet."

# 4

At nineteen, Aly already was living at top speed. London was his oyster and he devoured it with restless, limitless appetite. He combined a disarming humility with bravado and charm; he was anxious to make everyone like him and he usually succeeded. In one sphere, at least, he felt confident.

His first big romance had been with the most celebrated debutante of the day. He now fell in love with a woman ten years older than himself, the strikingly beautiful wife of a man whose family was one of the most powerful and wealthy in Britain. Her Christian name was Peggy.

They met for the first time at a Court ball for the Queen of Rumania. Aly, resplendent as usual in tunic and turban, was standing behind Queen Mary. A few days later they were both at the racecourse. Aly turned his back to the race and spent the afternoon staring fixedly up at Peggy in the stands. It was the kind of unabashed attention that flatters any woman. And it was so un-English. To Peggy, Aly appeared like an exotic Prince Charming whose flowery language and liquid admiring eyes carried her far from the brusque realities of an unhappy marriage. He had a softness and sweetness lacking in the British aristocrats with whom she spent her life. "He was most generous," she recalls today, "kind to all people without any class distinction whatsoever. You couldn't call him good-looking, but he had the most beautiful face."

Peggy's family and friends were scandalized. It was not so much that she had fallen in love with a man not her husband. That happened all the time in the upper-class British society of the day. But the rules of the game must be observed; it must all be done within the right circles, with casual British unconcern and, above all, with no scandal. How could Peggy risk her reputation and her future and that of her family with this son of the Aga Khan, ten years her junior? She seemed to have taken leave of her senses. Peggy was deaf to their protests. She was living a romance out of Omar Khayyam. Even when friends pointed out that Aly was not only highly unsuitable—but often unfaithful—she turned a deaf ear. Aly could convince her he loved only her. And it is true that though he dallied along the way, again and again he returned to Peggy.

# Chapter VIII

> ". . . Mention shall now be made of the
> Old Man of the Mountain. . . . In a beautiful
> valley enclosed between two lofty mountains,
> he had formed a luxurious garden, stored with
> every delicious fruit and every fragrant shrub
> that could be procured. Palaces of various sizes
> and forms were erected in different parts of the
> grounds. . . . The inhabitants of these palaces
> were elegant and beautiful damsels, accom-
> plished in the arts of singing, playing upon all
> sorts of musical instruments, dancing, and espe-
> cially those of dalliance and amorous allure-
> ment. . . ."
>                                    —MARCO POLO, *A Description of the World,*
>                                    1296 A.D.

It was six centuries after Marco Polo that a young and dapper Aly, fresh from his social triumphs in London, set sail for the curious world of the Old Man of the Mountain. His father had decided to send him on a tour of the Ismaili communities of the East. The Aga himself had not visited them in years although his mother, Lady Ali Shah, kept urging him to come home. He was busy in London, this time with a Round Table

Conference on India's future which the British government had convoked; as one of the Aga's biographers, Harry J. Greenwall, has remarked, the Aga always found it more agreeable to represent the East to the West than vice versa.

It was Aly's first grand tour as *Waliahad*—heir apparent— and Lady Ali Shah volunteered to meet him and act as his mentor and guide. Syria, one of the most ancient Ismaili settlements, was picked as their rendezvous.

It was difficult to guess what kind of welcome Aly would receive there. Although Syria was a country in which some of Ismailism's most romantic history had been made and where small pockets of Ismailis had held out through all the vicissitudes of their history, no Imam had visited the community since 1256.

The Syrian Ismailis had their own customs, their own leaders, their own languages—one of which, fortunately, happened to be French, which Aly spoke fluently. They had been cut off from the experiences that bound together the Indian Khojas. They were of another heritage and another race. The sudden arrival now, of a half-Italian *Waliahad*, educated in England, a habitué of the Embassy Club, the racecourses and the fashionable debutante balls of London, could have been a blunder. Except that religion flows by its own inviolable tides. When Aly's ship docked in Beirut, dozens of Ismailis, rough men in Arab headdresses, sweeping mustaches, and horny hands, strode with the bow-legged walk of horsemen aboard the ship. They made their way toward his cabin, and—suddenly losing all confidence— prostrated themselves on the deck as Aly emerged. The braver crept forward to touch his sacred person. Then they escorted him in wild jubilation to meet his grandmother. From the first moment they claimed him as their own. Aly was swept up in their exuberance. They were the kind of free, demonstrative people that appealed to him—handsome, great horsemen, some of them blue-eyed and blond, a reminder of Crusader ancestors. They had adopted the dress and swashbuckling manners of the Bedouins among whom they lived.

Aly's first visit set the pattern for the many that followed. As soon as it became known that he was due in the vicinity,

Salamiya, the principal Ismaili town in Syria, and its surroundings erupted with joy. The roads were lined for twenty miles with people awaiting his arrival. Men dashed up and down firing rifles into the air, while the women split the air with a weird tremolo wailing. Thousands converged on the town, camping in tents in an orchard of apricot trees near his house. At night they lit huge glimmering bonfires. Aly, cloaked and daggered like a Bedouin sheik, went out to join them, listening to their songs and taking part in their rugged sword dances. During the day, he rode with the men, racing them across the countryside, competing in their daring feats of horsemanship and proving—to them and to himself—whose blood ran in his veins.

Aly didn't encounter in Syria any of the "elegant damsels" described by Marco Polo—he usually brought his own—but he did learn about one of the strangest chapters of his family's past: the story of the Old Man of the Mountain and his Order of Assassins, a group whose name has become synonymous with cool, premeditated political murder and whose fantastic history has intrigued people ever since Marco Polo brought back his account of their extraordinary doings.

In the course of its bloody career, the Order of the Assassins was headed by several Old Men of the Mountain. But the first and most celebrated was Hassan-bin-Sabbah, a brilliant and brooding Persian convert to Ismailism who wandered through Syria and Persia at the beginning of the eleventh century, during the waning days of the Fatimite Caliphate, preaching and picking up followers. Needing a headquarters to accommodate his growing army of disciples, he captured the fortress of Alamut in Persia, south of the Caspian Sea.

For the next thirty-four years, Hassan closeted himself in his room in Alamut, spending his days in prayer, in compiling his religious theories, and in plotting warfare to expand his authority. His military tactics were daring; he depended on a small, highly-trained mobile force—his *fidaya*—which appeared suddenly in the enemy's midst, caused terrible havoc by assassinating a leader or two, and then quickly disappeared.

His recruiting methods were original, too. According to

Marco Polo, when Hassan spotted some likely young men in the neighborhood, he would invite them up to Alamut and ply them with hashish. While they were in a stupor, he would have them transported to his luxurious gardens and palaces peopled by beautiful damsels where, awakening, "each believed himself assuredly in Paradise." After several days of amorous dalliance, they were drugged again and brought before Hassan who assured them they had, indeed been in Paradise, and promised: "If you show yourselves devoted to the obedience of my orders, that happy lot awaits you."

Marco Polo's account may have been fanciful—and, in any case, was based on hearsay, as the Assassins had disappeared by the time he got to their land. But he seems to have been correct in at least one detail: the name "assassin" is accepted as a corruption of the word hashish—the drug made from hemp which, probably more than any elaborate arrangement of gardens and palaces, held the *fidaya* enthralled.

The Assassins spread their influence into one realm after another in Persia, Iraq and Syria, holding at their peak a string of 105 fortresses, exacting, with their threats of sudden death, tribute from as far away as Germany. The Syrian fortresses, especially, became powerful and were ruled by their own Old Man of the Mountain.

But all of this was just the means to an end, as far as Hassan-bin-Sabbah was concerned. He was, first and last, a theologian. It was he, alone in his isolated room in Alamut, who evolved the Ismailis' most remarkable religious belief—that their Imam is God, ". . . the Lord of all things in existence. He . . . possesses all the open and hidden properties of God."

It remained only for Pir Sadruddin, four centuries later, to discover that the Imam was also an incarnation of the Hindu god Vishnu, and the groundwork was complete for the fanatical adulation which Aly was encountering during his first trip as *Waliahad*.

Hassan-bin-Sabbah never claimed to be the Imam himself, nor did he try to found a dynasty (he put his own two sons to death—one charged with, of all things, murder, the other because he drank wine). But one of his successors, the fourth Old Man of the Mountain—Hassan II—was not such an ascetic. A wine-drinker himself, he found the concept of an earthly divinity irresistible. He proclaimed himself Imam, claiming he had been spirited into Alamut as a baby and was really the great-grandson of an Imam who had lost out during one of the periodic disputes about the succession a century before. He had no trouble in making his claim stick and the Ismailis accept it today. It is from him, the fourth Grand Master of the Order of Assassins, that the present family of Aga Khans, including Aly, stem. Their descent from Mohammed, their aureole of divinity, their leadership of the Ismailis, all rest on Hassan II's belated discovery of his illustrious parentage.

## 2

Despite this vital link, Aly's father always took pains to deride the story of the Assassins as a legend without historical foundation: "Assassin" was hardly a word he wanted connected in the public mind with the Ismailis.

Some Ismaili scholars, following the Aga's lead, have tried valiantly to rehabilitate Hassan-bin-Sabbah and the Order of the Assassins. Professor Jawad al-Muscati is "inclined to believe" that the word assassin comes from the name "given to the community on account of their belief in Asas, that is, the Imam." Other Ismaili writers assert that Hassan never existed or that, if he did, he was of no more consequence than a harmless crank and his followers peaceful agrarian reformers.

The word "*fidaya*" has suffered similar scrubbings. Professor al-Muscati defines it as "redeemer"; it has also been defined as "volunteer, self-offering, or devoted." But other authorities contend it means "avenger," and it was with this connotation in recent years, that Egyptian irregulars raiding Israel, and Algerian nationalists staging commando operations against the French army, have called themselves *fidaya*.

Unlike his father, Aly never disparaged Hassan-bin-Sabbah and his *fidaya* once he knew about them. Their history amused him in much the same way that English noblemen, taking visitors through their ancestral portrait galleries, like to point out which ones took mistresses and which ones were executed for treason.

Aly named his private airplane and one of his horses "Avenger." When asked about his ancestors, Hassan-bin-Sabbah's was the first name he would mention after Mohammed's.

Aly never got to visit Alamut, which lies within the borders of present-day Iran, but he did make his way to Massyat, the principal Assassin fortress in Syria. No Ismailis live in Alamut any more. When the fortress was overrun by the armies of Genghis Khan, just 178 years after its founding, it was completely destroyed along with its large library, an observatory, and a collection of scientific instruments. Eighty thousand Ismailis were killed; women and children were captured and sold into slavery. The survivors dispersed, to repeat their legends and revere their Imam in secret. The ruins, overgrown with wild grapevines, perhaps planted by the wine-drinking Hassan II, stand less than one hundred miles from Teheran, in a primitive mountainous region. The poor farmers in the vicinity know little about its history. But they have heard tales that an "artificial paradise" once existed there and they believe that the rock of Alamut itself is hollow and its interior filled with gold. When Wladimir Ivanow, a Russian who has become one of the world's leading authorities on the Ismailis, suggested to some of them that they drill into the rock to verify the legend and thereby become rich, they said a *Ganj-Nama*, an occult certificate, was needed and would be difficult to obtain. But they did wish somebody would show up with a gadget they had heard about, that saw things underground. Ivanow surmised they were talking about a mine detector.

It will take more than remoteness, time, or the efforts of embarrassed historians to banish the memory of Hassan-bin-Sabbah. He keeps cropping up in the most unexpected places. Hitler's "Eagle's Nest" above Berchtesgaden in Bavaria, bore an eerie resemblance to Hassan's Alamut, which also means "Eagle's Nest." There is a family resemblance in all the madmen who inhabit fortresses and command armies of dehumanized bogeymen in our fiction and films, Dr. Frankenstein's monster no less than James Bond's Dr. No. And, not long ago, the avant-garde author, William Burroughs, explained how he had written his fantastic account of drug addiction, *Naked Lunch*. It had been "dictated" to him, Burroughs solemnly said, by no other than Hassan-bin-Sabbah.

# Chapter IX

*"I am sending my beloved son to you, you should consider him as tantamount to my own coming. I am sending the prince in capacity of my Heir Apparent."*

—AGA KHAN III, in a message to the Ismailis of Syria, 1930

Aly went on from Syria to Bombay. Rousing sport among the descendants of the Assassins was not as important as wooing the Indian section of the Ismaili community, the Khojas, those descendants of fifteenth century Hindu converts who were now by far the most numerous and influential branch of the Ismaili community.

No one knew—or knows today—exactly how many Ismailis there are in the world; it is one of those rubber band statistics that can go as high as 80,000,000 (in a Swiss newspaper) and as low as 1,000,000 (the estimate of an Islamic scholar, Dr. Asaf A. A. Fyzee). The Aga, knowing the Westerners' penchant for dining on plump round numbers, had sometimes fixed the total at 20,000,000. This figure got no argument from the West, which always thought of Asia in terms of teeming millions out there, somewhere. Whatever the actual figure—and 2,000,000 seems generous—the Khojas whom Aly now set out to visit were the most active and prosperous of his father's visible followers.

In Bombay, Aly discovered a new kind of Ismaili. There was none of the nostalgic romance of Syria. The Khojas were a hard-headed business community. This outcast sect which his great-grandfather had moved in upon for bed-board-and-bets in 1845 had been transformed by its own energy, his grandmother's astute management, and his father's shrewd public relations among the British overlords into a flourishing hive of traders. Settled through Western India, including what is now Pakistan, they lived in compact and aloof groups among their Sunni Moslem and Hindu neighbors, who despised them as religious heretics and envied them for their industry. This corner of Western India had become the seed bed for new Ismaili communities as far away as the West Indies, Argentina, and Hong Kong. Thousands more had emigrated to the British colonies of Africa, encouraged by the Aga, who felt that Africa was India's "America," and even urged his people to intermarry with the natives to secure their position in the new homeland. The African immigrants had progressed from stoop laborers to small shop-keepers to substantial traders. Like other isolated minorities around the world, the Khojas had stuck together, helped one another, and demonstrated a tenacious ability to surmount hardship. They had concentrated on retail trade and import-export businesses where their international connections could do them the most good. When Aly got to Bombay in 1930, the city's trade in ivory, horn, cotton, hide, mother-of-pearl, grain, spices, shark fins, furniture, silk, and even opium was carried on, to a large extent, by Ismaili firms. Later they branched out into electronics, automobile franchises, insurance companies, and department stores.

In a way, Aly's presence took note of the fact that the Khojas had "arrived." Climbing higher in the economic pecking order, they were showing less interest in the droning, wailing, and teeth-gnashing of traditional Islamic worship. The successful operator of a Bombay import-export business, with branches in Nairobi and Dar-es-Salaam, with his own car, a Western wardrobe, and a son aspiring to study at Oxford, needed something new to rally his interest. Aly—of all people—supplied that need. His first trip was so successful that the Aga decided to send him every year. With his upper class accent and quite the right degree of stammer, his was the voice of the Imperial ruling class. Ismailis who read the illustrated magazines and the Sunday newspapers knew of his exploits in the Mayfair smart set, on the race tracks, and on the week-end domains of the English aristocracy— and were secretly pleased. *They* might be excluded from the English clubs, but their *Waliahad* got into some of the most amazing places. Above all, glowing like the midday sun, was Aly's charm. His breathless effusiveness might be caused by a last-minute sprint to get there on time, but once on the scene, whether it was a banquet, a mass marriage, or an inaugural visit to the far reaches of some proud Ismaili merchant's new warehouse, Aly would brighten, throw back his shoulders, and literally bound into the arena.

Wherever Aly was scheduled to appear, an adoring throng turned out, even if they couldn't understand English, the only language in which he could address them. "It was astonishing," recalls a leading Ismaili woman in Bombay, Mrs. Zarina E. C. Currimbhoy, "what faith the people had in anything Aly said or did, particularly the unlettered and illiterate people. When he entered a room, his personality simply lit it up." An Ismaili girl remembers the time Aly presented her with a medal for her work with the community's youth groups: "I was wearing a Girl Guide costume, trousers and a long shirt. He had to pin the medal on my shirt and he did it so carefully, just holding it out so I didn't feel anything. I was looking at him all the time and he was looking at the medal with so much concentration as if he was thinking only of that and that was his attitude for anything he did. Whenever he came to the prayer house, we would garland him with a big wreath of flowers; he would wear it so happily and then at the end of his walk he might jump over the ropes which were holding back the crowds and pick out some old woman over in the corner who could not even see him properly and give her the flowers."

Aly's appearances always sent the marriage rate soaring. Young men would speed their courting; young women would overcome their shyness; parents would time their negotiations so that all details could be settled in time for Aly to perform the ceremony. "Aly did it so sweetly," one girl has recalled, "never mechanically the way the Aga Khan did. He always had something special to say to each couple." It was hard work. Once, after a mass marriage in Bombay, Aly returned to his hotel and remarked to his friend, Viscount Astor, who was accompanying him: "I'm exhausted. I just married four hundred women."

Behind the Ismailis' adoration of their personable *Waliahad* there loomed, of course, the omnipotence of his father which one day would be transmitted to him—the singular Ismaili belief that their Imam is divine.

Unlike the austere bare-walled mosques of other Moslem sects where images are forbidden, the *jamat-khanas* of the Ismailis are festooned with pictures of the Imam. An Ismaili addresses his prayers, not to Allah, but to the Aga. Three times a day, at sunrise, sunset, and before retiring, he runs through the entire catalogue of forty-eight Imams, starting with Ali, Mohammed's son-in-law, and—just in case he missed one—ends by imploring: "Oh, Master Aga Khan, forgive the mistakes I may have committed in the prayers."

Ismailism is based on the Koran, but Ismailis do not study it. One young Khoja explained with a candor seldom found among his sect, and with just a touch of irony: "Our religion comes direct from the Imam, who is supposed to keep it alive and up to date through his modifications." When Aly's father visited India or Pakistan, young Ismailis were assigned in relays to write down every word he said for careful preservation and study. Ismaili spokesmen, embarrassed before Westerners by this unquestioning worship of the all-too-mortal figure of the Aga Khan, often try to explain him in terms of the Vatican and Pope. But there is a world of difference. To Catholics, Pope Paul XI is the Vicar of Christ on earth; to Ismailis the Imam *is* God.

The wily old Aga didn't set much store by religious ritual and was more interested in making sure his followers took vitamins and compounded their interest rates accurately. However, being God was a handy device for rallying the faithful. His critics insist that, far from the sceptical eyes of the West, the Aga did lay claim to divinity with such titles for himself as *Malik i yaum-il din* (Master of the Heavens).

According to one story, the Aga gave the especially meritorious among his followers letters of introduction to the Archangel Gabriel to ensure their comfort in the next world. Jawaharlal Nehru, the late Prime Minister of India, but in 1935 a political prisoner, writing from the Almora District jail for the *Modern Review*, a British publication, said: "I do hope it [the story] is based on fact. There is little romance left in this drab and dreary world, and to correspond with an Archangel is a captivating idea. It seems to bring heaven nearer, and even our life down here below assumes a rosier hue. . . ." He concludes by musing that he had often wondered "what curious quality the Aga possesses which enables him to fill with distinction so many and such varied roles, combining the thirteenth century with the twentieth, Mecca and Newmarket, this world and the next, spirituality and racing, politics and pleasure."

2

In 1932 aviation still bordered on the miraculous to the peoples of the Orient. There were flying clubs in the major cities composed of helmeted and goggled sportsmen who flew by the seat of their jodphurs in tiny fabric-and-canvas planes whose names—Puss Moth, Gypsy Moth, Leopard Moth—testified to their fragility. A British airline had flung the Imperial lifeline to Karachi and hoped eventually to reach Australia. But to the ordinary man-in-the-bazaar, flying suggested the fabulous, like the Flying Gandharvas of Hindu mythology. In this atmosphere, Aly undertook a flight from Bombay to Singapore that made every Ismaili's spirit soar. It was a trip of ten thousand miles over deserts, mountains, jungles, and rough water—"at the time,"

Aly once said, "the longest civil flight done out of India." Three planes set out, ostensibly to promote air mail service. Aly's plane was a single-engined Puss Moth. It had a professional pilot—a Major Vetch, chief instructor of the Bombay Flying Club. Aly, who had taken some flying lessons, was copilot. The third man crammed into the tiny cabin was an elderly Parsi, Naoroji M. Dumasia, an assistant editor of *The Times of India*, who on this occasion and others served as a public relations adviser for the Aga and his family. The two other planes were Leopard Moths, open-cockpit jobs, each carrying a pilot and a passenger.

They took off from Bombay, backtracked to Karachi, and then headed east across India to Calcutta. There they refueled for the leap across the Bay of Bengal to Rangoon. At each stop, giant crowds of Ismailis gasped as their *Waliahad* dropped out of the clouds like some heavenly messenger. In Rangoon, the two Leopard Moths turned back, their mission accomplished. But Aly's plane went on.

Aly told the story of his hazardous flight on many occasions, but never made it clear why his plane had been the only one to continue. He had just been trying to make people air-minded, that was all. Thirty years later in London, Peggy revealed that more than aviation had been on Aly's mind: she had been waiting for him in Penang; he had flown all those miles across the jungle simply to keep a date.


## 3

Despite the cheering crowds that greeted Aly everywhere, he was aware of a rumbling undercurrent of discontent among the Ismailis. For many years, a pugnacious little band of rebels who called themselves the Khoja Reformers, had been firing protests to and about the Aga, complaining of his long absences in Europe, his luxurious way of life there, his excessive demands for money, and the doctrine that put him in the place of God.

The Aga had never taken the Reformers seriously. Branches had popped up in various communities and, discouraged, afraid even to reveal who belonged, had disappeared. But in Karachi, a well-educated young businessman, Karim Goolimali, had become secretary of the Karachi branch and publicly emerged as a fiery pamphleteer. In November, 1932, by-passing the Aga, he took the Reformers' grievances directly to Aly, who by then was the familiar and the darling of the community. In a bitter and caustic seven-page booklet entitled *An Appeal to Mr. Ali Solomon Khan son of H. H. The Aga Khan*, Goolimali told Aly that he was being "used as a pawn in the game that your father . . . is playing." It recalled the "cult of the dagger practiced under the reign of the 'Old Man of the Mountain' at Alamut," and asserted that the history of the Assassins "is neither a fairy tale nor a thing of the forgotten past." As proof it cited several recent murders and attacks against dissenters, including two beatings suffered by Goolimali himself. It asked Aly to give up all claim to divinity and ended with the hope that "the true Almighty God may guide you."

Aly did not reply to this *Appeal*, but he undoubtedly saw that it got to the Aga. Lady Ali Shah added her own warnings. She had been successfully holding the community together. Through a secret women's organization, the *Moto Punth* (Great Religion), which she headed, she had built up so effective a network of informers that the Aga could boast that "I have a private secretary in every home," and the Reformers would complain that they were endangered "through the women of their own houses." But Lady Ali Shah was getting old (she was in her eighties) and she reminded her son that, after her death, no one would know the details of the community's affairs. Once again, she insisted he come home, but the Aga could not be budged. He had his own plans for the Ismailis; he was planning to build a giant *jamat-khana* near London and operate the community from there. Meanwhile he was preoccupied with larger matters, such as arguing India's future with Mohandas Gandhi at the second Round Table Conference in London. Finally, Lady Ali Shah made the long trip to London, her first visit to the West, to bring him home.

The Aga's long delayed visit to his people was marked by

unpleasant incidents. Indian nationalists of Gandhi's Congress Party attacked his pro-British speeches. The Khoja Reformers distributed pamphlets denouncing him and discouraged attendance at his ceremonies. There were even, according to one of the Aga's biographers, Stanley Jackson, threats to murder him. Thoroughly alarmed at last, the Aga returned to London and began casting around for a solution.

Other Eastern leaders were bargaining—even fighting in the streets—for autonomy for their people. At the Round Table Conferences and other meetings, the Aga saw the handwriting on the wall: Independence for India was inevitable and even if it came within the framework of the British Commonwealth, he and his Ismailis would be left in a minor role. They could never swing as much power as the Hindu and Moslem majorities; the Aga's influence could only decrease as new and aggressive Indian politicians came forward from the major factions.

The Ismailis, too, had their nationalistic dreams. They remembered the glorious days of the Fatimite Caliphate, and studied with interest the aspirations of another homeless religious group— the Jews. The Aga had watched as the Zionist leader, Chaim Weizmann, almost single-handedly wrested from the British the Balfour declaration that Britain "views with favour the establishment of a Jewish National Home in Palestine." He was inspired too by his racing friends, the Rothschilds, who were active in the Jewish colonization of Palestine. (On their behalf he had once approached the Sultan of Turkey when Palestine was part of the Ottoman Empire and Baron Edmond de Rothschild was seeking permission for Jewish colonization.)

The Aga decided that the Ismailis, too, needed a country of their own, some part of India which they could call home. In 1934 he raised the idea with the Indian Viceroy, Lord Willingdon. Willingdon passed the Aga's request on to London but no action was taken and Sir Samuel Hoare, Secretary of State for India, refused to discuss it when questions were asked in the House of Commons. It was a pre-emptory dismissal for the Aga Khan, who was much more intent on realizing his dream than the British suspected. For all the fine honors the British had given him—a title, artillery salutes, receptions at Buckingham Palace—he had no territory and his people had no country: both were dependent on the sufferance of others.

The Aga's fiftieth anniversary as Imam was approaching. He decided to celebrate it in a manner that would give his followers a lift and catch the world's eye.

He would be weighed against gold.

It was, he says in his autobiography, "an ancient ritual." Its antiquity among the Ismailis can be questioned. But the Maharajah of Gondal, ruler of the princely state of Kathiawar, had been weighed on the occasion of his Jubilee two years before, and the Aga was determined to give his Ismailis an even more impressive spectacle.

The "weighing-against" took place in Bombay on January 19, 1936. The wherewithal to furnish the Aga with his weight in gold had been collected from every Ismaili community in cash, checks, and pledges. The actual gold bars were borrowed for the day from Bombay banks.

At 11 A.M. the Aga, resplendent in a crimson tunic and green turban, appeared, cheered by more than thirty thousand spectators, and mounted a golden throne. On his right sat Lady Ali Shah, on his left Princess Andrée. The scales were set up under a fringed canopy and the Aga climbed up, with the help of a footstool, and slid his massive bottom on to a lavender cushion in one of the scale's trays. The gold bars were piled on another lavender cushion in the opposite tray. At 220 pounds the trays swung level. The Aga's worth in gold was 335,000 rupees ($128,800). The crowd watched, pop-eyed, but the climax of the ceremony was yet to come. After he had been helped off his lavender cushion, the Aga advanced to a microphone and announced that all the gold piled in the scale would be donated by him "for the uplift of my spiritual children." The money, he said, would be used for "all kinds of scholarships, relief by emigration from congested districts, infant welfare and other beneficial work." With one dramatic gesture, he met the most telling argument of his critics: that he impoverished his followers to support his own extravagant life.

The Khoja Reformers were not impressed. Goolimali called the ceremony a "hoax . . . it amounts to nothing short of the angler's investment of venturing a small fish to catch a big one," and pointed out that the Ismaili people had contributed the money in the first place. But to most of the Aga's followers it was final proof of their Imam's love and magnanimity.

# Chapter X

"*None of the duties of God on man is
more important than the return of the money
belonging to God from your property. Many
people are ruined by the neglect of this duty.
See that you put this money in the hands of the
Imam of your time. It is not part of your
property.*"

—IMAM JAFAR SADIQ

The source of the Aga's wealth, and Aly's, was as
mysterious to Westerners as everything else about them. They
were obviously rich—the Aga was reputed to be one of the
wealthiest men in the world—but where did the money come
from? No one knew for sure. Now there seemed to be an explanation in those mounds of gold heaped up for the Aga's Jubilee.
Newspaper photos and newsreels showed their old friend of Ascot
and the Ritz sitting in a green turban on a giant scale surrounded
by a mob of ecstatic donors.

Actually, the elaborate "weighing-against" ceremony did no
more than dramatize the age-old Ismaili custom of paying stiff

and regular tribute to the Imam. For centuries the faithful had been making long and dangerous journeys, by camel caravan if necessary, to take the Imam their gold. Ismailis in Hindustan and Turkestan had been known to throw their tribute in the sea rather than keep it, when they were unable to get it to the Imam.

The reason for this spendthrift fanaticism: An Ismaili's most important religious obligation is to make generous contributions to the Imam. He is constantly exhorted to save his soul and improve his fortunes by giving more. For every rupee he gives, he is told, he will receive: "125,000 times the return of . . . wealth in the next world." If he doesn't pay he will know hell right here on earth: of his income, "one-tenth turns into fire and the other nine parts into wood and they together burn everything . . . to ashes."

For Ismailis, religion and money, sanctity and tribute are inextricably intertwined. They have limitless faith in the Imam's divine powers and are ready to pay for them or even for the sight of his face, which they are convinced brings them good luck. When the Imam travels, granting his *didar*, collectors pass among the crowd with white bed sheets on which are tossed the tributes of the grateful. Devout Ismaili women send the tastiest morsels from their kitchens to the *jamat-khana* to be auctioned off for the Aga. Jewelry, clothing, and furniture are similarly offered and auctioned.

A young Ismaili described how he had been schooled from childhood to pay the monthly *dasoond*, or tithe, which every Ismaili gives to the Imam. It is the mainstay of Ismaili finances and brings in untold millions of dollars a year. *Dasoond* means one tenth, but the actual proportion of income a man pays may be less if he is poor or much more if he is rich or particularly pious. The young man paid one fourth, which entitled him to meet once or twice a month with the "one-fourth group" to discuss religion and ponder the Aga's latest *firmans* (admonitions). "Day by day, you got lost in the religion," he said, "and you thought that religion was the end of life and whether you lived poor or rich was no matter, you will sacrifice everything. When you are in the one-fourth group you want to be in the one-half group. Yes, there are people who give one half of all their income to the Imam. Some people give everything, they give even their homes and their dishes and their clothing. And everyone admires them. I would sit thinking: 'If only I had the courage, if only I were devoted enough to give more.' "

The money is collected at the *jamat-khana* by the two community leaders, the *mukhi*, or chief, and the *kamaria*, or treasurer, both the Imam's appointees, who total the income and dispose of it according to the instructions of the Imam. But the *dasoond* by no means exhausts an Ismaili's opportunities for proving his devotion to his Imam. According to the Khoja Reformers he gets about 275 other chances during his lifetime. There is the *chati mandu*, paid six days after the birth of a child; the *gulf* fee paid when a boy's head is shaved in his eighth or ninth year. An Ismaili can be solicited for funds when he embarks on a sea voyage and when he returns, when he becomes ill and when he recovers. If he wants to be considered a modern-day *fidaya*, he joins the *Mota Kamno Panjebhai* (Great Works Association), a secret, semireligious order, with five degrees of initiation. Its symbol, appropriately enough, is the open hand. Any Ismaili who can raise the entrance fee ($15 to $1000 depending on the degree) and keep up his payments can ascend the scale of ranks—membership can even be bought posthumously, for dead relatives. All who can afford it join, for it is at Panjebhai meetings, sitting on straw mats on the floor of the *jamat-khana*, the men on one side, the women on the other, or chatting on the verandah afterward, that a striving businessman meets the wholesalers and contractors who can do him the most good, where a doting father drops hints about his intelligent son who would like a community scholarship, and where a conscientious mother scouts suitable husbands for her marriageable daughters. The higher the degree, the better the contacts.

On his deathbed, an Ismaili gets a final chance to pay financial tribute to the Imam as the *mukhi* moistens his lips with water mixed with dust from the holy city of Kerbela, and reads about the Hindu god Vishnu's ten incarnations from *Das Avatar*.

All of these tithes, fees, and gifts are the Imam's to dispose of as he pleases. The point is explicitly made in Ismaili dogma, which repeats over and over again that all offerings are "an absolute gift to His Highness personally." It has been confirmed in the courts in a number of law suits brought—unsuccessfully—by restive fee-payers. Starting with Judge Arnould's famous decision in 1866, the courts of India and East Africa have held that the offerings "were intended . . . to be for his [the Imam's] own personal use and benefit," and he need not account for them. If, as at the epochal Golden Jubilee, the Aga decided to use them for the benefit of the community, that was a bit of personal generosity for which his followers humbly thanked him.

The sums collected are enormous. No one knows—or is disclosing—the total. Ismailis are as secretive about community financing as they are about every other aspect of their religion. Their custom has been to say nothing, except for occasional denials of such rumors as that the Imam sells his bath water. A reliable source recently estimated that today in Pakistan alone, the take amounts to 100,000 rupees ($20,000) a day—or $7,200,000 a year.

The Aga's wealth was once estimated at something between $100,000,000 and $150,000,000. The Aga himself never said how much money he had except to deny that it was as much as everyone imagined. Certainly the tithes he received from the Ismailis were only a beginning. He was a shrewd investor. He acted on tips from British friends and bought stocks like Hudson's Bay, Canadian Pacific, and British-American Tobacco. One of his biggest coups was made on Wall Street after its devastating crash of October, 1929. An American friend advised him to buy securities at their depressed prices, and the Aga, a wealthy bull in a field of wounded bears, picked up bargains like Standard of Jersey and A.T.&T. When taxes became a nuisance, he became a resident of Switzerland, and advised his sons and grandsons to do the same.

Any calculation of the Imam's personal wealth is confused by the almost incredible fact that all of the property of all the Ismaili communities all over the world is held in his name. He owns, as custodian for his sect, *jamat-khanas*, schools, hospitals, apartment houses, insurance companies, banks, jute mills, import-export houses. No outsider really knows what distinction, if any, the Imam and his followers make between the community's holdings and his own or how much of the flow of tithes stays with him and how much is funneled back to the community. Karim Goolamili recently estimated that less than one quarter got back to the people. Less sceptical Ismailis have said they didn't know and didn't care; their faith in the Aga was implicit. They regarded his lavish scale of living in Europe as no more than befits a god; they loved to see photographs of his luxurious villas on the Riviera and chuckled with delight over the news that the Aga had won again at Ascot or that Aly was buying a private airplane to ferry him about the world. Cannily, many of the Aga's followers felt they got their money's worth, for they had prospered along with their Imam. When he set up shop in London and the Riviera as social lion, diplomat, and friend of the powerful, he won for them international prestige and protection beyond anything they could have achieved by themselves in Bombay. His shrewd direction of their economic development and philanthropies raised them up out of the morass of poverty that was most men's lot in some of the poorest countries in the world. A non-Ismaili Bombay journalist, Adi N. Confectioner, recently remarked that "of India's millions of beggars, slum dwellers and destitutes, not one is a Khoja."

By the time the Aga's seven-decade reign had ended, the Shiah Imami Ismaili sect was a triumph of paternal organization and modern bookkeeping. From the cradle to the grave, from marriage dowry to convenience cooking, everything was taken care of. An Ismaili could be born in an Ismaili hospital, go to an Ismaili school, live in an all-Ismaili neighborhood in an apartment constructed by a co-operative Ismaili building society, buy it on easy terms with low-interest financing from an Ismaili bank which also would help him get started in business. Unless he lived in Syria or Afghanistan or some other place of ancient Ismaili settlement where traditional customs and local chieftains were left untouched, his life would be governed by federal, supreme, and local councils, all of whose members were appointed by the

Imam, and all of whose actions could be vetoed by the Imam. A constitution, written in English, specified how he should behave down to such details as the number of guests he might invite to a betrothal party for his daughter (ten) and what he might serve (milk or sherbet). A recent listing of Ismaili organizations in Karachi included boards of education, boards of health, Boy Scouts, (started, incidentally, by Aly, who as a lonely boy had burst into tears when Professor Grin showed him a picture of Swiss Scouts), Girl Guides, men's clubs, women's clubs, and two volunteer organizations with very specialized functions: to take care of footwear during prayer meetings and to provide fresh drinking water at community affairs.

Business and religion, politics and piety, overlapped and meshed in a warm and cosy cocoon. If some of the younger, Western-educated Ismailis chafed under the godly paternalism of the Aga and fretted at the tithes and homage exacted by him, they repressed their doubts, for the consequences of rebellion are severe. The councils conduct what amount to full-scale court hearings of charges against those who flaunt the laws and decrees of the community and hand down sentences which begin with a "calling for explanations" and range through fines to the most dreaded sentence of all: excommunication.

To a person who has been excommunicated, all doors are closed. He cannot enter the *jamat-khana* or be buried in an Ismaili graveyard. He cannot use any Ismaili institution and is forbidden to take part in communal functions and religious ceremonies. His relatives are ordered to shun him, his children will not make good marriages and his business will languish. Perhaps worst of all, he is left adrift in a hostile, or at best strange, society, for the outside world still holds terrors for Ismailis.

A young Ismaili woman from Pakistan, a Moslem nation so religiously and ethnically like the Ismailis that an Ismaili might expect to have more in common with his neighbors there than in, say, Hindu India or black Africa, recently explained that it was almost impossible for her to walk, unescorted, from her home in the Garden section of Karachi, one of the Ismaili neighborhoods, to the bus stop ten minutes away. Like other Ismaili women, she is not in purdah; therefore she is regarded "as if I were a woman of the street. When I walk down a street, often my hair is pulled, my sari tugged at, and bicycles and motor scooters purposely come straight toward me. I am even spat upon."

It takes courage to be an Ismaili but it takes even more courage to stop being one. The Khoja Reformers claim that every sort of threat and harassment, up to and including murder, have been used against would-be seceders. However, most Ismailis have no desire to secede and will do almost anything to avoid excommunication. For all but the most exceptional (like Mohammed Ali Jinnah, the "father" of Pakistan, who was born an Ismaili but drifted away from the faith), to leave the Ismaili fold is a step backward, away from the progressive social views and institutions of the sect, the advantageous business deals, the banks, co-operatives and shiny new apartment houses, the mobile pharmacies, the coeducational schools, the emancipated position of Ismaili women. It means, also, the abandonment of the cosy camaraderie of the *jamat-khana* and the sense of kinship with Ismailis all over the world. A young Ismaili student in London explained that although he no longer believed in many of the tenets of his faith, he would never consider leaving the community. "As an Ismaili," he said, sitting in one of the deep armchairs of the Ismaili Centre in London, "I can go anywhere and I will be welcomed as a brother by other Ismailis."

*Chapter XI*

"*Edward VIII might still be on the throne
of England today if not for Aly.*"

—ELSA MAXWELL

Old friends still believe that Peggy was the "great
love" of Aly's life. He was very much under the spell of
this beautiful woman, so at ease in society, so knowing in her
tastes. He learned a great deal from her. She was the first "adult"
since his mother who really seemed to care. He must also have
been secretly pleased at the sensation his romance was creating
in London—and the consternation it was causing the Aga.
Peggy was to say years later that Aly never really loved anyone
but his mother. But in London, in the 1930's, he gave every
appearance of being deeply in love with her. He begged her to
marry him; she hesitatingly asked her husband for a divorce.
But her father-in-law refused to permit it.

All London—the London privileged to know such things—
knew about Peggy and Aly, and kept it a secret from the press
and unprivileged public. The same London knew when Aly
strayed from Peggy and in one way or another let her know
about it. Friends, sentimental one moment, malicious the next,

watched to see how it would all turn out. Against all odds, the romance lasted for four years, but finally moved to a dismal end.

One day a friend called Peggy from the Hotel Berkeley. "Come right over," she said. "From my room you can see Aly with another woman across the street at the Ritz."

Peggy asked Aly about it later. He blandly denied that any such thing had happened. She gave him two weeks to confess. When he didn't, she finally and sadly broke with him.

The Aga was so relieved to see the romance end quietly without a scandal that, partly as reward, partly as consolation, he sent Aly off on a trip to the United States. He hoped Aly would forget Peggy; he never dreamed that the woman who would replace her in Aly's affections would represent an even greater danger to his reputation in England.

2

Lady Thelma Furness was in the United States visiting her twin sister, Mrs. Gloria Vanderbilt, that cold winter of 1934. While waiting in New York for a ship to take her back to England, she went to a small dinner party given by Mrs. Frank Storrs. On her right sat Aly, a heartbroken Aly, perhaps, but not too distraught to respond to a pretty woman. In *Double Exposure*, the witty autobiography which she published jointly with her sister, Gloria, in 1958, she recalls that he immediately "turned his battery of charm on me." A few days later Lady Furness sailed for England; Aly had told her he would be in Florida. When she got to her cabin, she found it massed with red roses, accompanied by a series of extravagant notes: "See you in London, Aly"; "Love, Aly"; "You left too soon, Aly."

The following morning she was having breakfast in bed when the telephone rang. "Hello, darling," said a voice she couldn't quite place. "This is Aly. Will you have lunch with me today?"

"Where will it be, Aly?" she replied. "Palm Beach or New York?"

"Right here," Aly said laughing. "I'm on board. I finished my business and flew back just in time to make the ship. Did you like the flowers?"

As the great ship plowed through the Atlantic, closer and closer to its rendezvous with history, it is important to locate the very special position held by Lady Thelma Furness at that moment in history. In March, 1934, she had been for four years the close companion of the Prince of Wales, the debonair bachelor who was heir to the throne of the British Empire. Slim, elegant, her raven hair pulled tightly into a bun, she reigned as the unofficial queen of London's smart set. She was an American, having been born Thelma Morgan in Lucerne, Switzerland, in 1905, one of the identical twin daughters of the American consul there. She shared with her sister Gloria a dark and Latin beauty, the gift of a Chilean grandmother, that launched her into society as neatly as if they had been Wall Street Morgans, and not relatively impoverished Morgans from Louisiana. At sixteen, Thelma had married James Vail Converse, a New York man about town; she had divorced him and tried Hollywood, where she counted Charlie Chaplin among her close friends. Meanwhile, sister Gloria at seventeen had married Reginald Vanderbilt of the New York Vanderbilts. Thelma moved on to England, where in 1926 she married Viscount Marmaduke Furness—Duke to his friends— the shipping heir and horseman who incidentally owned Gilltown, an Irish stud which the Aga was later to buy. They had a son, Tony, but the marriage was going badly, by her account, when she met the Prince of Wales at the Leicester Fair "pinning rosettes on cows." He invited her up to London for dinner. She recalls her feelings when she entered his private sitting room in St. James's Palace: "It marked officially the beginning of the break-up of my marriage to Duke, although it was not until many months later, when I was sitting with the Prince beside a campfire deep in the African veldt, that this fact became clear to me."

In Africa, while Duke busied himself elsewhere, the Prince and Thelma stalked animals and each other. "This was our Eden," Thelma wrote (there were forty persons in the party), "and we were alone in it. His arms about me were the only reality; his words of love my only bridge to life. Borne along on the mounting tide of his ardour, I felt myself being inexorably swept from the accustomed moorings of caution. Each night I felt more completely possessed by our love, carried ever more swiftly into uncharted seas of feeling, content to let the Prince chart the course, heedless of where the voyage would end."

Back in London, Thelma and the Prince spent long week ends at Fort Belvedere, his retreat near Windsor Castle where he "pottered in the garden, pruned his trees, blew on his bagpipes" while she did petit point. Thelma taught him how to do it too; his first project was a paperweight for his mother, Queen Mary. The Prince was a frequent guest at Thelma's London apartment; at cocktails one day, he met two of her new acquaintances: Ernest Simpson, an American-educated English businessman, and his American wife Wallis. It is "nonsense," asserts Lady Furness, that there was an immediate attraction between the Prince and Mrs. Simpson. "I came to regard her as one of my best friends in England, and the Prince and I often would include Wallis and her husband in our parties. The Prince, consequently, saw her at least once a week for the next three and a half years."

In 1934, Thelma decided to visit the United States to see her sister Gloria, now a widow. It would be her first long separation from the Prince since their romance began. She lunched with Wallis at the Ritz just before sailing. "Oh, Thelma, the little man is going to be so lonely," Mrs. Simpson said. "Well, dear," Thelma remembers replying, "you look after him for me while I'm away. See that he does not get into any mischief."

Now she was returning to her Prince in a stateroom studded with roses from Aly Khan and with Aly himself on board. Aly, not yet twenty-three (Thelma was twenty-nine), had cockily taken on the most formidable competition that England, if not the world, had to offer. The Prince of Wales was "the most eligible bachelor in the world," a man of thirty-nine years, considerable experience, and celebrated charm, whose title and position in those balmy days of Empire held as much prestige and glamour and promise as any man could offer a woman.

Aly was not abashed. Far from it. That kind of contest with

a stronger man challenged him. Lady Furness recalls that "Aly
was always untroubled. He gave me the impression that he
thought himself tops—the best rider, the best dancer, the most
attractive man on the international scene." She bade him farewell
and went to meet the Prince of Wales. But not for a romantic
reunion. The Prince seemed distracted; their conversation stumbled until, over coffee, the Prince suddenly said: "I hear Aly
Khan has been very attentive to you."

"Are you jealous, darling?" Lady Furness replied. She said
later: "There could have been no possible basis for any real
jealousy." The Prince didn't answer and they parted coolly.
Thelma went to see Wallis, seeking "a friend's advice," and was
assured: "Darling, you know the little man loves you very much.
The little man was just lost without you." Just then the telephone
rang, and Wallis's maid announced that the Prince of Wales was
calling.

There was one more week end at the Fort, where the Simp-
sons, as usual, were guests. No petit point this time. Thelma
watched the Prince and Wallis closely until the point struck her
like a darning needle. "Wallis—Wallis, of all people."

That was the end of Thelma and the Prince, at least that
prince. She rejoined Aly in Paris and proposed they go to Spain.
"I don't know what made me think of Spain, but I wanted to go
somewhere quickly. And I knew Aly—part of his attraction was
that he was one of the few men in the world ready to do anything
anywhere, any time. He had no ties, and he was adventurous.
My gesture at this moment was one of defiance more than anything else, and I'm sure Aly knew it."

The following morning they left for Barcelona, Aly driving
at his usual breakneck speed, sometimes more than a hundred miles
an hour. Thelma loved it: "Aly was the ideal person with whom
to do all this. He was gay, attentive, impetuous, jealous. There
is in Aly, however, a strong Eastern quality that is not realized
except by women who have known him well. His ways of thinking, his desires are, in his mind, unquestionably 'right' where
women are concerned. He makes demands that he expects to have
unquestioningly accepted."

They went on to Paris, Ireland and Deauville, where Thelma took over Aly's villa for the season while he became her house guest. Gloria was there too. They spent mornings on the beach, evenings in the Casino. At the Deauville sales, Aly bought Thelma a horse—a gesture he was to make to other women in later years. But by the end of the summer, the romance had cooled. Aly had won the contest but he did not claim the prize.

Thelma rushed off to New York, where her sister Gloria had been accused by their mother, Mrs. Harry Hays Morgan, and her sister-in-law, Mrs. Harry Payne Whitney, one of America's richest women, of being unfit to have custody of her ten-year-old daughter by Vanderbilt, Gloria Laura. With names like Vanderbilt and Morgan involved, the case became the most sensational custody suit of the decade. After several of Gloria's servants had trooped to the stand and given a keyhole view of high society which included insinuations of adultery and Lesbianism, the court gave custody of little Gloria to her aunt, Mrs. Whitney, although her mother was found fit enough to have the child on week ends.

By December, 1936, when King Edward VIII broadcast that he was giving up his throne for Mrs. Simpson, the Morgan twins, Gloria and Thelma, were in the dress business in New York. Years later, after World War II, Aly and the Duke of Windsor became neighbors in the South of France, where they struck up a friendship, drawn together by similarities in their lives that outweighed past differences.

# Chapter XII

> *"Aly started off more or less like other people with the thought of founding a family and settling down. But that was not being sincere with himself; that was not his true nature."*
>
> —MARIO MAGLIANO

Thelma Furness was not the only woman Aly had been seeing in Deauville that summer of 1934. At a dinner party he met the woman he was to marry. The fact that she was already married, and to a member of Parliament who came from a distinguished English family, may only have whetted his interest. There is a story, probably apocryphal, that Aly ignored the tall, blonde, haughty-looking Mrs. Thomas Loel E. B. Guinness during most of that dinner party, but that at one point when the company suddenly fell silent, he turned around to face her and, perhaps to cover the silence, perhaps on some prescient impulse, said in a loud voice: "Darling, will you marry me?" She is said to have smiled, and the others to have laughed, at Aly's wit.

The laughing soon ceased and turned into horrified reactions among Mayfair's smart set. The gossip about Aly and Joan Guinness sent shivers of anticipation (female) and apprehension (male) up and down some of England's proudest spines. There were mutterings in the best clubs that Aly, though a fine chap, of course, and the old Aga's boy, was after all a colored man, probably possessed of some mystic Oriental charm not available to the best bred Englishman.

Joan was three years older than Aly, a shade taller in high heels; she wore her hair in a bun and a prim expression on her face—at first glance, an incongruous choice for Aly. But he saw in her the epitome of the elusive aristocratic Englishwoman he had been taught to admire by his father, the Waddingtons, and his life in the counties and London. As for Joan, she was all that she appeared to be—poised, impeccable, mature for her twenty-six years—and yet, there was in her background an indication, a cluster of genes, perhaps, that made her susceptible to the kind of excitement and gaiety that Aly promised and, given the opportunity, delivered.

On her father's side, it was all martial ruffles and drums extending back into England's history. She was the eldest of six children of Lord Churston, a former aide-de-camp to the Viceroy of India. On her mother's side, the music took on a livelier beat. Mother, before her marriage to Churston, had been Denise Orme, the Gaiety Girl—born Jessie Smithers, the daughter of a bartender. Denise Orme had captivated her music-hall audiences with her tiny waist, long eyelashes, and coquettish singing of "No One Ever Marries Me." (As it turned out, three men did—first Lord Churston; then, after twenty-one years of marriage, he divorced her naming as corespondent Theodore Wessel, who became her next husband; that marriage was dissolved six years later in Tahiti, and in 1946, at the age of sixty-one, she married the Duke of Leinster, six years her junior, who later was to sell his life story under the title, *My Forty Years of Folly*.) As one friend said: "Joan wasn't really as stuffy as she appeared." At nineteen, she had married Guinness, whose family were bankers and related to the Anglo-Irish brewing family. He had been educated in the United States and, for a short time after their marriage, they lived in New York where he was serving a young banker's apprenticeship. In 1932 they had a son, Patrick. As was expected of bright young men like Loel Guinness, he had embarked on a political career and been elected to Parliament as a Conservative member for Bath. He was a busy man, too busy in August 1934 to spend the entire holiday with his wife in Deauville.

What ensued was explained with an expressive Gallic shrug by Julien Duclos, the tall, urbane Frenchman who presided, omnisciently, over the Casino at Deauville in those days as he still does today: "Mr. Guinness was a charming, very charming, very amiable gentleman. And his wife, Mrs. Guinness, she was gentle, very English. You know, English morals are somewhat reserved. But we are not saints. Men are not saints. Women are not saints. Sometimes women have faults. They are like everybody else. They have their tendencies; they have their leanings. She was no exception to the rule; she was like everybody else."

Guinness was unsuspecting at first. But in January, 1935, he later told a London divorce court, he went to Australia on business and, as a thoughtful husband would, arranged for his wife to spend a holiday in Switzerland with a party of friends. He returned via Milan and learned there that his wife hadn't gone to Switzerland, but to South America.

In April, Guinness testified, he met with his wife at her mother's house in London. She told him that she "had formed an attachment" for Aly Khan and wanted Guinness to divorce her. Guinness said he did everything he could to persuade her to give up the prince, but he was unsuccessful. They parted, and she went on to her new life.

Between April 17 and April 20, Guinness testified, his wife and Aly Khan were in Paris, sharing a hotel suite. In June, Guinness filed suit for divorce, naming Aly as corespondent. It was case Number 936 on the court's docket—the divorce rate was rising in England—and there were several months of waiting before it came up for a hearing in November. Joan did not defend herself. Judge Bucknill heard Guinness's testimony and read an affidavit sent by Joan's attorneys from Paris. Then he granted

Guinness a *decree nisi*, which meant that it became absolute in six months. Guinness won custody of little Patrick. Aly was ordered to pay all the costs of the suit.

While waiting for the divorce to become final, Aly and Joan went to Nassau, leaving their numerous friends to speculate about what would happen next. An incredulous London could not believe that the freewheeling Aly really planned to slow down. There were rumors that other scandals involving Aly were about to explode. He later told a friend: "I had been involved with several women. I was tired of trouble. Joan was a sane and solid sort of girl and I thought if I married her, I would stay out of trouble." He was also much more committed emotionally than people imagined.

The week after Joan's divorce became final, she and Aly were married in Paris. Although the ceremony was supposed to be secret, someone alerted the press and the usual contingent of reporters showed up. The bride, in a green dress with a white collar, carried no flowers. Aly wore a blue pin-striped suit, with a flower in his lapel. They drove to the *mairie* (town hall) of the Sixteenth Arrondissement, Paris's most sophisticated quarter, followed by another limousine carrying the Aga and his wife, their two-year old son, Sadruddin, and Mrs. Guinness's mother, now married to Theodore Wessel. The mayor sped through the ceremony, pausing only to praise the Aga's work in India and Geneva. The wedding party posed for pictures and then got into their cars and drove to the Paris Mosque. There, they removed their shoes and entered the Hall of Prayers. Years later, Joan remembered sitting on her haunches on the deep carpet while a *mullah*, Ben Kalifa, intoned a service in Arabic. She had no idea what he was saying. She did remember that just as the ceremony was beginning, Aly realized he had forgotten some papers, and rushed out to the car to retrieve them. She sat there, bewildered, peering around the dimly lit room, her legs cramped.

The Aga paraded out of the Mosque, holding Sadruddin's hand, and grinning broadly. He told reporters that the couple would go to India for their honeymoon and while there, a third— Ismaili—ceremony would take place. But within months it became evident the trip would have to be postponed. Joan was pregnant. She and Aly went instead to the Riviera to visit the Aga and his Princess at Villa Jane-Andrée. (The Aga's pet name for his wife was "Jane.") An ornate luncheon was planned in their honor. Joan arrived on time—and alone. One of those present noted "how English she looked. She wore sports clothes. She was friendly, but very reserved." It was a massive French luncheon. Course after course was served. Yet it was over before Aly arrived, out of breath and grinning. "Nothing had really changed, I remember thinking," the long-memoried luncheon guest recalls. "Aly was still being detained for mysterious reasons and still had the most elaborate excuses."

2

If Naples was the place to die, Geneva was the place to be born, at least for members of the international set. The hygiene of Swiss hospitals, like the scholastic polish of Swiss schools later on, was considered indispensable to the young. A room was reserved for Joan in a fashionable private clinic in Geneva. On December 13, 1936, a son was born. (Two days before, Edward VIII had abdicated.) The baby was described as premature; the marriage was eight months old. He had a crown of black curly hair. His skin was ivory despite all the whispers that Aly might well father a "black" baby. Only the baby's eyes, with their slight almond cast, gave the slightest clue that one of his paternal grandparents had come from somewhere east of Mayfair. He was named Karim, which means generous and is one of the ninety-nine names for God on the Moslem tabir, or rosary.

Aly had rented a ten-room chalet in Gstaad, a winter resort which had been developed by the Rothschilds and had immediately replaced St. Moritz as the place to go if you wanted to stay ahead of the crowd. But after two months there, Aly was restless. The honeymoon he and Joan had never taken, a grand voyage to the East, seemed possible now. In fact, it had to be taken right away, for Joan was pregnant again.

Karim was left behind in Gstaad with his English nurse as his parents sailed for Karachi. There and in Bombay, and Nairobi, Joan got a demonstration of what it was like to be a *Waliahad*'s wife. She and Aly were greeted with parades and by mobs of people who whooped with joy, prostrated themselves in the path of their car, and stood for hours for a glimpse of them. Surrounded by the shouting crowds, Joan, in her picture hats and flowered dresses, sometimes looked like an English lady tourist who had been swept up in a riot.

They returned to Switzerland where their second child, another boy, was born on September 13, 1937, nine months to the day after Karim. As Aly was frequently to point out: "Premature babies run in our family." The new baby was even fairer than Karim and had a fuzz of reddish-blond hair. He was named Amyn, one of the nicknames Mohammed bore before he became the Prophet. Soon afterward, Joan and Aly left on another trip, this time to Egypt, Turkey, and Syria. The Syrian Ismailis greeted them deliriously, remembering Aly's first visit; Aly was their very own.

Joan took her marriage seriously from the start. She was sympathetic and curious about her husband's people. She became a Moslem, taking the name of Tajudowlah, and studied Persian and Arabic. She also shared Aly's interest in horses and, a week after their return to England, registered her own colors: green with a red crescent; Aly's were green with a red sash. As Viscount Astor, who knew her well and later became one of Aly's close friends, said: "She was an admirable wife."

The Aga and Andrée came to Gstaad at midwinter to help celebrate the birthday of one of the lesser prophets of Islam. "Christmas always was a big event," recalls Halldis Poppe, a stout and jolly Norwegian nurse, known affectionately as "Poppy," who had come home from the hospital with Sadruddin when he was born and stayed on as nurse, comforter, and companion to all the family. Poppy and Andrée spent weeks assembling the decorations and gifts for the big Christmas party given for all the family's friends. Aly would dress up as Father Christmas and arrive at the house in a sleigh. "Everyone left with his arms full," a former playmate of Sadruddin's recalls. Sometimes the role of Santa Claus was taken by Aly's chauffeur, Emrys Williams. Aly would then captivate the children by going up to him and, in a wee small voice, inquiring: "What have you got for me this year, Father Christmas?" Santa would reply: "I have nothing for you because you've been a naughty boy." The children would roar with laughter while the adults just shook their heads.

Neither the Aga nor Aly found anything incongruous about their celebrations of Christmas. Jesus, after all, was recognized as one of the prophets of Islam. And in any case, they were never parochial in their attitude toward religion—or anything else. They moved with equal aplomb from a meeting at Newmarket to a *durbar* in a *jamat-khana*. Their friends included people of every religion and color. Paradoxical as it may sound, Aly was almost oblivious to religion, certainly to religious differences. A woman who happened to spend a Christmas, years later, with Aly and Rita Hayworth recalls with amusement and amazement that on Christmas morning, Aly presented her with a gift. "I'm Jewish," she said, "and Aly was a Moslem. What do you suppose he gave me? A crucifix set with amethysts."

When the season waned at Gstaad, Aly and Joan moved on. They might briefly separate as in early 1939, when she went to Greece, he to Cairo. They met again in Nairobi where they visited the Aga Khan Girls' School, the Aga Khan Night School for Boys, the Aga Khan Library, the Aga Khan Ladies' Library, the Aga Khan Child Welfare Centre, the Aga Khan Dispensary, the Aga Khan Club, and the Aga Khan Ladies' Club. Aly also dropped by the Aga Khan Bungalow, which the community had given his father.

Then they went on safari into the Masai Reserve, where Aly got a lion and a leopard. They flew back to Gstaad to see the boys and then on to Paris and London for the opening of the Season. Their headquarters, for Paris, was the rambling country house of Aly's training farm at Maisons-Lafitte, outside the city. Summers they spent in Deauville at the Villa Gorizia. There were still women in Aly's life besides Joan, like the blonde, tubercular French actress, Corinne Luchaire, who rose to stardom on the strength of her role in *Prison Without Bars.* Some Joan did not know about; others she may have forgiven. None were serious and she understood Aly. They were compatible in many ways and she was the kind of woman who, having made up her mind to something, would stick to it.

She shared Aly's friendship for Peter Beatty, the second son of the late Admiral of the Fleet, a tall, thin bachelor who had inherited a fortune of nearly a million and a half dollars (mostly from his mother, who was related to Marshall Field, the Chicago department store magnate). Aly and Beatty got together when-ever Aly was in London. Through Beatty, Aly met the handsome family of Joseph P. Kennedy, then U.S. Ambassador to the Court of St. James. (Beatty was attentive to Eunice, one of Kennedy's daughters who eventually married R. Sargent Shriver, a wealthy young Yale graduate and one of her brother John's most effective aides in his 1960 Presidential campaign.) Beatty became Aly's closest friend since the gardener's son of his Cimiez childhood.

Beatty, although a year older than Aly, was taken by Aly's sophistication and worldliness, and especially by his knowledge of horses. Beatty was a horseman too, and frequently came to Aly for advice. The Aga's stable was by now one of the best in Europe and Aly was in large measure responsible. In 1938 Aly made one of the most sensational purchases of his career, Bois Roussel, an unknown three-year-old which three months later romped away with the Derby. Unfortunately, Aly had not bought the horse for himself, but for Beatty. The Aga was furious.

Later in the same 1938 season, Aly sold Beatty one of his own horses, Foxglove II. Twenty-four hours later, Foxglove came home ahead in the Ascot Gold Vase. Said Aly afterward, above the roars of the crowd: "I am perfectly delighted. My father begged and implored me not to sell him, and told me I was a damned fool to do so. But why not? It is my fun and sport to buy horses and sell them. . . . I tell you I get a hell of a kick out of it. Besides I backed him for quite a bit myself, although I could not get better than three to one. Anyway, Peter Beatty is a great friend of mine."

Aly professed never to have regretted the Bois Roussel or Foxglove II deals. In part it was pride; he never liked to admit disappointment or acknowledge mistakes, a trait which sometimes made him seem cavalier in the face of much graver situations. But in large part it was the way he felt about friends, a kind of spontaneous generosity, on a grand scale, that was particularly endearing. Aly, his close friends felt, was a man who would give them the shirt off his back and, while there is no record of exactly such a gift, he came close. Once, Jean Cocteau, the French author and artist, admired a pair of red evening shoes Aly was wearing. Aly slipped them off and handed them to him.

## 3

In 1937 the Aga was unanimously elected president of the League of Nations Assembly. In one sense, it was the culmination of his career as a world statesman. In another, it marked the beginning of a series of events that still remain a conundrum. Back in 1931 he had been one of several prominent men invited by the BBC to tell what they would do "If I Were a Dictator." The Aga had said he would rectify the errors of the Versailles Treaty and unite Germany and Austria, among a list of other things about which few persons could argue. In May, 1936, in an article published in the London *Sunday Express*, the Aga again speculated on "If I Were a Dictator," again declaring that he would "make of Germany and Austria one nation, restoring to them such truly Germanic territory as has been acquired by others." The Aga's views hadn't changed, it seems, but circumstances had. What had been a clever broadcasting stunt in 1931 had become a dangerous game in 1936, with Hitler threatening to do that very same thing by force in an uneasy Europe. Certainly the Aga's views, so prominently restated at this time, were noticed by the Nazis, who were seeking friends wherever they could. In October of 1937, just after the Aga had been elected League president, he accepted an invitation to visit "the New Germany" and meet face-to-face with Hitler. He conferred also with Propaganda Minister Paul Joseph Goebbels, clue enough as to what use the Nazis were making of this visit by a leading Moslem dignitary, longtime ally of the British in the East, and officer of the League of Nations.

At Berchtesgaden, the Aga and Hitler fell to discussing horse racing, and the Fuehrer was astonished to learn that one of the Aga's stallions was worth more than forty German automobiles. (When war came, Hitler's agents got a better bargain; they simply stole all the stock in the Aga's French stables.) The Aga came away bearing a framed and autographed portrait of Hitler and what can only be described as a benevolent view of the Nazi dictator: "Hitler is a very great man." He wrote the *London Times* that Hitler was "a firm pillar of peace. Why not take him at his word?"

The Aga was not so naïve that the Germans could have subverted him with a signed snapshot and some heel-clicking. Something had happened to damage his affection for the British. All the signs point to his pique over their rejection of his request for a territory, however modest, of his own. In October, 1938, the month after Prime Minister Chamberlain had flown to Munich to help Hitler slice up Czechoslovakia for the sake of "peace in our time," the Aga raised the nagging issue again in a long memorandum to the then Viceroy of India, Lord Linlithgow.

If he did not get a territory in which he was sovereign, the Aga wrote the Viceroy, he feared that "my heirs, if not myself, may be subjected to annoyance and attack by possibly unfriendly local governments in the future, by way of penalizing the loyalty of my House to the British Government for a century past."

Nothing ever came of the Aga's memorandum.

When war came on that balmy Sunday in September, 1939, the Aga's reaction was, to put it mildly, puzzling. In Deauville for his annual holiday, he cabled his Ismailis: "Heartfelt loyal unstinted service must now be given to the cause of the Empire, which is the protector of our faith and liberty."

He himself packed up Andrée, Sadruddin, and Poppy and headed for Switzerland. He had decided this was not to be his war. "There was no occasion for diplomatic or political activity on my part such as I had undertaken in the First World

War," he wrote later. "No great Muslim power was involved . . . my duties and my responsibilities were no more and no less than those of any other private citizen."

Yet the Nazis, if some of their captured documents are to be believed, still considered him a possible ally. In July, 1940, probably the low point of the war for the Allied cause, a German agent, Prince Max Hohenlohe, sent a letter to Berlin about a conversation he had had with the Aga in Switzerland. The letter, sent to Walther Hewel, the German Foreign Office's liaison officer with Hitler, reported: "He [the Aga] asked me to convey to you the following with a request that you relay it to the Fuehrer. The Khedive of Egypt, who is also here, had agreed with him that on the day when the Fuehrer puts up for the night in Windsor, they would drink a bottle of champagne together. He knew that the King of Egypt would do likewise with them if he were present."

Other captured Nazi letters indicate that Von Ribbentrop, the German Foreign Minister, was interested in using the Aga as a vehicle for German propaganda. But Hewel finally decided that "while the Aga Khan's views were of interest, his financial interests were so bound up with the interests of Britain that he could hardly be used."

When the correspondence was published by the United States government after the war, and after the Aga's death, Aly called it "nonsensical. My father fought all his life for Britain."

# Chapter XIII

*"You shouldn't say you were happiest*
*while there was a war going on, but I think*
*that's a sentiment a lot of men feel. Those were*
*some of the happiest years of my life."*

—ALY KHAN

There was no question in Aly's mind where his sympathies lay. He had always considered himself a victim of injustice—all kinds of injustice—and he was as aroused by the Nazis as if they had singled him out. "I thought it was essential that the world should be rid of Hitlerism," he later explained.

Not since the death of his mother and the Aga's remarriage had he taken such sharp issue with his father. The Aga was waiting it out in Switzerland. Aly headed for Paris and joined the Foreign Legion. He had visions of rugged basic training at Sidi-bel-Abbès, the Legion's headquarters in Algeria where a mixed bag of six thousand volunteers, mostly anti-fascist Germans, Spaniards, and Italians, were being indoctrinated in the Legion's motto: *"Legio Patria Nostra"*—"The Legion is our homeland," and readied for battle against their former homelands.

But when you are the son of the Aga Khan, you are seldom

allowed to do things the hard way. And when you are as fond of good living as Aly, you seldom push your good intentions to the limit. Aly was posted to Beirut to the headquarters of the Commanding General of the Army of the Levant. His Legion record—a meager document, stored in the archives at Aubagne, the small French town near Marseilles where the Legion has taken refuge now that Algeria is independent—gives no evidence that Sub-Lieutenant Aly Khan, serial number 4702, ever got near the dusty streets of Sidi-bel-Abbès. While the French Army of the Levant prepared to attack Germany, Aly enjoyed what pleasures Beirut had to offer. His frequent companion was Count Charles de Breteuil, a big bear of a man who had taken leave of his publishing ventures in Africa to become a Spahi cavalry officer. After the war, he loved to regale friends with a story more revealing in its gaps than in its few details, of a mad midnight chase with Aly through the corridors and over the balconies of a Beirut apartment house. It seems impossible, but Aly was carrying a saddle as they fled.

The war was going badly. France fell to the Germans and some of the French officers in Syria wanted to surrender there too. Others, convinced that the British had betrayed them, were ready to go over to the Axis side, taking the forty-five thousand French troops in Syria with them. Everyone waited for orders from the tremulous Vichy government of Marshal Pétain.

Aly, shocked by the turn of events, argued against surrender. He was not even a Frenchman, but he was committed to the defeat of Hitlerism. When it became obvious that the Legion was not going to fight (the French forces did surrender), he resigned his commission and joined a motley stream of anti-Nazi officers and men moving south from Syria and the Lebanon into British-held Palestine. Besides other disenchanted Legionnaires, there were Madagascans, Annamites from Indo-China, Algerians, Tahitians, a Lebanese camel corps, Spahi cavalry and troops from metropolitan France. Aly made his way to a reception camp at El Mansûra on the Mediterranean, which the British had set up to receive those who wanted to switch sides. There, in the shade of an old Roman aqueduct, Aly found the Royal Wiltshire Yeo-

manry encamped. It was an elite outfit of English country gentlemen and farmers, the descendants of yeomen who had banded
together in 1794 against Napoleon. Among its officers were old
friends like Lord Weymouth, whose wife, Daphne, an adolescent
and eager Aly had once taken to a country fair, and the Earl of
Cadogan, who had married Joan's sister. It was like old times.
They took Aly in hand and got him a commission in the Royal
Wilts, and Second Lieutenant The Prince Aly Khan (No. 157269)
was promptly posted to military intelligence in Cairo.

2

One of the most eccentric figures an army ever nourished
headed the section of British intelligence in Cairo to which Aly
was assigned. He was Major Alfred D. Wintle of the Royal
Dragoons, a bantam, wiry professional cavalry officer who had
lost an eye and part of a hand in the First World War. Wintle
spoke German and French so faultlessly that he could pass for
either. The monocle he wore turned his face into a sceptical dart
aimed at the world.

When France had fallen, Wintle, still in Britain, had decided
to save the French air force by himself. He had posed as a British
Air Ministry official and ordered a plane to fly him to France
where he was sure he could persuade unhappy French pilots to fly
back to Britain with him. Before he could get off the ground,
his ruse was discovered, he was sent to the Tower of London for
court-martial and shipped off to Cairo as punishment.

He and Aly took to one another on sight. Both were indi-
vidualists, fearless, pledged to no cause that they had not chosen
for themselves. Wintle found Aly a "natural" intelligence officer.
"The real meaning of intelligence," he recently explained, "is to
know what the enemy is going to do. You have to be in their
frame of mind. You have to be capable of intuition. The ordinary
child remains in his nursery until he goes to a preparatory school
where he meets people exactly like himself. He reaches the age of
eighteen or twenty without ever having left the particular en-
vironment in which he was born. Now I was born in Russia and
lived in Germany and France. Aly was the same. From infancy he

was traveling, seeing new faces, sizing up new situations. He had that lifelong habit of expecting and noticing any change."

Wintle's principal concern soon after Aly arrived was to learn if and when the Germans might send troops to reinforce the beaten Italians in the Western Desert. The British could not afford to be caught unprepared. Aly and Wintle discussed the prospect endlessly. "One day," recalls Wintle, "I said to myself: 'If I were a German I should now be in the Western Desert.' I had nothing to prove it to my commanding officer, nothing to show and say, 'Here are their footprints.' I just knew."

Wintle was sitting in his office, his intuition turned on full, when Aly walked in. "You know," Aly began, "I think the Germans must be in the Western Desert by now." The two men fell to examining every scrap of enemy material British patrols had picked up on the desert. "We finally found a cartridge with a K stamped on it," recalls Wintle. "I said, 'That's it.' The Italian alphabet has no letter K."

Unbeknownst to the British, the first units of General Rommel's Deutches Afrika Korps had indeed been moving up under the cover of a large Italian force. The British stopped reducing their forces in the Western Desert. Even so, the Afrika Korps was able to smash ahead into Egypt, almost to Suez, before General Montgomery's Eighth Army counterattack at El Alamein finally ended the Axis threat. But that lay in the future. In the meantime, Wintle moved up to Jerusalem to take part in another British move in the Middle East. He took Aly along, since two intuitions might be better than one.

The British were planning to attack Syria. This was home ground to Aly. His friends of London days, even his fellow officers of the Royal Wilts, never saw in him a potential Lawrence of Arabia, but he now gave it a try. Under Wintle's supervision, he organized a cloak-and-dagger outfit which used Ismailis as scouts. It was a small, hit-and-run reconnaissance force, and Wintle, whose heart still belongs to the Dragoons, shrugs it off as nothing much. If it did nothing else, it temporarily turned the Syrian Ismailis into Assassins again.

On June 8, 1941, the British crossed the Palestine border. They expected little resistance. Instead, the Vichy French fought fiercely, offering stiff opposition as British, Indian, Australian, and Free French troops moved over the corkscrew roads that ran below the steep cliffs of Lebanon's mountains.

Ahead and on the flanks of the advancing Allied troops roamed Aly's Ismailis, reporting on enemy troop movements, blowing up bridges, holding vital road crossings. Whenever Aly could get away from his desk in Jerusalem, he joined the unit, often with Wintle. The front was fluid and never far away, Wintle recalls. "We would just get in a car and head north. Everything was so confused. We knew when we had crossed into Syria only because the neat rows of telegraph poles which the British had put up in Palestine suddenly went off in all directions, leaning over, with old bottles for insulators. We would drive along and then get off the main road looking for sport."

Once three Syrian Ismailis came all the way down to Jerusalem, infiltrating the British lines as if they didn't exist, to see Aly. The British officers with whom Aly shared a bungalow were dumbfounded when the swarthy men, catching sight of Aly, prostrated themselves at his feet. What made the scene remarkable was not the Ismailis' veneration for their *Waliahad*, but Aly's aplomb—except for a bath towel, which he clutched about him, he was stark naked. He had just stepped out of the tub.

Finally Damascus fell, British troops pierced Syria all the way to the Turkish frontier, and the Vichy commander asked for an armistice. Before returning to Cairo, Aly organized the Ismailis who lived on the Mediterranean coast into a network of coast-watchers to give warning of any attempts by Axis forces to land in Syria for subversion or sabotage.

Wintle, now retired and living in Kent, England, where he writes novels and children's stories, gives Aly his highest accolade: "Old Aly was a bit of a Zulu, but he would have made an excellent cavalryman."

3

Aly, who moved as easily from one army to another as from one social group to the next, got permission from the British to join General Georges Catroux, the Free French commander

and High Commissioner in Syria as the General's *chef de cabinet.*
Joan joined him in Beirut; the boys were in Nairobi with their
English nurse, Doris Maude Lyon. Catroux assigned Aly a sumptuous villa which had once been the governor's residence. The
days were warm, the nights cool; the views of sea and mountains
refreshing; after a while, it was hard to see the war. Aly felt
himself sinking into a familiar slough. Restless, he returned to
Cairo with its sweltering climate and teeming intrigue. But Cairo
was a dichotomous city: at war and at peace, pro-British and
pro-Axis, civilian and military; its intense and ingrown social life
divided into hundreds of fragments, each redividing and breeding
new intrigues. It was like life in Lawrence Durrell's Alexandria.
(Durrell also was in British intelligence in Cairo during the war,
but he never met Aly.) The city's prewar foreign colony had
been augmented and then overwhelmed by refugee Poles, Greeks,
French—thousands of bored, desperate people who sought release
from their frustrations in one another. England shuddered under
the Nazi blitz, Russia was aflame, but in Egypt—officially neutral
and uncommitted, but a principal Allied base and headquarters—
there was plenty of food, oil, pleasure cars, social clubs and
horse races.

For Aly and Joan, who joined him there with the boys, life
was not much different than in Paris and London. They took a
house on Gezira island, a pleasant residential suburb with wide
streets lined with flame trees and elegant private homes. The
Gezira Sporting Club had a race course, polo grounds, a golf
course and swimming pools. Aly acquired several horses and rode
there every morning. Karim and Amyn swam with the other
officers' children.

In the prevailing manner of Cairo in 1941, Aly and Joan
entertained lavishly. Huge tents were erected in their garden
over bounteous buffet tables; orchestras played for dancing on
portable wooden dance floors. Old friends kept turning up. New
ones, some destined to become close and lifelong, were made.
Peter Beatty arrived, in navy uniform, a volunteer in the Commando Brigade in the Middle East, as dangerous a job as a man
could ask. At a party one evening, Aly noticed Beatty doing
something odd; he was holding up one hand in front of his face,

as if trying to make sure he could see it. He repeated the gesture curiously all evening. Yet he was cold sober.

Through Beatty, Aly encountered William Waldorf Astor, a lieutenant-commander in Naval Intelligence, the eldest son of Virginia-born Lady Nancy Astor, who had been Britain's first woman M.P. Astor and Aly had met casually before the war, but Astor, four years older, had found Aly "gay" and "irresponsible, rather like the public image one had of him in the newspapers." In Cairo, and later, Astor reappraised him: "I realised how basically serious and intelligent he was. His father had been immensely overeducated and as a reaction had given Aly a poor education. Aly was really like old King Edward the Seventh: he knew everything except what was written in books."

Other new friends were Nigel Campbell, a tall and sandy-haired lieutenant in the King's Royal Rifle Corps, and Major Alexander ("Xan") Fielding, an intelligence officer who had just returned from organizing anti-Nazi resistance in Crete. Fielding later married Lady Daphne Weymouth, whom Aly, at sixteen, had so impressed at the county fair and whose first husband had helped him get into the Royal Wilts.

Then came "The Flap." General Rommel's Afrika Korps was advancing, while British General Montgomery's newly formed Eighth Army, for all its Lend-Lease equipment, was still untested. Nothing seemed to be able to save Egypt and Suez. Cairo's fitful gaiety squealed to a sudden, frightening stop. Its Allied colonies overnight found themselves in the thick of things, surrounded by hostile, loot-hungry Egyptians waiting for the Germans to arrive. Families were hurriedly evacuated to South Africa, India, and Kenya—to wherever they could get passage and find safety. Joan fled with Karim, Amyn, and their nurse to Nairobi.

Cairo waited, like a drunken prostitute between customers. At El Alamein, Montgomery's Eighth Army met the Afrika Korps and turned it back, smashing not only Rommel but, once and for all, the Axis threat to the Middle East. Before 1942 had ended, the Americans had landed in North Africa to meet up with the British in a vast pincers movement that reopened the Mediterranean. The Russians stopped the Germans at Stalingrad.

Nazi Europe's southern coastline became, as Winston Churchill called it, a soft underbelly.

Alone in Cairo, Aly put in long days as an intelligence officer, and longer and longer evenings as Cairo's optimism revived its social life. The son of the Aga Khan had entree everywhere.

He was particularly attracted to the Polish colony, where the women were especially beautiful, the men especially adventurous, and good talk flowed like vodka. They were brave, even fool-hardy people, frustrated and rebellious, their homeland lost, their pride tingling, an island of Slavic emotionalism in a sea of British calm. One of the Poles with whom Aly became friendly was a remarkable woman whose name, at least when she was born, was Krystyna Gizycka: her married name was usually given as Countess Skarbeck, but in Cairo she was known as Christine Granville. Slim, dark-haired, and deep-voiced, she looked and dressed like Greta Garbo. She had won a beauty contest in Poland at the age of twenty and gone to England to compete for an international beauty prize. There she had married and moved to East Africa. When Poland fell and Britain entered the war, she had joined another of those deceptively named British organizations, "First Aid Nursing Yeomanry," or FANY, which trained her for things other than bandaging the wounded. She was sent into Hungary, a German ally but a corruptible one, to establish an escape route across the Carpathians into conquered Poland. She made her way into Poland to lead out fugitive Polish soldiers and escaped British prisoners of war who then went on to Turkey and freedom. Twice the Gestapo arrested her; both times she got away. She was between missions in Cairo when Aly met her. He was to meet her again during the Allied invasion of Southern France when they both were working with the French underground. On that occasion, she brought him news of "Xan" Fielding who, on a secret mission, had been captured by the Vichy French and sentenced to death. Christine had learned where Fielding and two other British prisoners were being held. First she had reconnoitered the building, whistling "Frankie and Johnnie" so Fielding would know she was near. Then she had boldly walked in the front door and confronted the commandant:

"The Allies are coming this way. If you want to escape a firing squad, you had better release your three British prisoners *tout de suite*." The Vichyite stared at the slender woman, flinched, and muttered an order to release the men.

After the war, Christine Granville sank out of sight, as if it had been her only reason for existence. When the British gave her the George Medal, with a citation calling her "one of the bravest women in the world" (she already had the French Croix de Guerre), she was working as a telephone operator in London. She then became a stewardess on ships, plying the Australian route. In 1952 she was strangled in a cheap hotel in Kensington by a porter whom she had met aboard a ship.

# 4

Joan's departure with the boys might have come anyway, even without the Nazi advance on Egypt. One of their close friends in Cairo recalls: "Aly and Joan were not getting along. There were difficult moments, better moments, difficult moments again. There were weeks when they seemed very cold to each other. Then everything was marvelous again—up to a point."

Karim, only five years old when they moved to Nairobi, knew that there was more to the separation from his father than the war. He had overheard gossip among the servants, and snatches of arguments between his parents, he told a friend years later. He was a sensitive child, easily upset, given to nightmares, restless at his lessons. Amyn was cheerful, elfin, as blond as Karim was dark. In Nairobi they occupied the large frame house with broad verandahs and wide lawns that the Aga's East African followers had given him so that he would have no housing problem during his visits to race-conscious Nairobi—there had been some unpleasant incidents in the past. The two youngsters were a handful. They rode their bicycles at top speed in the garden, hurdling ditches and hedges; Karim once prevailed upon the chauffeur to let him "drive" the car and promptly steered it onto the front lawn. They had their own playhouse, an elaborate affair, electric trains, and a giant collection of lead soldiers the Aga had sent from Switzerland. Joan, to her credit, managed to discharge her responsibilities to the Ismaili community as the wife of its *Waliahad*, and to stay on good terms with the English colony.

Karim and Amyn took part in special ceremonies at the Nairobi *jamat-khana*, sometimes wearing the miniature officers' uniforms, complete with insignia, Sam Browne belt, and saber, of the Ismaili Volunteer Corps, a para-military organization that reflected the spirit of the times. Sometimes Nairobi's leading Ismaili businessman, Count Sir Eboo Pirbhai, sent his son, Badruddin, over to play with them. Badruddin Eboo now is a law student in London and the president of the Ismaili community in Great Britain.

Aly seldom got to Nairobi to see Joan and the boys. Whenever he had leave he visited the Ismaili communities in Africa and India, for with the Aga neutralized in Switzerland, Aly was Imam in everything but name. He relished his new importance, giving dignified, statesmanlike interviews which reflected the propaganda broadcasts he was also making for the British to the Middle East. "One thing which must be realized—and which cannot be too strongly emphasized—is that the Eastern races, which have had in the past great civilizations, will never cooperate fully with any form of government which begins and ends by putting racial inferiority in any governmental programme—an avowed tenet of the Nazi creed of a dominant '*Herrenvolk*.' " He himself was a handsome symbol of tolerance in his British major's uniform, crisscrossing the lines of racial and religious demarcation.

Aly, also, throughout the war, managed to keep half an eye on the family's racing business. The Aga, expecting a long war and possibly an Allied defeat, had wanted to sell out the stables. Shortly after the outbreak of war he had telephoned his old friend, the Earl of Carnarvon, in London and asked him to sell all of his bloodstock to an American buyer for £300,000. "It didn't come off, for one reason only," Lord Carnarvon recalls. "The American who would have bought the lot didn't come; his wife wouldn't let him because the first neutral ship to try to cross the Atlantic got torpedoed." It seemed up to Aly to keep things going. In Bombay, he would dash out of an Ismaili *jamat-khana* to get to a bloodstock sale. In Ireland, his old guardian, Charles Waddington, who had come out of retirement when the young men left, to manage the Aga's stud farm, helped Aly buy—anonymously—a stud farm at Clonsilla, County Dublin, which, added to his other properties, gave him an impressive Irish estate for future expansion.

In 1943 Aly was sent to Tripolitania as the military mayor of a small area, a job where his charm with people stood him in as good stead as it had in Cairo's drawing rooms. Again he demonstrated his ability to change hats without mussing a hair; he got on famously with his Arab townspeople. Years later, when he was making arrangements to marry Rita Hayworth in the little French Riviera town of Vallauris, he interrupted the long and complicated negotiations to swap experiences with Vallauris's Communist mayor, Paul Derigon. "We discussed housing and water supplies," Derigon recalls. "The Prince was very interested in all of our problems. He said he'd enjoyed being a mayor and would like to do it again sometime."

# 5

It was during his wartime tour in Cairo that Aly entered into one of the more enigmatic and enduring relationships of his complicated life. When Aly's will was read in 1960, his friends and family were astonished to learn that he had left $14,000 to a Mrs. Sybilla Szczeniowska and $56,000 to her son, Marek Szczeniowski, then sixteen. There was no bequest for an older son, Matthew, then nineteen. With Bettina and Viscount Astor, Mrs. Szczeniowska and Marek were the only persons outside of Aly's immediate family and employees to be named in the will. Their surnames were even misspelled. Aly's London solicitor declared that Mrs. Szczeniowska was "a complete mystery: I only know her name and address." Karim refused to discuss the bequest, saying: "It concerns the private life of my father and I prefer not to speak of it."

Only a very few intimates from Cairo days recalled her as the shapely blonde wife of a minor Polish diplomat, whom Aly had met in 1941 at a party given by the Polish Minister. She was twenty-one years old at the time and had recently arrived with her husband from Hungary. Of medium height with narrow-set blue eyes, fair complexion, and a Roman nose, she wasn't beautiful but was electrically attractive. She had a low, almost husky, voice and a charming manner. She made friends easily; she was the kind of woman whom men take to immediately—warm and witty, interested in their problems, high-spirited, and, at the same time, sensual. She was an ebullient talker and an excellent listener. She also had an easy, amused tolerance of mankind's peccadilloes. She didn't demand perfection of her friends nor of herself.

Aly was attracted immediately and he and Sybilla were seen together in the swirl of Cairo's social life. They met again in Heidelberg in 1945 where Aly was serving with still another army, the American, and Sybilla was working for the Polish Red Cross. The following year she visited him in Paris. Until 1953 when Sybilla, having separated from George Szczeniowski, left Egypt to emigrate to the United States, Aly visited her whenever he was passing through Cairo. In 1948 he stopped long enough to sit for his portrait. Sybilla was painting then and she did a serious, rather poignant picture of Aly. He didn't like it, but she did; she felt she had caught the real Aly. Reminiscing recently in her East Side Manhattan apartment, Sybilla, now a dress designer, was still lively and attractive. Marek, now called Mark, was away at Kenyon College in Ohio; he plans to use his inheritance from Aly to study medicine. Sybilla was remarried in 1958, to a businessman named Jorge Sorondo; they recently had a baby girl.

"Aly was a serious person, really," Sybilla said, "and a little sad; that's what I tried to catch in the portrait. He was happiest when he was completely caught up in the war or when he was with his Ismaili people. Then he would work from morning to night, he would be relaxed and content. Sometimes, stopping off in Cairo after visiting his people in Syria, he would spend all night talking about them, how beautiful it was there and how interesting they were. He was extremely happy when he was on his horse farms with the people who looked up to horses. This was something that would put him at ease too; it was one of his worlds.

"He needed something to get completely locked in. Socializing was not it. It had no depth to it. It was fun, kept him busy, but I don't think it made him very happy. I remember in Paris in 1946, he was a different person than I had known during the war. There were always twelve or sixteen or eighteen people around. He was in a constant rush. He couldn't seem to be quiet. He could not be alone. I talked to him about this, but I never got any answer. He went to bed late. He was up at eight. Often I had telephone conversations with him at eight in the morning. He couldn't sleep more than two or three hours, he was—like—pushed.

"I don't think he made real friends easily. He had lots of people who liked him. There were always women; he loved beautiful women. The men who were his friends were completely devoted to him and he was devoted to them. To him, this kind of friendship was the most important thing. He depended on it. He wanted to be able to count on people come hell or high water. He would get very angry if someone he trusted let him down. Even if he had invited you for dinner and you called and said, 'I can't possibly do it, because of something or other,' he would be angry, even though he might do the same thing to you sometime.

"What stands out when I think of him is his tremendous warmth, his being a friend above everything. I always had the feeling that if anything went wrong with my life, he was one person who would never turn me down, whatever it was I needed."

In 1957 Aly visited Sybilla in New York. He was then divorced from Joan, had married and divorced Rita Hayworth, and was Pakistan ambassador to the United Nations. He suddenly remembered his portrait. "Do you still have it?" he asked. Sybilla brought it out. Aly studied the sensitive, serious face for a while. "Finally he saw it was a good portrait and he wanted absolutely to have it," she remembers. "I gave it to him and he hung it in his New York apartment."

When Aly's bequest to Sybilla and her son was made public, they explained to inquiring newspaper reporters that when Marek was born in Cairo in 1944, Aly had wanted to be named godfather but it was impossible because the family was Catholic and Aly a Moslem. So Aly had become his "spiritual godfather"; he had remembered Marek every Christmas and given him occasional gifts. The $56,000 trust fund would be his when he reached the age of twenty-one.

The obvious conclusions about Aly and Marek were drawn by some, and flatly denied by Mrs. Sorondo when interviewed for this book. "I know a lot of people would like to think that two and two makes four," she said. "I always considered Aly my best friend. That is all there is to it." Why had he left such a large sum of money to her and Marek? "It is typical of Aly's generosity. He always said he wanted to pay for the portrait. I think that in this way he finally paid what he thought to be his debt."

# Chapter XIV

*"You could send Aly out on a mission
where he'd have to be out all night in the snow
and ice and it would never get him down. He
was not deferred to and he was not looked
down upon either. He was just treated as
another man, which is what he liked."*

—Henry Cabot Lodge

At dawn of an August morning in 1944, an Allied
armada descended upon the Riviera like a guest without a reserva-
tion. The Nazi occupiers fled after only token resistance.

Streaming off their landing craft, the Americans, Free
Frenchmen and Canadians pushed north in the hope of linking
with the invasion force that had landed in Normandy from
England nine weeks earlier, thus springing a trap on the German
armies in France. As the war moved past with hardly a glance,
the long, curvesome, luscious, golden body of the Côte d'Azur
lay naked and unwanted in the August sun. But to Major Aly
Khan it was home.

Shortly after D-day, he had arrived in St. Tropez, assigned

at his own request to serve with yet another army, the American—
his third since the war had begun. Behind the tank traps on the
beaches and the shuttered camouflaged buildings along the coast,
Aly saw his old familiar haunts. And, as usual, he had a few
personal, as well as military, objectives in mind. As soon as he
could he headed for Cannes, which was wildly welcoming its
liberators. Stopping at the Carlton Hotel, which was closed, its
entrance barred by a Nazi blockhouse, Aly banged on a side door
until a porter emerged.

"Have you a room?" Aly demanded, marching into the
office of the hotel's director, his old friend, Jean Mero.

Mero fell on Aly as if he were a one-man army of liberation.
Here, in steel helmet and battle dress, was visible proof that the
gay old times were back.

"I'll open up the royal suite for you!" Mero cried. He told
Aly where he could find his tennis pro of prewar days, Tommy
Burke, who as an Irishman, and therefore a neutral, had been able
to stay in Cannes throughout the German occupation. Aly
rounded up Burke and confided that he had a private mission to
perform before getting on with the war. In a jeep they set out
along the coast road toward Golfe Juan until they came to a
bridge which bore the sign "Chateau de l'Horizon."

"Let's take a look," Aly said, and drove across a bridge over
the railroad tracks into the Chateau's grounds, overrun with
weeds and coiled with barbed wire. Aly walked around, ignoring
the danger of mines, and looked at the sea side of the house with
its shiplike decks and giant swimming pool; he studied the windows of the house as if trying to divine the number of rooms
inside. Satisfied, he got back into the jeep and they drove on to
Cap d'Antibes. All the houses on the Cap had been taken over
by the enemy, first the Italians and then the Germans, with one
exception: Villa Jane-Andrée, the Aga's home, which they now
approached.

Aly sped past a sputtering gardener at the gate and stopped
in front of the house, where a handsome blonde woman stood
on the terrace steps, looking as indomitable as a lioness defending
her cubs. She was Ketty Bréant, a friend of Andrée's who

had come down from Paris in 1943 to live in the house and keep an eye on it. She warily watched the intruders, one in helmet and battle dress, the other in shabby civilian clothes.

"I want to occupy the villa," the uniformed man shouted at her. Her face froze.

"The Italians didn't," she replied. "The Germans didn't." She smiled and turned on the flattery. "Certainly the Americans are not going to."

The man whooped and bounded up the stairs. Only then did she recognize Aly and fall weeping into his arms.

Aly visited her several more times. But soon it was time to move on. Aly had been assigned to a special intelligence unit of the American Sixth Army Group that would have the prickly job of maintaining liaison with the Free French troops and with local resistance groups that had sprung out of the underground when the landings began. At Ramatuelle, in back of St. Tropez, he reported to his new commanding officer, a former United States senator from Massachusetts who had resigned his office to serve in the army—Lieutenant-Colonel Henry Cabot Lodge.

The meeting of Aly and Lodge was a confrontation of two worlds. Lodge, a tall and imposing Boston Brahmin, a distillation of America's austere Puritan tradition, was the grandson of an isolationist United States senator who had led the fight to keep the United States out of the League of Nations; Aly, a man of no particular country, at home in all, undisciplined and sensual, was the son of a Moslem internationalist who had been president of the League of Nations Assembly.

Aly eyed his new commander uncertainly. The charm so successfully deployed in civilian life would not work here. He would have to prove himself in tougher terrain. He found an opportunity as the unit raced up the Rhone Valley alongside the combat troops, on its mission of co-ordinating French and American military movements. It was tricky work. The French were sensitive. They had their own political scores to settle, some of which at times took precedence over the American desire to push on through France into Germany. Lodge soon discovered that Aly's knowledge of the countryside, his fluent French, and his

*1) His mother was the center of young Aly's universe.*

*2a & 2b)*
*The dreamy boy who sat in a tree for hours became heir-apparent to a god's throne.*

*3a & 3b) 1938 . . . In the Aga's shadow . . . 1954*

*2c) The scandal was over, but the principals at Aly's wedding to Joan nonetheless looked distracted. (Andrée is between Aly and Joan; the Aga is at the right.)*

4a) *Joan was out in the cold . . .* 4b) *. . . on Rita's wedding day.*

4c) *Chateau de l'Horizon: Women took pot-luck with Aly.*

*5a) With Gene Tierney . . .*

*5b) with Bettina . . .*

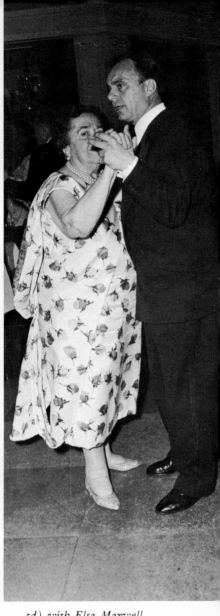

*5d) with Elsa Maxwell.*

*5c) with Kim Novak . . .*

*6) Eastern Aly . . .*

7) . . . and Western Aly

8a) *Funeral march: Aly, Karim, and the Begum took the Aga's body to Aswan for burial.*

8b, 8c, 8d) *Aly's friends: Juliette Greco . . . Lise Bourdin . . . Bettina.*

8e) *As painted by Sybilla Szczeniowska: "Aly was a serious person, really, and a little sad; that's what I tried to catch in the portrait."*

uncanny ability to set up waves of sympathy between himself and whomsoever he met, from whatever country or walk of life, were invaluable. He particularly remembers Aly's help on a complicated co-ordinated attack which required the full co-operation of the Free French units in the area: "We had to do a delicate job of persuasion. Aly was extraordinary." It was the kind of excitement that Aly thrived on. His physical hardiness astonished his fellow officers. Lodge recalls that "he hardly ever slept but he never got tired." Any initial apprehensions the Americans might have felt at having a Moslem prince in their midst were quickly dispelled. This prince put on no airs, and expected no favors.

During that frigid winter, as the American campaign stalled in the Vosges mountains, Aly, Lodge, and Lodge's executive officer, Major Chandler Bigelow, also of Boston and today the president of the South Boston Savings Bank, shared a small house called *Sapin Bleu* (Blue Pine) in Vittel. One evening they decided to entertain their commanding officer, General Jacob L. Devers. The house had a fireplace and, knowing that the general would enjoy an open fire, Lodge "detailed Aly to clean the chimney, secure the wood, and be sure that the fireplace did not smoke," Devers recalled. "Aly discovered that the chimney needed cleaning so he proceeded to get some advice on how to go about this task. He was told he needed a rope, a small tree, and that with a man on the roof pulling the tree up through the chimney by means of the rope—he would have the job in hand. Aly couldn't find anyone to get on the roof, so he climbed up there and finished the job himself."

When things let up a little, Lodge arranged a special leave so that Aly could visit the Ismaili community in India. He came back laden with gifts: gold earrings mounted with sapphires for Bigelow's wife, a large bracelet studded with small sapphires for Mrs. Lodge, and an armload of trinkets for the enlisted men to send to their families.

By then one of his closest friends was yet another American officer, Major Gordon Grand. One of the things that drew them together was a love of riding. During the closing days of the war they captured some Italians who were on horseback. "We rigged up a van and hitched it to the back of a jeep," recalls Grand. "The Italians took care of the horses. Every morning at about five we'd have a little ride. I can see Aly now in his British uniform, riding those captured horses in the Black Forest. He would assume the racing position and we'd go like the wind. We took the horses with us when we crossed the Rhine. We still had them with us when we went into Heidelberg at the end of the war."

Grand, now a vice-president of the Olin Chemical Corporation, says flatly that, "of all my friends, I enjoyed Aly the most. He was a real man. He had three qualities: physical vitality, humility, and love of people. If you and he were congenial, then you were friends. He didn't care whether you were rich or poor. Money meant nothing to him. He was completely unpretentious himself. I remember one day Aly was sitting outside the door of Cabot Lodge's office waiting to see him. It was freezing. I said: 'Why don't you ask Cabot if you can wait in his warm office?' But that would never have occurred to Aly."

When in June, 1945, General Devers was ordered back to the United States, Aly came into his office to say good-bye. "He had tears in his eyes," Devers remembers. "He said, 'I wish to tell you personally that my service with the Sixth Army Group has been for me the happiest days of my life.'" Devers later awarded Aly the Bronze Star. The French gave him the Legion of Honour and the Croix de Guerre with palm. The American citation notes that he showed "tireless energy, marked industry and constant willingness to undertake any task, regardless of its hazards or its irksomeness."

Aly had not been in close touch with his father since the war began. He knew almost nothing about the Aga's living conditions in Switzerland. They were luxurious as always, but boring. Switzerland, a haven to thousands of refugees during the war, was zealous about its neutrality. The Aga, a voluntary refugee, was in the position of an amateur house painter who, setting out to do a floor, paints himself into a corner. The Swiss had requested him to give up all political activity. He was cut off from his influential friends and from his usual sources of income. He had nothing to do but wait.

He had rented a chalet in Gstaad but, with Andrée and Sadruddin, spent part of every year at St. Moritz, and in that way kept up at least the illusion of a change of scene. But the Aga's life followed what for him was a stultifying round. At St. Moritz, for instance, where he took half a floor of the Palace Hotel, one apartment for himself, his secretary, and his valet and another for Andrée, Sadruddin, their servants, and friends, he would send for "Sadri" each morning at nine—he never entered the family apartment himself—and spend and hour or two talking to him about politics and world affairs. Then he played golf at the Samedan links, trailed by Sadri and a young French schoolmate, Patrick Fuchs, who often vacationed with the family. Fuchs recalls the Aga with some awe: "The first time I saw him, the Aga was completely nude. I met him in the hall. He wasn't embarrassed. He wasn't anything. He just said, 'Hello.' "

When the Aga's golf game was finished, he and the boys ate lunch in the hotel dining room at a small table in an alcove reserved for them. After lunch they played chess.

Sadri, a plump, conscientious youngster, was seeing a good deal more of his father than Aly had, and enjoying a much more normal childhood. He attended a small private school, Taurnesol (Sunflower), with a dozen select students who received almost individual tutoring and spent as much of their time in rugged outdoor athletics as studying. At home the Aga employed a full-time coach for Sadri, a former ski instructor named Alfred Tochterman who took the boy and his friends skiing in the winter and mountain climbing in the summer. Andrée, aided by the indomitable Poppy, busied herself with the household and such social life as wartime Switzerland had to offer.

There was another, seldom seen and never mentioned, member of the Aga's entourage in Switzerland too, a tall young woman from prewar Cannes, Yvette Blanche Labrousse, the winner of the "Miss France" beauty contest in 1930. Relations between Yvette and the Aga had been close for some time. In 1938 he had built her a twenty-one-room mansion on a hillside in Le Cannet, above Cannes, romantically named Yakimour to combine their names with the French word for love, *amour*. In

1943 the Aga suddenly announced that he intended to divorce Andrée to marry Yvette. The following year they were wed. The news must have shocked Aly. He had met Yvette before the war and disliked her instantly.

For some time now Aly had been worrying about his peace-time future. The war had brought him a measure of maturity and independence he had never known before. He felt he had been accepted on his own; he had never been happier. He considered staying on in whatever army would have him; he and Lodge talked of volunteering for service in the Pacific together. There were other times when he thought of throwing everything over and getting a job after the war. But his resolve weakened as his unit moved north, closer to Switzerland. Face to face, Aly had never been able to stand up to the Aga. His father always could dominate him with his towering presence, seduce him with the lure, so magnetic to Aly, of the wealth, fame, and power at his command.

A few weeks before the German surrender, Aly took a short leave and went to Geneva. In the bounteous atmosphere of neutral Switzerland, so remindful of the good things in life to be enjoyed after the war, father and son confronted one another for the first time in six years. There must have been a lot to talk about: the Ismaili community, with which Aly had kept in touch all through the war—a foretaste of the increasing responsibilities he would have in the future; the stables in which the Aga had promised Aly full partnership; the family interests around the world which should flourish again once the war was over.

Aly returned to his unit in Germany and thought no more about cutting loose.

# Chapter XV

*"I once left Aly at four in the morning in Deauville. When I got back to his house late that same day, he had ridden a horse in the morning, played tennis, flown to England to watch one of his horses run, flown back, and then we played bridge until three the next morning. Meanwhile, he had a few girls around to relax to. At three in the morning, he took his car and drove off to the Casino. He came back at seven and slept until nine."*

—M. JEAN FAYARD

Shortly after V-E day, Aly heard that some of the horses the Nazis had looted from the Aga's stables in France were at the German National Stud at Altefelt. He had had those horses on his mind ever since joining up with the Americans. General Devers recalls that "General Maitland Wilson, my British commander, requested me to take Aly on my staff for the invasion of the south of France, for the Germans had captured about a half-million dollars' worth of horses."

Aly now saw his opportunity. He went to Metz and hunted

up Robert Muller, who had been the assistant manager of the Aga's French stables. Muller had been captured while serving with the French army; the Germans had put him in charge of the Aga's horses at Altefelt as soon as they learned who he was. It was Muller, immediately after his liberation, who had informed Aly where the stolen horses were.

They divided forces. Muller stayed on in Metz to find a temporary stable, while Aly sped into Germany at the wheel of a jeep pulling a makeshift horse van. The countryside was in chaos as Aly bounced over bombed roads like a miniature Red-Ball Express. He could only take two horses at a time, so he had to make several trips between Altefelt and Metz. Then Muller took them all back to the Aga's farm in Normandy.

Whenever he could get away from Heidelberg after that, Aly went looking for more horses. Grand accompanied him on a couple of these forays. "We would pass a field and Aly would say, 'That horse is mine.'" Sometimes Aly insisted on taking the horse immediately to Normandy. "We drove all night and I was dead but Aly wasn't. He had inexhaustible energy."

By now a lieutenant-colonel, Aly stayed on in Heidelberg, performing routine occupation chores at Sixth Army Group headquarters. "We were just waiting to get sent home," Lodge recalls. Whenever he could, Aly got away. He went to England with Grand to see the first postwar runnings of two great races, the Derby and the One Thousand Guineas. He had a visitor from Cairo in the person of Sybilla Szczeniowska, who came to Germany as a representative of the Polish Red Cross.

In August, 1945, Aly returned to London to be demobilized.

His personal life was in limbo. Joan had returned from Nairobi with the boys but she and Aly had no illusions about their marriage. It was over. It had ended, in fact, in Cairo.

Joan decided to make her home in England, near her mother, who had become the Duchess of Leinster; her three sisters, the Countess of Cadogan, the Duchess of Bedford, and Lady Edbury; and her brother, John Yarde-Buller. She moved into London's Belgravia and settled into a discreet social life, exactly the sort of existence Aly had long ago decided to avoid.

The boys were nine and eight now, both handsome; Karim dark and husky like his father, Amyn slim and frail. They spent some time in Ireland with Aly, who found, to his dismay, that neither of his sons liked horses.

Aly and Joan exchanged recriminations about the boys. Joan wanted to bring them up as young Englishmen. Aly wanted them to have an international education, to travel and meet people of as many nationalities as possible. "I am a tremendous believer in that," he once explained. "I think one of the best ways to get over a lot of the problems of the world is by constantly meeting people from other parts of the world. I tried to bring up both of my sons that way."

Aly's arguments prevailed and the boys went to Le Rosey, a Swiss boys' school which has been called *l'école des rois* (the school of kings), so many fledgling monarchs have been numbered among its student body.

Aly next turned his attention to his finances. The Aga, at first informally, later by a transfer of shares, carried out his promise. Aly became his partner, with almost complete working control of the stud farms, stables, and stock. The Aga retained a hand in breeding selections, based on his beloved charts and an elaborate theory worked out by his French stable manager, Colonel Jean Vuillier. Together the Aga and Aly owned three thousand acres of prime land and eight million dollars' worth of bloodstock, a big business that went far beyond the layman's notion of a rich man's hobby.

Aly's purchases of additional stud farms brought their total to four in France and seven in Ireland. He commuted frenetically between Maisons-Lafitte, Normandy, and Ireland. He flew to the United States and to South America to sell bloodstock, for there was a world-wide shortage and the Aga Khan's stables still had a reputation as one of the best. As a salesman, Aly was incomparable; all his charm, eagerness, and volubility coalesced to one purpose, as he delivered his halting, flowery monologues on the horses he had for sale. "Aly loved buying and selling; it was the breath of life to him," recalls the Earl of Carnarvon, one of Aly's lifelong friends.

Horse trading, after all, was what the racing business came down to. The big winners like Blenheim and Bahram were, above all, glamorous advertisements which won buyers for the Aga's bloodstock, either in stud fees or the purchase of foals. Aly's enthusiasm and charm, and his reputation as a daredevil jockey who rode his own merchandise to victory, could mesmerize people.

The Aga always claimed that racing was, for him, merely a hobby, but one with noble aims: "A source of pleasure not only to ourselves but for thousands, indeed for millions, who follow our colors on the turf."

Aly, however, pretended to nothing nobler than the profit motive: "After all, Father and I are just a couple of horse traders. Some people are in this business for fun; we're in it for profit."

It was a tough and competitive business. Aly explained on several occasions: "The winning margins in European racing are so narrow that in breeding winners every little thing is important. You've got to have the best trainer and the best jockey and then, on top of it all, you've got to have luck."

With Aly's freshet of enthusiasm, the stables made a spectacular comeback. By 1948 they were at the top of the racing world. That year the Aga's horses—the Aga still took the public bows—won the Derby, the Irish Oaks and several other races for a season's stake money of £46,000 (nearly $135,000). In 1949 they took prize money of £68,916 (about $200,000). Tidy sums, but even more important, the prestige brought more buyers to listen to Aly's persuasive sales talks as he peddled stock around the world.

Lord Carnarvon, himself an outstanding horseman, has estimated that at their peak, the Aga's and Aly's stables were worth between $12,000,000 and $15,000,000 and brought a net return of 5 per cent, with perhaps 20 per cent in capital appreciation—a total profit of over $3,000,000 a year.

But by the time the stables had made their comeback Aly's zeal was fading. He would remain interested in horses, and a good salesman for the stables, but his personal dream of the postwar good life would take over.

2

The Riviera represented Aly's grass roots, if anything did. It had changed from the days of La Belle Epoque. Now, middle-class Frenchmen, enjoying their *congé payé* (paid vacation), thronged south by train, car and motorcycle to put up in small hotels or try the new outdoor sport called *Le Camping*. The Côte d'Azur was no longer an exclusive winter resort of European society. But it was still a good place to meet girls.

Aly had kept in mind the house he and Tommy Burke had visited, ignoring barbed wire and mine fields, after the invasion of Southern France. The Chateau de l'Horizon, designed by the American architect, Barry Dierks, for the American actress, Maxine Elliott, was unprepossessing from the highway, but intimate and charming on its sea side. Big windows gulped in the view; a broad terrace, with gardens at either end, stretched across the beige rocks; below that was another terrace supporting a giant swimming pool, and below the pool, as below a ship, lapped the sea.

Aly bought it from Miss Elliott's heirs for only $87,000, bidding for it anonymously.

It was not the grandest estate on the Riviera; it was of another sort entirely from the stately villas of La Belle Epoque with their mirrored Louis XVI decor and formal gardens. It was modern, informal, and spectacular. It caught the sun like a tilted mirror and Aly loved to lunch on its terrace, stripped to the waist to enjoy the winter sun. So much sun had its dangers, he found. One of his new friends was the former daughter-in-law of a celebrated statesman. Red-haired, freckled, translucent-skinned, she once came to the Chateau for a visit and foolishly fell asleep on the terrace. The resulting sunburn put her in bed for the rest of her visit while Aly, furious with frustration, sulked alone. But Aly loved the sun, and the swimming pool with its chute that went into the sea. And he loved l'Horizon's size. With ten bedrooms and seven baths, it was possible to have a houseful of guests without their bumping into one another in the halls.

Two of the Chateau's bedrooms were on the main floor, one

of them known as the Winston Churchill room from the days when he had been Maxine Elliott's guest. Nearby was Aly's office, which looked out on one side to the sea and on the other to a triangle of green lawn, with twisted evergreens, that ended at the high white wall which shielded the house from the railroad. Next to the office was the long living room with a wall of French doors on the terrace side and a large Provençal fireplace opposite them.

The Chateau was furnished with soft, deep sofas covered in beige linen, low coffee tables, and bookshelves full of books which, like some of the furniture, had come with the house. The few books Aly owned disappeared among them. The dining room held a long table hewn out of one slab of marble, which dominated its arched doors and windows and stone floors. On one wall hung the brooding portrait of Aga Khan I, Aly's great-grandfather.

Aly collected paintings for the Chateau with the help of a knowledgeable art dealer in Nice named Henri Gaffié. He built up a first-rate collection, especially of French impressionists. "He was very excited then about the Chateau," Gaffié recalls. "I remember visiting him one day; he was down on all fours with a hammer in hand, driving in nails."

Aly kept his retinue to a minimum. His inseparable "all-around man" was Tutti, otherwise A. Hussein, an Ismaili from Bombay who began as Aly's valet, but, like everyone close to Aly, soon was enlisted for a variety of other duties.

Aly's chauffeur was a Welshman, Emrys Williams, whose job came to include that of bodyguard. Williams left to run a pub in England when his health gave out. While he lasted he was an excellent driver; moreover he could be a steel-nerved passenger when Aly took over the wheel. Cars were among Aly's passions; he always owned six or eight. A series of secretaries handled Aly's correspondence and appointments. An off-and-on member of Aly's entourage was his uncle, Mario Magliano, who had spent so much time with him during his childhood. Mario's relations with Aly seesawed wildly. Sometimes they were very close, at other times they treated each other like employer and servant. Gianni Agnelli remembers driving back from lunch at l'Horizon one day and asking his chauffeur if he had been given lunch also. "Yes,

sir," said the chauffeur. "I lunched with the uncle of the Prince."
"His uncle?" Agnelli asked in disbelief. "Yes, and very charming
too," said the chauffeur.

Aly was a master at creating an ambiance, but he was poor
at keeping it in good working order. That was Mario's job; he
occupied himself with the repair and redecoration of the house.
As he explained it: "How could you expect Aly with his upbringing and personality to understand a household budget?
When a bill was presented to him for payment, he was astonished.
He didn't know that one had to pay for things like kitchen
repairs." Aly was never a man to fuss over household details.
A succession of servants came and went; those that stayed often
became slovenly because there was no set routine. Occasionally a
girl friend of Aly's, moving in, took an interest in the household
management, firing and hiring servants, buying new linens, planning menus. But it was a dangerous game. She might find herself
taken for granted, and soon would be planning menus for a rival.

# Chapter XVI

*"If you are going to help people in their lives, you've got to know something about life instead of talking about things you haven't experienced and know nothing about."*
—ALY KHAN

The way Aly drove, Cannes was only five minutes from the Chateau de l'Horizon, so that the Carlton Hotel there, with its adjacent tennis courts, served as a handy annex. It often became, by appointment or by chance, a kind of wayside inn for young ladies on the road to the Chateau. Aly would speed in to play tennis or meet friends, dressed in blue jeans and a black leather jacket, his hat tilted characteristically over his forehead. He usually played with Tommy Burke, who found the postwar Aly "overweight and without much style, but still he played well."

As he played, windows might open in the hotel. "The girls would look out," Burke recalled, in his rich brogue. "They knew who Aly was and they would telephone over here to my office and ask to talk to him. He would hang up with a smile and say,

'Well, I'll have to go and see that person.' Or maybe he would invite her to come down to watch him play. They were all after him."

Sometimes he would stop in the Carlton bar, alone or accompanied, after a tennis match. The head barman, Jules Moschietto, "Jules" to the international set, would serve him mineral water or fruit juice or, on very rare occasions, a Pimms Cup No. 1 which "Aly liked because of all the fruit in it." He had no taste for alcohol. At a night club he often took champagne to be companionable, but he didn't really like it. Nor did he like his woman companions to drink very much. He behaved as if they needed no other stimulant but his charm; he never felt that liquor was quicker.

When at the Chateau, Aly was host to a dozen or more guests for lunch almost every day, some of whom he knew, others whom he had met barely or not at all. Friends of friends would call, announce they were on the Riviera and, if they sounded interesting, be invited to lunch the following day. Evenings he usually dined out. When he was with a companion who particularly interested him, he forgot about food. He often missed dinner entirely; he might be diverted by a bridge game or a drive to visit somebody or even an early-evening look at the moon. He would eat later, from a tray the butler left for him and his companion in the kitchen.

Although he tried to emulate his father in employing first-rate chefs and setting an excellent table for guests, he didn't share the Aga's epicurean interest in food. Aly would pick his way through a large meal, talking more than he ate. What he liked were desserts. "I never saw anyone who liked ice cream so much," said one friend. "He ate it every day, and every day he had a different flavor. His favorites were orange and tangerine sherbet. He was like a child. Once he gave a luncheon with ten different desserts."

Aly never slept more than three or four hours a night. He could sleep anywhere and always insisted that ten minutes was as refreshing to him as five hours to anybody else. He slept on airplanes, in theatres, at the movies, on the back seats of cars when Williams was driving. At the Chateau he sometimes excused himself for a nap after lunch but this always brought knowing winks and discreet avoidance by the servants. Aly didn't really think of bed as a place to sleep.

He still lived out of a suitcase. The Chateau was his headquarters, but he didn't occupy it more than two or three months a year, although it was kept open all the time. Villa Gorizia at Deauville was open all summer. In Paris, the town house on rue de Prony was kept staffed. Outside Paris, he had houses at Maisons-Lafitte and at Chantilly, both training farms for horses. It took only a phone call from his secretary that the prince was en route to put either one in operation. A similar call to the Gilltown Stud in Ireland's County Kildare sent red-cheeked maids scattering to dust up the big manor house. At the Normandy stud, there was a rustic hideaway without a telephone. There were other houses in Venezuela, in India, and in Syria. Later there would be a duplex apartment in New York, a lakeside villa in Switzerland, and another house, never lived in, in the private colony of Castelleras, on the Riviera.

Wherever Aly alighted there were house guests, luncheon parties, excursions to the races, sudden trips to attend a theatre opening in London or Paris. His one big formal entertainment of the year was the ball he gave each June in Paris at the Pré Catalan restaurant in the Bois de Boulogne, following the running of the Grand Prix de Paris at Longchamps racecourse. The balls were reminiscent of Edgar Wallace's parties in London. "Nobody but Aly could have put together such a mixture of people," said Agnelli, who attended most of them. "Among the guests would be a former Premier of France and his wife, an Indian prince, horse people from England, and movie stars. Some of the girls went down to the level of tarts."

Aly was very proud of these parties and went to a great deal of trouble to make each one an event. He worked on them for months in advance, often designing himself the decorations and ladies' favors—a Hermes scarf inscribed with the names of famous horses, or a perfume named Yla.

But the Grand Prix ball was only one night a year. The rest of the time Aly was on the move and to him, perhaps, belongs the distinction of introducing the modern miracle of aviation to the ancient art of love.

Just after Aly had returned to London from the army, he met a demobbed and dashing RAF veteran named John Lancaster, a former squadron leader in the Middle East, who was setting up shop as a free-lance pilot. Lancaster began flying for Aly. At first they hired planes, then Aly decided he needed a plane of his own. The De Havilland factory in England began building a two-engined Dove monoplane, a descendant of the Puss Moth of his Bombay-to-Singapore adventure, to his specifications. He had it painted in his colors, green and red, and named it *The Avenger*.

Just before he was to take delivery, Aly canceled the order. He had lost fifteen thousand pounds gambling; his debts were piling up and he was on one of his periodic economy waves. It didn't last. One day Aly wanted to get to Newmarket in a hurry; Lancaster cannily offered to borrow a plane from De Havilland. They dropped by the plant and there was *The Avenger*, sleek, freshly painted, ready to fly. Aly was ushered inside for a look. On the control panel fascia was a plate—H.H. Prince Aly Khan. It was too much to resist. *The Avenger* was towed out and took off with its new owner sitting in the copilot's seat.

The plane gave Aly the mobility he had dreamed of. Now it was possible to enjoy an afternoon nap at l'Horizon, fly to Paris for dinner with a friend, and go on to a race in London the next morning. Friends could be picked up anywhere and delivered to wherever Aly had temporarily alighted.

The switchboard at the London Ritz supplied the necessary lines of communication. Wherever he was, Aly used the Ritz switchboard as his personal telephone answering service. It worked like this: The Ritz's telephone operators, and particularly Lydia Scalia, the senior operator, whom Aly nicknamed "Flo," took messages for him whether he was there or not. Aly telephoned the Ritz regularly to pick up messages and let the operators know where he could be reached. If a call seemed sufficiently interesting or urgent, the Ritz switchboard transferred it. *The Avenger* waited, ready to close the circuit.

How handy the plane was to pick up a Broadway showgirl

who had come to London armed with Aly's name and dialed the Ritz telephone number, had been switched to him in Paris, and promptly been invited to drop over for a week end. For one Englishwoman in particular, the wife of a distinguished member of the royal circle, the plane ended the isolation of her country life. When business took her husband away, *The Avenger* would land at an airdrome near her home, and whisk her off to wherever Aly was staying at the moment. That same evening, she might change from her sensible tweeds to a Paris gown to play hostess at an intimate dinner party on the rue de Prony. Or, just a few hours after she had stepped, bundled and befurred against the North Sea wind, into the plane, she might be sunning herself on the terrace of l'Horizon.

It is true that she sometimes sunned alone. *The Avenger* made Aly no more punctual than he ever had been, and often his guests found themselves dining in one of his houses without him. Since Aly never liked to be by himself and never liked to be kept waiting, he always made more dates than he possibly could keep. He was eternally optimistic about the elasticity of time. One afternoon, after a long lunch and his usual nap at the Chateau, Aly, Nigel Campbell, and Lancaster took off for Paris where Aly had a dinner engagement. Campbell says: "We had hoped to leave at two-thirty to reach Paris before dark. Instead, we left at four. So instead of going up the Rhone Valley, Aly insisted on going over the Alps. We ran into very bad weather at about fifteen thousand feet and black ice, the most dangerous kind, started forming. In order to try and avoid this, we had to climb higher and finally attained a height of twenty-one thousand feet. The airplane was being tossed about like a cork in a rough sea. The plane had no oxygen on board and after a time, at this height, we began getting splitting headaches; any movement was a tremendous effort. Suddenly the radio operator passed out cold and Aly and I were dreading the same thing would happen to Lancaster. Apart from all other discomforts, it was extremely cold and I remember scraping the ice off the inside of the windows which formed almost as quickly again."

Aly and Campbell kept thinking of the tragic accident that

had befallen a similar plane just a short time before. It had crashed in central France, on the way to Cannes, killing the Earl of Fitzwilliam and the Marchioness of Hartington, the former Kathleen Kennedy, one of the gay brood of Kennedy children whom Aly had known in his prewar London days.

"It was all the more frightening," Campbell recalls, "when darkness descended as both aerials had been swept away and we were flying without wireless communications with the ground, but Lancaster was magnificent and after a nightmare journey of over four hours, we finally reached Paris." They had two litres of petrol left. "My narrowest escape from death," Aly shouted to Lancaster as he leaped into a taxi to keep his date.

## 2

His visits to London coincided with race meetings or the Newmarket sales. For the Derby he usually rented a house for a week. Otherwise he took a fourth floor corner suite at the Ritz, overlooking Piccadilly on one side and Green Park on the other. George, the head porter, booked his bets. Always short of ready cash, always hopeful of a quick killing—or several of them—he bet heavily on the races but his expertise didn't always help him. He lost enormous sums and for years was heavily in debt to bookmakers.

On every trip to London, he saw Peter Beatty, who had been invalided out of the Commandos because of an eye disease and was now almost blind. He wore heavy glasses and when he came down to London from Mereworth Castle, his valet had to accompany him everywhere, leading him by the arm. Beatty used to lunch with Aly and Campbell. "Peter would peer through those thick glasses as if the food was fading out of sight," Campbell recalls. "Aly would glance at me with the most pained and sympathetic look on his face but he would keep right on talking about horses as if nothing had changed."

Aly was so busy he sometimes spent days in the suite without going out, even for meals. These sieges were devoted to his two interests, horse dealing and women. He would have something sent up to the room: a carefully ordered dinner with champagne if it was a tête-à-tête with a lady; roast beef and a vegetable, topped off by a couple of flavors of ice cream, if he had invited one or another of his man friends to join him, greeting him with his battle cry: "Any new blood?" The telephone rang incessantly. A friend of those days remembers: "Everything was always in a mad rush. We would be talking about horses, and the phone would ring and he would shout at me, 'Answer it.' I would pick it up and the operator would say, 'Mrs. So-and-so is waiting in the lobby. Shall I send her up?' And Aly would say to keep her waiting a few minutes longer. Before Mrs. So-and-so had come up, another woman was calling. There was a steady procession. I wonder how many Mrs. So-and-sos cooled their heels in the Ritz lobby?" Another friend of Aly's recalls being jolted by the greeting he got upon arriving in the suite. A young woman demurely extended her hand and said: "Aly says you're terribly keen on women and reasonably good in bed."

The Aga once became furious when a delegation of Ismailis, in London on a visit from India, were kept waiting in the lobby for over an hour, while Aly entertained a young lady upstairs.

Some of the women Aly saw were old friends of prewar days. As one friend said: "He hated breaking up with any woman. He liked to keep the pot boiling. He liked them to think he might be interested again at some future date." Another friend, more Freudian-minded, felt that "Aly wanted to be the one who said good-bye. He never wanted a woman to walk out on him. He never wanted to be rejected. It was a game with him to keep them interested." Then there was a continuous stream of new recruits, introduced by friends, male and female, or spotted by Aly at a theatre, night club, or restaurant. When he saw a woman he found attractive, he arranged, at once, to be introduced, perhaps by the head waiter. Or he simply introduced himself. He assumed the lady would know who he was and it mattered not at all to him that she might already have an escort. One young Parisian recalls going to the theatre with his striking blonde Danish bride. Aly, seated in the row in front of them, turned his back to the stage, rested his chin on his hand and stared at her throughout

the performance. His conduct at theatres was seldom encouraging
to the performers. He was always late; the clatter of Aly's entrance became part of the first night scene in London, Paris, and
New York. But then he didn't come to the theatre primarily to
see the show on the stage.

Aly liked what he called "going out in a pair"—double-
dating. But his Freudian-oriented friend felt he was envious, even
destructive, of other men's seductions. He vividly remembers an
evening when he and Aly were dining in a restaurant with two
very pretty girls. "My date was obviously in a much more
romantic mood than his. He winked and mugged at me, as if
urging me to get out of there with her. Halfway through dinner
he left the table and I saw him having a long consultation with
the head waiter.

"I was staying with Aly in one of the bedrooms of his Ritz
suite. As soon as possible after dinner, I went there with the girl.
When we entered the room, a horrible smell nearly knocked us
down. The girl didn't say anything, just looked annoyed. I pretended there was nothing wrong. We didn't stay very long; we
just couldn't stand it. I took her home. When I got back to the
suite Aly was sitting there grinning. I mentioned the smell and
he went into a fit of laughter. Then he recovered enough to tell
me what he had done. He had arranged to have a whole Lim-
burger cheese put under my bed."

Aly never got over his boyhood penchant for practical jokes.
He loved to go to the shops in London and Paris that sell magic
tricks and gag articles. He laughed until tears came at the
Chateau one day over a whoopee cushion which, when sat upon,
emitted an embarrassing squeal. It was a strange quirk for a man
who was usually so gallant.

Aly was always discreet. Otto Preminger, the movie producer, said that although he had known Aly for many years,
he had never known him well, and explained why: "Aly had only
two real interests, horses and women. I don't know anything
about horses and Aly never discussed his women."

One rare exception to his rule of silence is worth mentioning if only as an indication of the epic scale of his romantic

adventures. One day he was at the races with a woman friend, one of the few persons with whom he discussed his most personal affairs. Moving close to her as they approached his box, he began whispering. "See that woman sitting over there. And that one. And that one." He went on, pointing out woman after woman with a flick of his chin. "He was pointing out his conquests," his companion said later. "Practically all the women in that section of the grandstand had been to bed with him."

In the precise and complex art of love, Aly had no peer. The woman's satisfaction came first with Aly. His concentration, his intuition, and his gentleness were not foregone as the affair reached a physical climax.

"Most men stay five minutes and then good-bye," one woman said. "That was not Aly's way. He had ideas; he had a lot of imagination." And another, typically reverting to the third-person pronoun, said: "The women he'd had always said what a marvelous lover he was and so the others would just say 'Yes' if he asked. He was marvelous for women and he knew his power over them."

There was, over the years, considerable speculation about Aly's technique. As one of Aly's friends said: "People couldn't help wondering. Six women a day? Impossible! Three women a day? No one could live very long at that pace." A story circulated in London for years that Aly, and the Aga too, plunged their elbows into cold water in the course of an evening of pleasure to rekindle their virility. This was so widely accepted that there were night-club habitués who swore they had seen Aly use a champagne bucket for the purpose.

The truth was neither so simple nor so obvious. Aly's extraordinary prowess was the result of a unique heritage and training which reached back to his Eastern ancestors. And once again he was beholden for what he was to his father. The Aga once confided the secret to an English friend, a peer, who passed it on years later:

"The Aga, so he told me himself, had gone as a young man to Cairo, to an old Arab doctor, an *hakim*, and spent six weeks with him. Then, when Aly was growing up, the Aga sent him to the same man or the man's son. Aly learned the same thing in Cairo."

For centuries a body of knowledge has circulated among the physicians of the East, often passed from father to son, for it is not the kind of thing that is taught in medical school. It is called, in Arabic, *Imsák*. More than a technique, it is a philosophy, one that Moslems can appreciate in their conviction that the art of love does not come naturally and automatically to a man but must be learned as a discipline. The ancient Taoists considered it an extension of man's vital force; even Dr. Kinsey touched on it in his surveys of American men. Yet, for the most part, it has remained underground, private, unwritten. Even Sir Richard Burton in his translation of the *Ananga Ranga* provided scant details: "This process is called in Arabian medicine *Imsák* which means 'holding' or 'retaining.'" In Burton's Terminal Essay to his translation of *The Book of a Thousand and One Nights* he elaborates only briefly: "The essence . . . is to avoid overtension of the muscles and to preoccupy the brain."

"My friend," the Aga told his English friend, "you must realize that to us, to Oriental people, it makes the whole difference."

Aly had learned to carry *Imsák* to its extreme. He could control himself indefinitely.

"No matter how many women Aly went with," marveled one of his friends, "he seldom reached a climax himself. He could make love by the hour, but he went the whole way himself not oftener than twice a week. He liked the effect it had on women. He liked to get them out of control, while he stayed in control— the master of the situation."

And a woman, especially candid, said: "He rarely went to the end. He could stay for five or seven hours with a woman, making love. That was his specialty. That was why he had so many women. Himself, he seldom finished. Otherwise his life would not have been possible. Because he only thought of that every night, and every day, too. He lived for that."

# Chapter XVII

*"Now I know how much I loved Aly."*

—The Begum Aga Khan

One woman whom Aly never charmed, not so he noticed, was Yvette Blanche Labrousse, the fourth Begum Aga Khan and Aly's second stepmother. She was—and is—just as overwhelming in her fashion as Aly was in his. She stands over six feet tall and, except for heavy ankles which have become more noticeable in recent years, she has the figure of an ample Venus. Wearing one of her snowy-white saris, she has been compared with the Matterhorn and, like it, she is magnificent and forbidding. Almost all men feel dwarfed in her presence; she does not bring out sensuality in them as much as a primal memory that disturbs and incites them. She is shrewd and determined, and gracious when she wants to be.

From the day in 1944 that Yvette married the Aga in Vevey, Switzerland, she took her new career as Begum seriously. Doubtless she had been rehearsing it in her imagination for years while waiting on the sidelines observing where her predecessor, Andrée, had gone wrong. Andrée had remained a Christian; Yvette became an Ismaili. She always called herself Begum, never Princess, as Andrée had done. She wore saris for public appearances, especially in the presence of her husband's people. She took the name of Ome Habiba, which had been the name of the Prophet's last wife. In later years, she even made a barefoot pilgrimage to Mecca. In her fascination with Islam, she has reminded some people of Lady Hester Stanhope, the granddaughter of one English prime minister and the niece of another, the two Pitts, who got herself involved in the intrigues of the Middle East in the early nineteenth century. But other people who know the Begum cast her in another image. They hold that in her climb from obscurity she never got past the middle class and that she is, in spite of the wealth that marriage to the Aga gave her, a typical bourgeois Frenchwoman, classic in her hard-headed practicality. One of the world's richest women, she is careful about her household accounts. "If her husband were a shopkeeper," says one acquaintance, "she'd be sitting behind the cash register." She owns one of the world's most magnificent collections of jewelry. Her wardrobe of Indian saris numbers in the hundreds and her Western clothes, which she often designs herself, fill closets and spill over into the basement of Yakimour, her Riviera villa, where they are stored in more closets and boxes. "She never gives anything away," explained a former employee. "Every pair of shoes, everything she is no longer wearing, is stored in the basement. Maybe she's afraid her money will vanish one day and she will find herself back where she began."

The daughter of a streetcar conductor, Yvette was born in the shabby Mediterranean seaport of Sète, west of Marseilles. Her family moved to Cannes, where she got a glimpse of the Riviera's rich world of adventurous men and lovely women. Next they moved to Lyons, where her mother worked as a dressmaker and apprenticed Yvette in the same trade. In 1929 Yvette was a twenty-four-year-old seamstress, unmarried, unhappy, distinguished only by her size and the scope of her dreams. Then she entered a beauty contest, became Miss Lyons, and then Miss France, and went to Rio de Janiero for a Miss World contest. She didn't win, but she had been applauded and ogled enough to learn that the tall, oversized figure that set her apart from other people was a negotiable asset. As Miss France, she got around to resorts, judged other beauty contests, modeled clothes, and bedecked parties. She met the Aga Khan, portly, twice her age, and very rich. The Aga, who had known many women, found her size provocative. She stood a good head taller than he. The Aga never seemed more Oriental than when he appeared with his lovely young friend, the caricature of a pasha and his odalisque.

### 2

The new Begum Yvette saw the source of the Aga's wealth and power for the first time when she accompanied him to Bombay in March, 1946, for his Diamond Jubilee, at which the Aga was to be weighed against diamonds. Aly had gone on ahead to help with the planning. The Aga's first visit to his people in nearly seven years was a sensitive one, for its aim was to reinstall him in their hearts, revive his prestige, and insure his reign.

The Indian community to which the Aga returned was not the same one that he had known before the war. The India of the British Raj, his India, was retreating before the irresistible tide of Indian independence, and his Ismailis were caught between the majority Hindus, led by Gandhi and Nehru, and the suddenly aggressive Moslems, led by Mohammed Ali Jinnah. The new leaders of India treated the Aga like a petty satrap. The Moslems, rejecting permanent minority status in a Hindu-dominated nation, had put forward the idea of Pakistan, a separate and independent Moslem state created of those portions of India where Moslems predominated. The Ismailis were secure in neither camp. Whether they stayed in India or fled with the other Moslems into the new Pakistan (as happened when partition came), they would remain a minority, depending upon their Imam to negotiate a better way of life for them.

The Aga's position had never been so shaky. The Ismailis, in the British colonies of East Africa as well as in India, had prospered during the war, and they had gained prestige by loyally supporting the Allies. It had all happened without him; his neutrality in Switzerland had embarrassed his local leaders, while Aly, turning up among them in British uniform, had rallied their pride, their cash contributions, and their young men and women.

The Aga thought of the vast amount of capital his Diamond Jubilee would raise among the entire community, and came up with an idea. He said nothing about it, except to his very top leadership, even after he had arrived in Bombay.

Aly, already a favorite of the crowds, seemed to be everywhere, greeting people in person or smiling out at them from pictures. There was "Lieutenant-Colonel Prince Aly Khan in British battle dress being awarded a Special Bronze Star Medal for Conspicuous Service." There was Aly in cowboy costume peering out from beneath a ten-gallon hat like a Hollywood hero. There was Aly in Arab costume, every robed inch a son of the desert. There was Aly, the fearless hunter, standing over the body of an eight-foot leopard he had shot in India. As one close associate of the Aga's observed, it looked as if Aly was running for some kind of office.

On the big day, he moved jauntily forward in the procession at Brabourne Stadium wearing a uniform of his own design: white tunic, white jodphurs and a black astrakhan hat tilted over one ear. As he, Sadruddin, and the Begum approached their front row seats, a band, which had been blaring wailing Oriental half-tones over the loudspeakers, switched to a rhythmic European melody in their honor.

The Begum wore a sari sewn with fifteen hundred diamonds, worth, according to one estimate, $180,000. Her eyes sparkled, too, as she drank in the excitement and adulation. She was eager to do everything required of a Begum. As a French writer said; "Sometimes she seemed to be ahead of the protocol chiefs in her desire to please."

Committee members wearing armbands and badges scurried to and fro. A crisis had erupted behind the scenes: the diamonds, borrowed from a London diamond syndicate, had not yet arrived. The ship carrying them had been diverted to another port. At the last moment, a Royal Navy flying boat whisked them to Bombay.

When word was flashed that they were in town, the Aga at last arrived at the stadium. Wearing a blue turban and long white silken caftan, he walked slowly and gravely under a green umbrella held by an aide-de-camp. A shifting, self-conscious, gorgeously dressed phalanx of the highest Ismaili dignitaries clustered behind him. Ahead marched Ismaili bagpipers from Karachi wearing tartan shawls and playing a Scottish air. The Aga slowly mounted the stage and sat down on a silken-pillowed *gadi*, which stood on an elaborate but businesslike scale. Giant blocks of ice, tinted red and green, had been set around it to cool the air.

The crowd of a hundred thousand which had been waiting for hours was impatient as Ismaili dignitaries made long flowery speeches, and the Aga scowled on his throne. Finally, the diamonds arrived. There was a murmur of disappointment when a *wazir* in a gold turban picked up a small, transparent plastic box containing what looked like lighter flints and set it on the balance. The crowd had been expecting a cascade of glittering gems; these were tiny industrial diamonds. But excitement mounted as box after box was piled on the scale. It reached a crescendo as the eightieth box went onto the pile. That was it: the Aga's weight stood at 243½ pounds. Against that had been set £640,000 ($3-200,000) worth of diamonds. The Aga rose, came forward to a microphone, and announced that except for a "negligible amount" which he would retain for himself as a "memento," all of the funds accruing from the ceremony would go into a Diamond Jubilee Investment Trust. At first, it sounded like the same gesture that he had made at his Golden Jubilee. Then it dawned on the crowd what an enormous difference there was. The weighing-against gold had yielded only $128,000, less than the value of the Begum's diamond-studded sari: this time there was $3,200,000. Then the money was used merely to support a few charities. Now the Aga envisioned "a totally new financial outlook among the Ismailis. Co-operative societies, corporations, and, I hope and believe very soon, building societies, too, will draw from the investment trust." In one grandiose gesture, the Aga had made available to the community more investment capital than could

be amassed by any individual businessman or even a *jamat-khana*
full of them. Everyone would benefit. Including, of course, the
Aga.

## 3

Jubilation was so intense throughout the community that the
Aga repeated the whole ceremony the following year in Dar-es-
Salaam so that the East African Ismailis could see and hear it for
themselves. If, on any of these occasions, Aly noticed the Begum's
interest in what was going on, he must have reacted with amusement. He had seen other European women, guests of his, become
fascinated with Ismaili rituals and then wilt in the heat and confusion. It wouldn't last. He wasn't even sure Yvette would last.
He knew better than most how impatient his father could become
with people who demanded too much of his attention.

Anyway, his own future seemed assured, and never more
so than when he and Lancaster flew to Syria early in 1948.

*The Avenger*, unmistakable in its red and green Ismaili colors,
first made a low-altitude tour of the towns and villages in central
Syria where most Ismailis live. By the time it put down at an
airport sixty-five miles from Salamiya, thirty cars and lorries had
gathered to welcome it. Lancaster, an observant, artistic man (he
is now a painter) provided a graphic account of the trip in a letter
to his wife:

> As we drove into the Salamiya country we came across
> groups of very excited Arabs who blocked the road and swarmed
> over the car, all wanting to kiss Aly's hand and touch him. Young,
> old, boys, girls; eventually we got to the small villa and a late
> lunch awaited us. I had visions of sheep's eyes and other horrors,
> but except that the cooking was Arab, the food was almost
> European. The furniture was what you'd expect in any house
> furnished by natives in what they consider the European style.
> But I had clean, new sheets and a comfortable bed with mosquito
> net and odd satin-covered pillows all over the top.

Aly was in his element. He drove from village to village
through fields of oats and barley, spangled with bright wild

flowers—dwarf iris, edelweiss, blood-red tulips—to inspect schools, watch the children do gymnastics, and make speeches.

A week later, Aly and Lancaster flew to Beirut, left *The Avenger*, and pushed on by car and horseback for a tour of even more remote mountain villages. Lancaster wrote his wife:

> On a night lit only by the stars and a few swinging lanterns, we mounted Arab horses for the ten-mile ride to our next camp, a school, built near the bottom of a ravine. Flashes from 'muskets,' dating from the Crimea, lit up the boulders and scrub and answering flashes and bangs echoed from hillside to hillside.
>
> The horses slipped and slithered and their hoofs clattered on the rocks. . . . I was to learn during the next few days how amazingly sure-footed these animals are. Aly first introduced them here and people said it was crazy. Now he himself is astonished at their capability.
>
> At intervals, the people of the nearest village would be collected waiting for God to pass and there would be much shouting and shooting from the men, while the women made that curious tremolo wail which seems to be common to all native women.

From Syria, Aly and Lancaster flew to Cairo where Aly, in an exultant mood, had his portrait painted by his friend of wartime days, Sybilla Szczeniowska. Everything was going well. *The Avenger* headed back to Cannes, the Chateau, the good life. The flight path seemed clear. But something was about to happen which would change Aly's course irrevocably.

# Chapter XVIII

*"When you're in love, you're living, you matter."*

—RITA HAYWORTH

In Cairo during the war Aly had gone to a cocktail party at the apartment, on the banks of the Nile, of Baron Adolph Bentinck, chargé d'affaires of the Dutch Embassy. Later in the evening, the Baron, his high-spirited blonde wife, Gaby, and some of their guests, including Aly, went to see the movie *Blood and Sand*, starring Rita Hayworth. The Bentinck party found its melodramatic plot amusing. "Everyone was making fun and joking," recalls the Baroness—except Aly. He was engrossed. "Don't disturb me," he hissed. "I want to see this wonderful girl." Eventually he saw the film three times.

It is likely that Aly was studying Miss Hayworth for his postwar plan. Every man in uniform had one. Aly was the kind who could seriously include a Hollywood star on his priorities list.

Their paths were almost certain to cross someday. Aly himself traveled enough to pick up the spoor of most of the beauties of the world. In 1948 Rita, too, was on the move and wandered right into Aly's own game preserve.

In May she sailed for Europe with her secretary, Shifra Haran. The first night out, they went to the first-class dining room where the captain invited them to join his table. All eyes were riveted on the red-haired "Love Goddess." It was too much for Rita; she retreated to her stateroom and ate there for the rest of the voyage.

Anita Colby, a celebrated cover girl, was also on board. A fellow passenger recalls that he could not help remarking the difference between the two famous women: Anita Colby, poised, sociable, sophisticated; Rita Hayworth, looking like "she would shrink to nothing if anyone spoke to her." His observations were acute. Rita Hayworth, that fateful spring, was a rich, famous, successful, glamorous, sought-after movie star who felt completely miserable, unworthy, and deprived of the one thing she wanted most: love.

It wasn't that she lacked men in her life; she had had two husbands and there had been a steady procession of suitors. "Rita is the kind of woman who always has to have a man around," explains one of her friends. But with none of them had she found the kind of romantic, schoolgirl bliss that was her ideal. The amorous experiences of the svelte screen star, Rita Hayworth, had never met the expectations of the plump, shy teen-age Spanish dancer, Margarita Carmen Cansino, she once had been.

There is no evidence that she ever wanted to become a movie star. In point of fact, no one ever asked her. The moment that she was born in New York in 1919, her father, Eduardo Cansino, a small, jug-eared man, son of a famous Spanish classical dancer, who had emigrated to the United States from Seville, decided she would be a dancer.

When Margarita was nine, the family moved to Los Angeles where Cansino, retired from the stage, opened a dancing school. It was hard going. Not many people could afford dancing lessons during the depression. Cansino concentrated on his most promising pupil—Margarita. When she was twelve, they began dancing as a team. They played Los Angeles theatres, worked briefly aboard one of the gambling ships anchored off the California coast and went below the border where they clicked as "The Dancing

Cansinos" at Agua Caliente, the famous Mexican gambling resort. With four shows a day to do, Margarita had no more time for school and playmates.

Lee Ellroy, a cashier at the Agua Caliente Casino in those days, remembers that Rita's mother, Volga Haworth, a former Ziegfield Follies girl of English descent, guarded her daughter ferociously in that ungirlish atmosphere. "After the evening show," he says, "a gang would get together for hamburgers or to go swimming, but most of the time Rita couldn't go. I can still see her mother sitting there, watching Rita rehearse and keeping her eye out."

A lot of Hollywood people patronized Agua Caliente and among them one evening in 1935 was a party which included Winfield Sheehan, head of the then Fox Film Company, and Louella O. Parsons, the Hollywood columnist. Miss Parsons recalls that Sheehan couldn't take his eyes off Margarita Cansino. On the way back to Hollywood he confided that he had signed her to a motion picture contract.

"What do you think about it?" he asked Miss Parsons.

"I'm afraid to say," she replied. "She's too plump."

"Oh, she'll diet," he said. "You wait and see. She'll be a great star."

As raven-haired Rita Cansino she had a run of bit parts, usually playing an exotic *femme fatale* in pictures like *Charlie Chan in Egypt*. But her career at Fox never got off the ground. One important event did take place. She met and married, at the age of eighteen, a car salesman twice her age, named Eddie Judson.

A veteran Hollywood press agent remembers that "Judson did all the talking for Rita. He was always buttonholing photographers, making deals for Rita to wear clothes from exclusive gown shops, borrowing jewelry. He was like a mother hen."

But for all of Judson's energetic promoting, Rita never would have amounted to anything if she hadn't been put on a studio assembly line by a tycoon the likes of Harry Cohn, the bluff, crude, hard-driving head of Columbia Pictures Corporation. He gave her a small part in a picture called *Only Angels Have Wings* with Richard Barthelmess. "They dressed her in a jersey dress," recalls one of Cohn's close associates. "And of course she was quite well developed. In her first scene she appeared walking down a stairway. Well, that was it. It wasn't just the dress; everything about her spelled sensuality. She had no personality off the screen but plenty of that special chemistry that shows up only on the screen. Cohn saw that and he started grooming her." Her name was changed from Cansino to a version of her mother's English surname, Hayworth. Her hairline was moved back, a hair at a time, by electrolysis, until nearly an inch more of her forehead was exposed. She became a redhead for *Strawberry Blonde* and henceforth spent hours of every week having her naturally coarse black hair bleached and tinted, and softened by oil and steam treatments. Her lackluster voice was corrected by a voice coach, Gertrude Fogler. She slimmed her waistline, lost twenty pounds.

Lou Smith, Columbia's publicity director, launched a campaign. "Whenever we wanted her to do anything, she always did it," recalls Smith. "I don't think she wanted stardom for the glamour but I think she wanted a certain security out of life, a good guy around the house. She came from very poor surroundings. Meat on the table one day and the next day, nothing." Another associate of those early days says that Rita took direction "better than anybody I ever knew. She always listened. She would never argue." The make-up men, wardrobe women, hairdressers, all the panoply of backstage technicians on whom the day's frustrations often are vented, received no temperamental treatment from Rita. "She was always punctual," recalls Helen Hunt, a hairdresser who worked on all of her pictures from the time Rita was eighteen. "She was kind, never mean. She never said a word against anyone. She never complained."

But in 1942, she revolted against Judson: "He had convinced me that I was helpless without him. He thought for me and dictated my every move. But he regarded me only as an investment. I had no fun," she explained. Judson insisted on a financial settlement. Cohn arranged it and himself took over as Rita's full-time mentor.

There were other men. Rita was nothing if not romantic.

"When she was in love," says Helen Hunt, "she was in another world. She would just sit and think about the fellow she was in love with. She was seldom out of love all the years I knew her." She fell in and out of love with Victor Mature, and, a year after her divorce became final, married Orson Welles. If Hollywood harbored an authentic genius at the time, it was Welles, a Renaissance man working in celluloid. He supplanted Cohn as Rita Hayworth's Pygmalion. He gave her a cram course in culture. They entertained his intellectual friends. They put on a magic show for the Hollywood Canteen. In December, 1944, their daughter, Rebecca, was born. But Rita was beginning to feel miscast as Galatea.

Musing recently about Rita's many unhappy romances, a woman who had known her intimately for many years said: "Rita is one of the most beautiful women in the world. She has more sex appeal than Marilyn Monroe ever had. She not only looks sensual, she is. She never talks about sex; she never tells an off-color story, but she lives it. Look at all the men she's been in love with. They all left her, eventually. I think it is because her curiosity is at such a low key. She never reads a newspaper. I doubt if she even reads her scripts, except for learning her own part. I don't know how she can enjoy life without knowing more."

Of Welles, Rita said later: "Orson stayed up all night writing. I couldn't live with his genius." Nevertheless, she wanted to keep their marriage together. They separated, reconciled, separated again. Welles wanted to make films in Europe, while she was bound to Hollywood by a long-term contract with Columbia.

Her agent, Johnny Hyde, an executive of the William Morris talent agency, set up the Beckworth (for Rebecca and Hayworth) Corporation to get her out from under the direct control of Columbia and to enable her to keep more of the money her pictures earned. Rita also took on as her business manager Lee Ellroy, the dapper, dark-haired man of French-Spanish descent she had known back in the Agua Caliente days. She had few friends; her mother recently had died; her intimates were her hairdressers, her secretaries, her dressmakers. In 1948, alone, uncertain in her new independence, still hoping for a reconciliation

with Welles, who was in Italy, Rita left for Europe. She went to
the Riviera, stopping at the Hotel du Cap d'Antibes. She was
depressed. "I'm just not well," she told Louella Parsons at a party
in Cannes. When Elsa Maxwell, the professional party-giver,
called a few days later to invite her to a party, she at first refused:
"Don't speak to me about a dinner or about anything else; my
heart is rather broken. I'm in all this trouble about Orson and
I can't think of parties." Miss Maxwell urged her to come; she
had a special reason for wanting her; "The Aly," as Elsa always
called him, just back from Syria, was going to be there. She had
promised him the presence of "some beautiful creature; the Aly
always adored a new and beautiful woman."

But Rita Hayworth demurred. She wasn't in the mood and,
furthermore, in the immemorial tradition of women everywhere,
she didn't have a thing to wear.

"Go and buy a dress," Elsa urged Rita. "Come in white and
come in late; make an entrance. I want you to meet a Persian
prince who is a real one, a wonderful person, and he will amuse
you and entertain you. It will cheer you up. You'll forget your
troubles for an evening."

And that won over Rita as it had so many of the people
who depended on Elsa Maxwell to brighten their rich but tedious
lives. She continued:

"I'll never forget. We sat there in the Cannes Summer Casino.
Everybody but Rita was there. We were playing a game. Rita
came in the door; everybody gasped. Aly said; 'My God! Who
is that?' I said, 'She's sitting next to you at dinner.' And that is all
I had time to say."

In the next few weeks, Rita was at Aly's l'Horizon almost
every day. Emrys Williams, Aly's chauffeur at the time, says that
to impress Rita, Aly ordered a quick Potemkin-village transformation of the haphazardly run Chateau. He hired a new chef,
brought down his best china and silver from his country house
outside Paris, and bought new table linen. His wooing became
even more frenzied when the Shah of Iran, who also was staying
at the Hotel du Cap, invited Rita to lunch. He was a powerful
adversary, even for Aly; he had plenty of charm, just as much
free time at the moment, and the lure of a throne to share. But

Aly's tactic of massing all of his artillery against a single target until it was leveled, immediately was brought into play. As soon as he learned of the Shah's invitation, he issued one of his own. Rita was invited, implored, begged to come to lunch. His telephone calls became more desperate, more flattering, more pathetic as the date of her luncheon with the Shah drew nearer. Few women can resist a man who is prepared, nay, poised, to kill himself if she does not appear that instant in the car he has sent around for her. Rita went, standing up the Shah, and proving to Aly that she could be won if he tried hard enough.

After that, Aly kept up the barrage. Every morning three dozen red roses arrived from the florist in Cannes where Uncle Mario got a discount because of the wholesale scale of the orders he placed for his nephew. Aly bombarded Rita with telephone calls: How was she feeling? Did she get home safely? Was she hungry, bored, lonely, in need of anything?

He was overwhelmed by her beauty. He also felt challenged by the competition: the Shah, Orson Welles, the leading men of Hollywood. It was not only the prize, it was the contest itself that was taking hold of his imagination.

## 2

Aly came up with idea after idea. If the day was rainy, there was a plane waiting to take Rita to a sunnier climate. If she wanted to forget Orson, there were diversions waiting in Paris, London, and Madrid. And, after a while, there was no question of "Why?" The only question, and it rings softer in any woman's mind as other things loom larger, was "Why not?"

Spain lay nearby. It was the country that appealed to Rita most, the home of her paternal ancestors, of the flamenco dancing she loved. In mid-August, a month after their meeting, Rita and Aly set off for Madrid, where they were recognized immediately.

They had hoped the newspapers would not find them, yet they always had reporters in mind, so much so that telepathy if nothing else would have drawn the attention of the press. On their second evening in Madrid, they went to a well-known outdoor restaurant. Their hotel had apprised the restaurant of their coming. They got an especially low bow from the head waiter; the chef came out and stood behind some latticework to take a look; the orchestra began playing songs from Rita's movies. She was expected to get up and dance, or take a bow. Instead she called over the head waiter and complained so bitterly that he immediately sensed there was more to their presence than a casual dinner date between two well-known people. And the hotel guessed because of the elaborate pains taken to let its staff know they had separate suites. So the newspapers heard about it, and the chase was on. It gave the newspapers something warm to tuck in among the long and disheartening reports on the cold war.

In Toledo, the bullfight crowd chanted "Rita" and "Aly" and ignored the bulls until the couple left.

In Madrid, they tiptoed out of the hotel through the kitchen and, at the back door, found so large a crowd waiting that Williams had to drive on the sidewalk to get them away.

They went to Lisbon and almost caused a riot.

They flew out in *The Avenger* to Biarritz. Crowds were waiting there too, so they went back to Cannes, where the press took up a vigil outside the Chateau and set up round-the-clock coverage of what promised to be the greatest love story since Edward VIII had renounced his throne for Mrs. Simpson. The reporters were helped, as usual, by hotel, restaurant, and night-club managers, and by press agents who offered friendly, indeed fervent, co-operation. As soon as Rita and Aly entered a restaurant, the head waiter's bland smile put the machinery into motion to notify the press. The system paid off in free publicity for the establishment.

Seeking some hidden aerie where the press was not about, Rita went in September to Hollywood, followed by Aly, who stopped off en route at the yearling sales in Saratoga. Hollywood has a press corps of 450 correspondents, more than cover the United Nations, supplemented by 350 press agents. The presence in their midst of a genuine Moslem prince, popularly regarded as one of the world's richest men, in company with America's "Love Goddess," left them gasping for copy. Ellroy helped Aly rent a pink stucco house on Rockingham Avenue, opposite Rita's red brick colonial on Hanover Street.

The press was omnipresent, popping up in the guise of plumbers, telephone repairmen, readers of gas meters. Rita's secretary, Miss Haran, and Aly's valet, Tutti, attempted to hold back the tide; they developed a sixth sense that could spot a reporter through a welder's mask. Rita and Aly gave up going to public places like night clubs. But even dinner at a friend's was difficult to arrange. They usually left in separate cars, then met at a garage where Rita would leave her car and go on with Aly or by cab. "We never knew where the cars were," recalls Ellroy, who also took on the job of transmitting telephone messages to foil eavesdroppers. Aly became uneasy; he looked around nervously for an exit and chose the closest foreign soil.

On November 1, Aly, Rita, and Shifra Haran took a midnight plane to Mexico City, unrecognized by their sleepy fellow-passengers. Aly was exhilarated by Mexico; he talked Spanish with Agosto, the driver he hired to show them around. He had Miss Haran take down the euphonious names of Mexico's towns and villages as possible names for his horses. When Miss Haran, not knowing just how she should address a Moslem prince, called him "Sir," he frowned: "Are you making fun of me?" He bought her a gold watch for intervening when he had had a spat with Rita and always identified himself to her when he telephoned Rita's suite by saying: "This is your little friend."

But the press learned they were there and donned a new set of disguises, exchanging uniforms with elevator operators, bellhops, and waiters. The backdoor getaways, stampedes, and wild automobile chases began again. They went to Acapulco and had a few days of relative quiet. Then Aly dropped out of sight. Rita returned to Mexico City again and held a press conference, alone. She discussed her past and future movies, while a Columbia Pictures representative nodded ecstatically. When a reporter asked the question for which all forty had come, she was primed. Would she marry Aly Khan while the two of them were in Mexico? "I'm not divorced yet," said Miss Hayworth. Where was the Prince at the moment? "I don't know," she replied.

Where was Aly? He had returned from Acapulco with Rita. But he was exhausted by the exigencies of so mobile and public a romance. He felt cut off from his old life and friends, and he was beginning to worry about his father's reaction to the publicity he was getting.

Both Aly and Rita might have been ready to let their romance simmer down a bit, at least enough to get some of the heat off. But as one Hollywood columnist, Sheilah Graham, wrote: "It would really hurt Rita, if the Prince ditches her. It would kill her reputation for glamorous sex appeal and without that, what has she?" Aly had his own reputation to think about. And so they clung to each other. They pushed on to Cuba; perhaps there at Varadero Beach they would get a few minutes of privacy in which to discover whether they were as much in love as the newspapers said they were. Aly went as "A. Kahn"; Rita as "Margarita Cansino de Welles," a half-hearted attempt at disguise. More night clubs, more Latin atmosphere; Rita's appetite for Spanish folkways seemed inexhaustible. Aly cheered up with the change of scene, as always, but in a few days he grew sullen again.

They made their way back to Hollywood where Rita picked up her final divorce decree from Welles, informed Columbia that she would not make the picture they had scheduled for her, and was promptly suspended, cutting off her salary of $248,000 a year. Hollywood columnist Herb Stein quipped that Rita had gone "from Cohn to Cannes to Khan to canned."

Rita was oblivious. When in love she thought only of the man in her life. And now she felt she had found the right man. He was handsome and charming. Hollywood money and fame meant nothing to him. He belonged to a different world, not the back-biting battle zone of the movie industry, but the land of jasmine and smog-free sunshine that was the French Riviera, the metropolis of champagne and gallantry that was Paris. He was gentle and understanding, and impassioned by her. Rita had worked since childhood, danced until she blacked out from fatigue, submerged all her feelings to be agreeable. Christmas was approaching, a time when all good Americans take inventory of their lives, and, taking stock of hers, she decided Aly was what she had been seeking ever since those long days when, plump and frightened, practicing hour after hour with her father, she had dreamed of something better.

# Chapter XIX

*"From the looks of things, would you say that Orson couldn't, but Aly Khan?"*
—HERB STEIN, Hollywood columnist

J ust before midnight of December 23, the liner *Britannic* hove to off Cobh in southern Ireland. A tender drew alongside the ship and a sleepy handful of passengers, huddled in heavy coats against the cold, got aboard. A winch lowered their luggage in a net. There was more luggage than usual; Mrs. Welles alone had sixty pieces. Her red hair tucked under a scarf, a mink coat over blue corduroy slacks, she took a seat in the tender's salon. Rebecca, wearing a snowsuit and rubbing her eyes, followed her, then climbed into the lap of Miss Haran and fell asleep. Several feet away sat Aly, coat collar up, his hat shoved low over his eyes. Two cars were waiting for them; outside of town, they all transferred to a powerful American sedan, to elude reporters.

Dawn was creeping into a pale sky when the car drove through the iron gate, adorned with two golden lion heads, of Aly's Gilltown Stud and up the curving road to the two-story beige and green house, with its cast-iron jockeys, painted in Aly's racing colors, standing as hitching posts before the front door.

Christmas Eve, Aly and Rita went shopping in Dublin. Rita bought him a dart board. Aly bought her a diamond bracelet. A traditional Christmas cake, filled with trinkets which were saved from year to year, was baked for Christmas day. A big Christmas tree sheltered the gifts. The holiday was celebrated as enthusiastically at this Islamic outpost in Ireland as it had been at the Aga's villa in Gstaad.

It was a quiet Christmas. Even the reporters who had been keeping vigil at the gate took a holiday after Aly had agreed to a stilted interview in which, while dodging the question everyone wanted answered, he managed to offer something of an alibi to calm things down at Villa Yakimour.

"I am glad to be back," he began. "Sometimes I think I am more Irish than the Irish." He always loved to tell visitors to his Irish home that his neighbors referred to him as Prince Alec McCann. And then he made his point, as though communicating directly with the Aga: "My trip to America was largely concerned with the racing affairs of my father and myself."

In Hollywood, a Columbia spokesman insisted: "At the moment there is no question of matrimony. Rita is fond of Aly, and he is of her, but he is a married man. Besides, Rita is a little soured on marriage. Aly has time to be attentive. Rita likes to be entertained." Every sentence was barbed; Harry McCohn was taking no chances on losing his multimillion-dollar creation to Alec McCann.


2


*The Avenger* flew them to London where they rushed through the Ritz lobby so hurriedly that Rebecca stumbled and fell. Aly picked her up and carried her into the elevator.

The next day they flew to Paris. Reporters met them at the airport. From Paris they went to Gstaad, the Swiss ski resort where Le Rosey moves for its winter school term. Aly's secretary wired the Palace Hotel for rooms. The press, of course, knew right away, and it knew something else that Aly did not. Already staying at the Palace Hotel was Joan Aly Khan, who so far had kept a discreet silence on the affair. As soon as she learned that Aly was coming, she packed and returned to England. "I'm surprised she left," said Aly, when he arrived a few hours later, still insisting he could not understand why anyone found his travels with Rita exceptional.

Back in London, Joan told reporters: "The whole business is a little too sordid." She stood in the entrance hall of her house in Belgravia, looking as though she expected Aly and Rita, trailed by Rebecca and the secretary, to come marching up at any moment. "I have no idea what my husband's plans are. If he wants to return here, well, the house is his."

That was the furthest thing from Aly's mind at the moment. While Rita took her first ski lessons, and Rebecca played with Karim and Amyn, he took stock.

The law of the sea also applies to great lovers in distress: women and children first. The London *Daily Express* had taken him to task over Rebecca, "this small sulky person in zip-sided boots and the same woolly ski suit being dragged by back door gangways, pushed out of side door exits, bundled into cars at midnight, lugged into one plane after another when she is too tired to walk."

Rita was under attack at home. Critical sermons were being preached in American churches, the Catholic Legion of Decency had commented, and the motion picture chairman of the General Federation of Women's Clubs had suggested a boycott of her movies. Hollywood had joined in the hue and cry against its errant goddess. Billy Wilkerson, publisher of the influential trade paper, *The Hollywood Reporter*, proposed that the industry "wash its hands of Rita Hayworth."

It was not only what was being printed, but what was being said among their friends that made the horizon look so black from Aly's vantage point in the Swiss Alps. In every celebrated love affair, there are always people who look for the flaw in the diamond bracelet, the bomb in the bouquet. Now it was being whispered that Rita was pregnant. Rumors like that travel with twice the speed of sound; undoubtedly, this one had reached Yakimour.

Aly's fears were heightened when the lofty figure of Begum Yvette appeared at Gstaad. At dinner she gave Rita and Aly news of the Aga. His health had been poor since the Diamond Jubilee. More and more, he sat—or rather, lay—on a rubber-wheeled chaise longue in the salon at Yakimour, reading his mail and the newspapers, dictating letters, and wondering if what he read and heard about Aly was true.

There was nothing else to do but head south for Yakimour. The Aga later wrote in his autobiography: "I asked them if they were really devoted to each other; they both said that they were, so I advised them to get married as soon as possible."

The reporters on duty outside the Chateau de l'Horizon were invited in for the big announcement. Aly shook hands with each one, chatting amiably in English, French, and Italian, pointing out a new Dufy painting over the fireplace and helping them identify some of the portraits of the generals under whom he had served in the war. The butler served whisky and aperitifs from a silver tray. Aly wore his blue blazer and old flannels. He explained why Rita wasn't there: "She has a touch of the flu." He handed out two typewritten statements and then sat silently as the reporters scanned them. One was His; the other, Hers.

Aly's tone was now one of injured innocence:

I have hitherto refrained from making any comment upon the uninformed and often scurrilous and vicious reports which have recently appeared in some sections of the press in connection with my domestic affairs. I should now like it to be made known that by mutual consent my wife and I have lived apart for over three years; that appropriate proceedings have been in progress for nearly a year; and that immediately these proceedings terminate steps will be taken to remedy a position which appears to have provided material for the press comment complained of.

I am going to marry Miss Hayworth as soon as I am free to do so. In the circumstances I hope that my private affairs will be treated with the consideration which is usually extended to the private affairs of individuals in general.

Hers read:

I am fully conversant with the statement which Prince Aly Khan has today issued to the press, and am in full agreement with what he says. I have only been waiting for him to be free to marry him.

The reporters looked up from their reading and cleared their throats. Aly smiled and nodded. The questions began:
When?
"I hope it will be as soon as possible. No date has been set."
Where?
"We haven't decided yet. Britain. France. Any place."
Now it was time for a show of family solidarity. Yakimour's gates were thrown open to the press and the Aga and the Begum, Aly and Rita, posed for pictures and chatted. The Aga concentrated on one small theme: "There are 150,000 divorces in Britain annually. Why should everyone criticize my son?"
The Begum wore a jeweled sari. Rita, wearing a black sweater and a full plaid skirt which deprived the journalists of grounds for further speculation, said she expected to be "very, very happy" in her new marriage but she didn't know when it would take place. In fact, she had no immediate plans, "only to vacation here a little longer." In January the marriage still seemed far away.
Joan was even more co-operative than Aly had expected. She arrived in Paris a day ahead of schedule to file her own divorce suit, which did not mention Rita but simply said her husband had shown "lack of consideration." The formalities had to be gone through. French law insists that the emphasis in a divorce hearing be on reconciliation, and French bureaucracy allows no short cuts. Accordingly, Judge Jacques Rousselet met first with Joan alone and then with Joan and Aly to try and talk them out of it. A humorist might have sport imagining the consequences if he had succeeded.
Aly and Rita returned to the Chateau. Marriage, at last, seemed imminent and Rita, at least, was in a hurry. On April 1, she said she expected to be married "within four weeks." But

Aly fell and broke his left ankle while playing with Karim and Amyn; the date was left indefinite.

They returned to Paris, to Jacques Fath's salon, to choose Rita's trousseau. His top model, a redhead with marvelous cheekbones who walked like a willow swishing back and forth, paraded gowns for them. Her name was Bettina.

# Chapter XX

*"It will be a very simple wedding, very intimate. Only close friends of Miss Hayworth and myself will be present."*

—ALY KHAN

With the announcement that they would wed, Rita's and Aly's romance took on a whole new fairy-tale aspect; forgotten were the harsh words of yesterday, replaced by allusions to Prince Charming and Cinderella. A storybook romance was just what the world needed in the spring of 1949, as a respite from all its crises. Those were the days of the Berlin airlift, the trial of Alger Hiss, Communist consolidations in China and Czechoslovakia. No wonder that newspaper editors, seeking to lighten the load of hard news, fell upon Rita and Aly and made their marriage plans the most talked-about trivia of the year. The watching reporters outside the Chateau were reinforced by colleagues from all over the world; they were watched in turn by clots of tourists who gaped from the highway, heedless of their safety.

The prospect of a wedding ceremony conducted before so

many prying and expertly inquisitive eyes began to worry Aly. French law requires that all marriages be performed in public at the *mairie*, or town hall, of the municipality in which the couple resides. Already several towns along the Riviera were vying for the wedding. Le Cannet, the Cannes suburb in which Yakimour is situated, pointed out that its town hall boasted an elevator, "and since the Aga Khan can't walk upstairs because of gout, the wedding should be held here." The Chateau was within the boundaries of the commune of Vallauris, a hill town which had experienced a whiff of fame when Picasso chose it for his pottery-making. A wedding, one almost royal, might be even more of a tourist attraction and the possibilities stirred the mind of Vallauris's Communist mayor, Paul Derigon, an agreeable man in whom Marxist materialism and capitalistic enterprise coexisted as happily as two Picasso doves.

Aly, fearing the worst, asked the French Ministry of Justice for special permission to have the civil wedding ceremony inside the Chateau. While he waited for a reply, and also for receipt of his final divorce decree from Joan, wedding plans went ahead with no one quite sure when or where the ceremony would take place. Invitations were printed with the date left blank, to be filled in later by hand, but the locale was optimistically given as the Chateau de l'Horizon.

Guests were coming from as far away as Hollywood and Brazil. Some of them had other appointments to keep, including the Aga, who was scheduled to be in Paris on May 28. The exact date of the wedding became more and more critical and still it wasn't set.

Aly had never been so busy. He liked planning parties and he did it expertly and imaginatively. Now he focused all of his inexhaustible energy on the details of the wedding: the guest list, the menu, the wines, the seating arrangements. As much as he feared the publicity, he was beginning to think of his wedding as a public event, like the Aga's Diamond Jubilee. He wanted it to go off perfectly. He recruited the Riviera's top professionals to help; all were old friends.

The luncheon at the Chateau, following the wedding ceremony, was put in charge of Jacques Duclos, suave director of the Cannes Casino, with advisory functions assigned to his boss, the redoubtable Monsieur André. Aly checked up on the shopping list: 40 lobsters, 110 pounds of cold meats, ten pounds of caviar, 25 pounds of salad, 1,500 cookies, 40 pounds of petits-fours, and a 120-pound wedding cake. He reminded chef Gondolfo not to serve ham.

Jules, the bar manager of the Carlton, was to be in charge of the bars at the Chateau. He promptly created a new cocktail, the Ritaly: two-thirds Canadian Club, one-third Italian vermouth, two drops of bitters, and a cherry.

Neither Aly's divorce nor permission to hold the wedding at the Chateau had come through but a date was set anyway, May 27, and the invitations were sent out to about ninety people, many of whom already had been invited by long-distance phone. Printed in English, the invitations read very simply: "MISS RITA HAYWORTH AND PRINCE ALY KHAN INVITE YOU TO THEIR WEDDING. . . ." They went to members of the family, including the Aga's ex-wife Princess Andrée; Aly's maternal aunt, Aimée, the former ballet dancer, and her third husband, a Nice dentist; a sprinkling of titled Indians like the Maharajah and Maharanee of Baroda; European royalty like the Prince and Princess de Bourbon-Parma (she was a sister of former King Umberto of Italy); wartime friends like Nigel Campbell; Paris society friends like Baron and Baroness James de Rothschild; family employees like Mme. Vuillier, who ran the French stables, and Nesbitt Waddington and Mrs. Nellie Smithwick, who ran the Irish Studs; art dealer Henri Gaffié and painter Maurice Utrillo; Tommy Burke, the tennis pro; Jacques Fath, the couturier; Edith Piaf, the singer; and, of course, Monsieur André. The guest list ranged the curious cross-section of people with whom Aly was intimate.

Rita's friends were a lonely few, reflecting what her life in Hollywood had been: Charles Vidor, the movie director, and his wife, who was the niece of Jack Warner, the Hollywood tycoon; Louella Parsons, the Hollywood columnist, whose invitation was the most publicized of all; Helen Morgan, who had just quit Columbia where she was Rita's personal press agent to cover the wedding for *Time* and *Life* magazines; Rita's agent, Johnny Hyde; and her business manager, Lee Ellroy, who brought along her cocker spaniel, Pookles, and a suitcase full of nylon stockings when he flew in from Hollywood.

The Duke and Duchess of Windsor were rumored to have been on the original invitation list but to have indicated in some ducal way that they would not accept. Harry Cohn was invited but, still sulking at Rita's insubordination, said he was too busy to make it. Rita's father, Eduardo Cansino, claimed he got his invitation too late to get there; nevertheless, Rita was hurt and in an eleventh-hour wave of family feeling, wept because none of her relatives had sent congratulations.

Forty-eight hours before the wedding, the French Ministry of Justice turned down Aly's request that it be held at the Chateau.

Mayor Derigon, the procurer of the Republic and the *sous-préfet* of the Alpes-Maritimes, went in person to the Chateau to give Aly the news. The procurer and the *sous-préfet* wore top hats and formal dress for the occasion. A startled Aly received them wearing what struck Derigon as "pyjamas." He recalls: "Both sides were rather embarrassed."

Derigon already had begun sprucing up his town hall, in case it should be needed. Now he pushed ahead with capitalist vigor. He decided that the ceremony would be held in a larger room on the ground floor where ration coupons had been distributed until recently, instead of in an upstairs room usually used for marriages. He ordered it painted and sent his assistant to borrow red carpets, green plants, chairs, a table, and some tapestries from local merchants. He printed special badges for the eighty-four wedding guests and others for the press. He began holding press conferences and, for forty-eight hours, became one of the most widely-quoted Communists in the world hierarchy as he announced his plans for greeting seven princes, four princesses, a maharajah, two generals and six other assorted title-holders, including a gaekwar and an emir. He consulted with Aly, who drove up to Vallauris to discuss the details. Together, they paced off the distance between the room and the front entrance, discussed where everyone should sit, and where the photographers should stand. Aly brought along a gift for the town: one million francs (about two thousand dollars) in thousand-franc notes, wrapped in a newspaper.

With the arrival in Cannes of Lee Ellroy and Helen Morgan, a semiofficial nod was given to the army of reporters camped outside the Chateau. Ellroy set up press headquarters in Suite 131 at the Carlton and announced that some of the press would be invited to the wedding luncheon. They would be issued special passes and be admitted to a lower terrace; the regular guests, for lunch in the garden, would get pink discs, designed and signed by Ellroy. The commotion which accompanied each of his statements—more often they were denials—was comparable to the rush of White House correspondents to their phones after a presidential press conference.

Aly had a full program of entertainment planned for his guests. A few days before the wedding he rented the Alexandre III theatre in Cannes to show Rita's latest picture, *The Loves of Carmen*. An afternoon showing was held for all the servants who could be spared from the Chateau and Yakimour, and for the tradespeople, craftsmen and caterers who were helping in the preparations for the wedding. On the eve of the wedding, a dinner was given for sixty persons at Les Terrasses, a restaurant in the little hill town of Mougins. The menu, chosen and titled by Aly, revealed him as more of a fan of his future wife's career than anyone had suspected. It began with Coupe "Cover Girl" and ended with Bombe "Gilda" and Strawberry "Blonde." Rita wore pink and a twelve-carat diamond ring that Aly had given her.

For several nights before the wedding, a task force of reporters scoured night clubs in Cannes, Nice and the towns in between. They couldn't believe that the bridegroom would not be out celebrating somewhere. When they failed to find him, they notified their newspapers that Aly was changing his ways.

They were wrong. Almost every night, at 3 or 4 A.M., when the scheduled festivities were over and everyone else at the Chateau had gone to sleep, Aly's car could be heard racing out of the driveway. A couple of hours later it would return. Two nights before the wedding, Aly invited Ellroy, who was staying at the Chateau, to accompany him on a 3 A.M. excursion. They went to the Casino at Cannes for some gambling. Aly turned to Ellroy. "You've been here a week or so now, haven't you?" he asked. Ellroy replied in the affirmative. Aly, the host who thought of everything, disappeared and came back in a few minutes with two attractive girls, one a breezy blonde. "Take your pick," he offered. When Ellroy declined, Aly shrugged and disappeared with the blonde.

## 2

And finally the wedding day dawned, clear and golden. Along the narrow main street of Vallauris, shutters flew open and children and housewives hurried along the sidewalk carrying long, fresh-baked loaves of bread. There was the sweet acrid smell of morning dust and strong coffee, and then, suddenly, the overpowering smell of exhaust fumes as trucks, jeeps, and cars full of white-gauntleted French policemen—the tough *Compagnie Républicaine de Sécurité*—swung up the street. Their radio aerials whipped the air like the riding crops of circus ringmasters. Behind them came reporters and photographers in cars and station wagons, crammed with ladders and flash bulbs. The police and journalists went to work, side by side, as though they were not enemies who in a few hours would be locked in mortal combat. The police strung rope barriers; the photographers sat on the church steps, checking their cameras; the reporters went into cafés for early morning cognac and coffee.

Derigon arrived at the *mairie*—a self-effacing man, bony as a deacon. Enough of a crowd had gathered for the police to take their posts, motioning people back with their white gauntlets. A police jeep parked ostentatiously at the steps of the *mairie*, its radio crackling as its passenger—a saturnine *commandant*—bent forward to listen to messages from another police jeep at the Chateau.

The crowd, thick now, numbering over a thousand, pressed forward, almost closing the narrow lane the police were trying to keep open for the wedding procession. Fathers held up children for a better view; Derigon had declared the day a holiday and the schools were closed. The journalists entered the *mairie*, flashing the badges Derigon had given them so sparingly, and went into the ground-floor room. A railing divided the front part of the room, where invited guests would stand, from the larger rear part where the journalists and members of the public had been allotted space. At about 10 A.M., an hour before the start of the ceremony, a grey Alfa-Romeo wheeled up to the *mairie*. It held Aly, with Sadri at the wheel. He wore a double-breasted black morning coat and grey striped trousers, newly tailored for him in England, but he looked ruffled, and his face was frozen with fatigue and impatience. He disappeared inside for a long and spirited discussion with Derigon. His running battle with the press, his fear of publicity and what the Aga might say about it, had been driving him desperately since daybreak. He had come to plead with Derigon, once more, to limit the movements of the journalists. What followed was this: The police unceremoniously herded the journalists out of the room and onto the stairway leading to the upper floors of the *mairie*. The journalists, principally the thirty Frenchmen among them, thereupon began muttering loudly and ominously. They argued with the police, with Derigon's secretary, and with Derigon himself, whenever he passed by. At the stroke of eleven, the Aga Khan and his Begum stepped out of their green Rolls-Royce to applause from the crowd. The Begum, towering above the Aga like a ship's figurehead, wore a pale blue sari, while her husband wore a cream-colored suit, with a giant rose in his buttonhole, dark glasses, and a fixed smile.

A cheer went up as a white Cadillac convertible came into view bringing Rita Hayworth in a blue dress and hat. The crowd grew to about three thousand, for the people who had been lining the road all the way from the Chateau up to the town, a distance of two miles, had trailed Rita's car up the hill. Rita joined Aly inside the big room while Derigon stood in the stairwell and tried to calm the reporters. They shouted reminders at him that their newspapers were influential, that France was a democracy,

and that French law required marriages to be held in public.
Inside the room, the wedding guests heard the fuss and smiled—
all except Aly, who was looking at the Aga, and who knew that
his hope of keeping the press inconspicuous had been defeated.
The journalists filed back into the rear of the big room, surly, suspicious, and arguing among themselves. Barely heard, Vallauris's
Secretary-General, Jean Rochas, read the marriage license.

Derigon stood up and asked Rita and Aly, who were sitting
opposite him, whether they accepted one another as husband and
wife. *"Oui, oui,"* said Aly. *"Oui, oui,"* said Rita. The guests
smiled, for the double affirmative was the fashionable thing to do,
a modern sign of passion barely held in check. Aly leaned forward
to sign the marriage register. Rita and the witnesses followed.
Eight minutes had passed. Aly slipped his arm around his bride's
waist and kissed her. The guests looked at one another and simultaneously raised their eyebrows—for he had kissed her on the
mouth, an Americanism not yet imported generally into France.

Derigon then stood up and read the speech on which he had
been laboring for three days. It was addressed primarily to Aly,
who shifted restlessly in his seat as the encomiums flowed on.
The wedding, the mayor said, was a "sensational event to which
the prestige and renown of your Highness had focused the attention of the entire world. By your grace, our little city where our
workmen fashion pottery and ceramics and our peasants reap
orange blossoms is honoured this day to have the name of
Vallauris spread throughout the universe with that of Prince Aly
Khan and the great artist, Rita Hayworth."

And so the lovers, legally linked at last, emerged into the
open air, half-blinded by flashbulbs, vaguely hearing the cheers
of the crowd, and fled into Aly's white convertible, which now
had its top down and was preceded and followed by motorcycle
police. The procession wound down the hillside roads and onto
the coastal highway, where hundreds of cars had stopped and
little clusters of people were waiting to wave and cheer. The fact
that it was over, that there had been no rioting in the streets, no
hurled cobblestones; that the Aga had not been injured, nor the
Begum outraged, and that everything had gone—was going—off

as well as could be expected, dawned on Aly and he, too, as Rita was doing, began to wave at the people on the road. He allowed himself a grin, the first of the day, and one of the few since he had left Gstaad for a meeting with his future. At the Chateau, everything was ready: thousands of fresh flowers had been wired into the ivy to embellish the garden; two hundred gallons of eau de cologne had been poured into the swimming pool, in which floated two giant floral wreaths in the shape of an A (for Aly) and an M (for Margarita).

As soon as Rita and Aly arrived, Jules offered each of them a Ritaly cocktail. "They each took a sip," he recalls. "I made over four hundred of my drink, the Ritaly, that day. The guests didn't drink much but the journalists, especially the Indian journalists, oh, the Indian journalists; they drank, some of them, seven or eight of my Ritalys. I lost my fountain pen writing the recipe for an Indian journalist. It was a gold Parker."

And so the afternoon slipped by, with the journalists penned on the lower terrace, crushed around Jules' bar, the uninvited hovering in boats offshore, while up above Yves Montand sang (Piaf had been unable to come), Aly read congratulatory telegrams, and Rita sat, tired, beneath her floppy picture hat. Tommy Burke remembers her sitting in an armchair, surrounded by "all these Indians. They all knelt down and kissed her foot. It was a very peculiar thing to see. Extraordinary! And each one had something to give her, pearls or a little gold object. She would take it and pass it over. It was extraordinary! She looked emotional about it, all these people whom she had never seen before, all different types, with women dressed in native costumes and some with rings in their noses, going on their knees to her."

A few feet away, the Begum sat smiling stiffly, as the Aga glumly conveyed spoonful after spoonful of caviar into his mouth. A guest who sat near him that day was still awed, years afterward, by the amount of caviar the Aga had consumed. It might have been due to his nerves. In his autobiography he said he hadn't had a good time: "This was a fantastic, semiroyal, semi-Hollywood affair; my wife and I played our part in the ceremony, much as we disapproved of the atmosphere with which it was surrounded."

Everyone agreed the bride and groom were very much in love. "With Aly," said Uncle Mario, "it was not that kind of strong love which lasts; it was perhaps superficial, it was a passion, but passion is part of love and he loved Rita very much. And Rita, surely she was in love with Aly."

# Chapter XXI

*"Aly wasn't exactly what you would call a homebody."*

—RITA HAYWORTH

As the last wedding guest left, so did Aly's high spirits. Once more, he felt, the Aga had had his way. After a small family dinner in the evening, the Aga and Begum left for Paris—mission accomplished. Aly was visibly edgy the next day as the Moslem marriage ceremony began, this time in the privacy of the Chateau, performed by two *mullahs* from the Paris Mosque. They read from the Koran, accepted Aly's assurance that he would provide his wife with a house and dowry, and toasted the newlyweds in fruit juice.

As soon as it was over, Aly slipped out of the house. Running into a night watch of reporters at the bridge, he stopped to tell them of the Moslem ceremony; it would make good reading in Nairobi, Bombay, and Karachi.

Whenever Aly felt the Aga had triumphed over him, he avenged his honor and soothed his pride in a burst of excitement. He sought comfort now wherever he could, visiting friends, playing tennis with Tommy Burke—Rita tried doubles, but soon gave up—and disappearing for unexplained periods of time. Gaffié, who was very close to him during this period, explains: "Aly was a tender man and a sentimental man, with an enormous affection for Rita. But he was of Oriental origin and to him it was of no great importance to 'pillage' a little one way or another. To see a woman on the side was of no importance at all. Rita ought to have accepted it because she had seen he was like that before the marriage."

Just how much Rita knew, she has never said. Asked recently how she had reacted to newspaper reports that Aly was seeing other women, she said: "I paid no attention because, well, what was I supposed to do?"

She settled into a routine as simple as Aly's was involved. She was determined to find tranquillity and security. She talked of retiring, of never being Rita Hayworth again. "I wanted to be a woman, not a man," she recalled. "I thought Aly would take over."

She let her hair go back to its natural color. Around the house, she wore blue jeans and little or no make-up. She slept late, breakfasted American-style on fruit juice, ham and eggs, toast, and coffee, and puttered around the terrace and her room, doing her nails and listening to records.

To Aly, such a routine meant boredom. He had married Rita Hayworth the film star. He had never asked her to give up her career. It never occurred to him that she was also Margarita Carmen Cansino, who had been working hard most of her life and now, more than anything, wanted a spell of quiet domesticity. Rita liked to spend evenings home alone. By alone, she meant with Aly. But Aly felt alone with anything less than a mob.

"His whole life was so different," Rita explained. "It was too difficult for me. I wasn't prepared for it and, who knows, he probably wasn't prepared for me."

She was baffled and discomfited by the international set. The gossip was about people and places she didn't know, and often in French. Although Aly hired a tutor to teach her the language, she found it slow going. Often she realized with a pang that guests at the Chateau knew the house better than she, and felt

more at home there. And so many of them were women, sophisticated women, the kind that always made her feel ill at ease.

To Aly's friends, she was disappointing—shy, unglamorous,
unworldly. They looked at her with all the knowledge they had
gained from gossip columns and fan magazines, and made no
further attempt to know her. "She was obviously out of her
depth," one of them recalls, "in a situation that did not please
her."

Soon there were arguments and sudden departures from the
luncheon table, headaches, and lunches on trays upstairs. There
were periods of sullen silence, until Aly was able to work his
charm again. Then there would be the sweet taste of reconciliation. But he kept up his pace. Some evenings Rita got so melancholy that, after several highballs, she would lock herself in her
room, put some Spanish music on the phonograph and dance for
hours all by herself.

Everyone assumed Rita was pregnant. Indeed, someone in the
Aga's entourage had been hinting at it since the wedding ceremony, as if impatient to prepare public opinion for an official
announcement. The trial balloons went up and lingered; soon
there was no reason to bring them down. But Rita and Aly kept
silent. They went to England for the racing at Epsom Downs
and stayed at Peter Beatty's Mereworth Castle. Aly was shocked
by his friend's appearance; he was nearly blind. They saw the
Derby with the Charles Vidors. The director took the opportunity to ask Rita if she would make another film with him. She
was vague but didn't rule out the possibility. The fact was, she
was in an embarrassing position for a Hollywood star married to
a wealthy prince. She needed money. She had never managed to
save much and she had received no income from movies since
her suspension almost a year before. Her father was asking for
money to buy a new dance studio and her brothers, Vernon and
Eduardo, wanted help. She had rented her Los Angeles house for
$600 a month but its maintenance and the salaries of her business
manager and secretary came to more than that. Aly had made a
$2,000 payment for her on her life insurance, a $100,000 policy,
of which Rebecca was the beneficiary. But he himself was short

of cash; as usual, his expenses were running ahead of his income. Even Rita's French teacher had not been paid and Helen Morgan had had to give her money for her fare back to Paris. After talking to Rita, Vidor was able to say: "She has no definite plans but I imagine she will do another picture, and I imagine I will direct it."

The newspapermen at Epsom Downs, noting Rita's loose fitting coat, again predicted she was expecting a child. A few weeks later, at Longchamps race track in Paris, she fainted. Marcel Boussac, the textile magnate, caught her in his arms and helped carry her into the Jockey Club. That convinced the Paris newspapers, and even Aly gave up denying the reports. The baby would be born in February, he said.

They went on to Deauville, which was having its greatest season since the war. Undoubtedly the highlight of the season was a Franco-Egyptian gala at the Casino. King Farouk, the guest of honor, gave the party a touch of exoticism that only a Chicago gangster could have matched, by bringing along a squad of food-tasters. As each course was brought out—melon, lobster, chicken, fruit, and ice cream—one of these hired tongues tried a morsel; the chief bodyguard studied him for adverse reactions before signaling to the King that it was edible. The Aga and Begum were in Farouk's party, presumably taking their chances on the menu along with everybody else. The Begum wore a solitaire diamond ring, diamond pendant earrings, a large diamond brooch, and a diamond necklace. A lot of the conversation at Farouk's table was about diamonds, for on their way to catch the plane from Cannes to Deauville, the Aga and Begum had been held up by a smartly disciplined gang of bandits, armed with Tommy guns, who took her jewel case containing $785,000 of valuable gems.

Aly and Rita were in the room, but not at Farouk's table. They stayed out of the limelight as much as possible. Rita in a maternity dress made by Jacques Fath, looked tired, and both she and Aly appeared bored. After dinner, Rita went home while Aly went into the private rooms to play *chemin de fer*. That night $2,400,000 changed hands, the Casino management reported, a record for Deauville.

"He was like quicksilver that summer at Deauville," a friend said of Aly. "He'd disappear in the morning, to see the horses. He'd come back for breakfast and disappear again. Suddenly Rita would find that twenty-five people had been invited to lunch. She'd sit at the head of the big table and look around. There would be six women there we all suspected Aly had been sleeping with. Everyone was watching her to see how she reacted, looking her up and down, laughing at her French. Evenings, she'd go to bed at ten after seeing that Rebecca, and Karim and Amyn who were staying there too, were in bed. Aly would be gone half the night."

Afternoons were sometimes better. Aly would play with Rebecca and the boys on the beach in front of the red brick villa. They built castles with tunnels, bridges, and runways, down which they rolled marbles. Rita joined them barefoot, in rolled-up blue jeans and a short red jacket, her hair pulled back with a ribbon. She looked like this one day when visitors from Hollywood arrived. Harry Cohn, the head of Rita's studio, and Jules Stein, the head of Music Corporation of America, the powerful talent agency to which Rita recently had switched from William Morris, flew in with their wives for what Rita described in a letter to a friend as "big business talks." Aly had never opposed her career; on the contrary, he was encouraging her to go back to it. "I don't think she wanted to come back," Mrs. Cohn recalls. "She liked being Princess Margarita. She and Aly seemed to be in love. They showed great affection toward one another. We had heard the talk about other women, of course; everyone had. I think Rita had found out. But women like Rita think that love conquers all and that they probably can handle any crisis and change things."

Aly and Rita spent autumn in Paris in a state of nerves induced by the Aga's insistence that the baby would be born at any moment. He announced, anonymously, on a couple of occasions that the birth was imminent, that a room had been reserved for Rita at a Swiss clinic; he even fixed on October as the likely date. Aly denied each report. The baby, he insisted, would be born in February. There was a lot of counting on fingers in Paris that fall.

And then came news that moved Aly more deeply than anything had in years. Peter Beatty had jumped from a sixth-floor window of the London Ritz and killed himself. Aly, his face grey, flew over in his own plane from Paris for the funeral. He hardly spoke and then unsmilingly: "He was my best friend, one of the nicest persons who ever lived."

No death since his mother's had affected Aly so much. He was thirty-eight; Beatty had been thirty-nine; and his own life suddenly seemed to be racing by. He had wanted to sample everything, enjoy everything, and suddenly he felt impaled by time. It was in this mood that he took off in *The Avenger* after the funeral. As the plane climbed, one of its two motors cut out. *The Avenger* heeled over and began a slow spiral descent. On the runway below an ambulance and fire trucks raced out to await the expected crash. The plane slipped a few more times, as if it was going into a spin, then straightened out and, turning slowly, drifted in for a bumpy landing. Aly got out and grinned. He was never a man to show fear. But the close call, coming on the heels of Beatty's death, had an effect that showed up in his future actions.

2

The Aga, following his own concept of public relations, was still making announcements as to when the baby's birth could be expected, apparently to let the world know, well in advance, that it would be "premature," although how he could foresee this, he didn't explain—to Westerners; Ismailis, of course, took it for granted that their Imam was prescient. Rita shrank more and more into herself as her pregnancy became more obvious, while Aly flung himself on the town. Having gotten past October, the month the Aga had decided would see the birth of the baby, they went off to Lausanne, where the most luxurious suite in the Clinique Montchoisi had been reserved. Known informally as the royal suite, it consisted of a bedroom and a drawing room, the latter fitted out for everything from a husband's catnaps to a full-scale cocktail party. Meanwhile, they installed themselves in a suite in the Lausanne Palace Hotel, and settled down to another game of hide-and-seek with the press. This was an unusual birthwatch since the date was so much in question. The Aga's and Aly's predictions ran as much as four months apart. Aly and Rita sent the ten American correspondents a case of Scotch for Christmas. They felt especially triumphant, for the Aga had been predicting the baby would be born before the holidays. Some newspapermen who had gone to Lausanne in response to the Aga's announcements already had left without a story when, three days after Christmas, at three in the morning, Rita's time came. Aly rushed her to the clinic. At 11 A.M. he emerged, looking exhausted, stammering out the news to waiting reporters: a girl had been born at 9:45 A.M. Five and a half pounds. The baby's name would be Yasmin, the Arabic name for jasmine. Rita had had a very tough time. She was very tired. So was her husband, he laughed. Someone handed him a cup of hot grog and he raised it to the men standing around him scribbling on their pads. "Let's all have a drink." He eyed one of the newsmen triumphantly: "I told you that premature babies run in our family." The early gossips—and the Aga—had been wrong. Eleven months had elapsed since Rita and Aly had announced in Cannes that they would wed. But they had been married for only seven months.

# Chapter XXII

"Mr. (Charles) Torem further stated that
if the defendant, Prince Aly Salomone Khan,
had wanted to stop the plaintiff, Margarita
Cansino Khan (also known as Rita Hayworth)
from leaving France it would have been easy
for him to do so, because of the influence and
power which said H.H. The Prince Aly Khan
and said H.H. The Aga Khan had with the
government and police authorities of France
. . . thus enabling the defendant to acquire
custody of their daughter, Princess Yasmin
Aga Khan."
          —BARTLEY C. CRUM, in an affidavit dated
          September 18, 1958

Rita relaxed after Yasmin's birth as she never had
since meeting Aly. He rented a chalet in Gstaad. Rebecca and
Rita's aunt, Frances Rosser, who had come over from Los
Angeles, were with them. Karim and Amyn came for school
holidays. Princess Andrée, with whom Rita had become chummy,
dropped in. "This was the happiest time of our life together,"
Rita has said. "Aly had to go to Paris on business very often, but

he was with us most of the time. It was the one time we were a family."

But Aly was not destined for a life of tranquillity. A ski accident snapped his right leg below the knee in three places. It required a cast and traction. Aly was immobilized in the tiny hospital at Saana. "It was in season so everybody was there," Poppy, who helped nurse him, recalls. He gave cocktail parties in his room. Aly's ingenuity in entertaining himself while flat on his back, his leg held up in the air by a fifteen-pound weight, is still talked of with wonder. In time he may become the hero of a Swiss folk legend like Wilhelm Tell, but for an older audience, of course. Finally the doctor said he could be moved and *The Avenger* flew the family to the Riviera with both Aly and Yasmin prostrate in the cabin and Poppy along to fuss over them.

At the Chateau, Aly was installed in his study. Rita kept busy with Rebecca and Yasmin, upstairs. Aly was seldom alone. An endless parade of visitors came to play bridge and backgammon, talk horses, bask in his charm, and, if they were beautiful women, respond to it. He conspired endlessly to get out of bed. Once he had Karim and his chauffeur rig up a canvas stretcher and borrow his father's folding wheelchair, so that he could fly in *The Avenger* to England to see his horse Palestine win the Two Thousand Guineas at Newmarket. When the doctor put his leg in a smaller cast and he could move around on light-weight aluminum crutches, Aly sped off to Paris. Soon a columnist reported that Katherine Dunham, the American Negro dancer, then in Paris, was wearing a diamond necklace from Aly. Miss Dunham replied tartly: "I think someone irked at his wife, Rita Hayworth, has been spreading those rumours." She said they had only been discussing real estate, and it was true. Aly was trying to sell his mother's old house on rue de Prony (he didn't—it became an Ismaili Cultural Centre), to help pay for a new house he was buying on the Boulevard Maurice Barrès, across the street from the Bois de Boulogne in suburban Neuilly. It was an elegant Paris town house, with a gold and white paneled sitting room on the second floor overlooking the Bois, a master bedroom and guest rooms on the third floor; and, on the fourth, a big study where Aly could work. It would be Rita's pied-à-terre in Paris—when she was in Paris. Aly had convinced himself that Rita would be happier if she returned to Hollywood now and then to make a movie.

He chartered Errol Flynn's schooner, *La Zaca*, for a holiday cruise and thoughtfully invited her old director, Charles Vidor, along to keep them company. Flynn, of course, had known Rita in Hollywood. He and Aly also were good friends; they had a lot in common, including the fact, confided in Flynn's autobiography, *My Wicked, Wicked Ways*, that Flynn's mother, Marcelle, had once had "a small fling" with the Aga Khan.

*La Zaca* looked like a pirate ship. Black, with a rooster painted on her bow, she bore the scars of several pitched battles, in which champagne bottles had been the weapons and young ladies the prizes. Below decks she looked more like a seraglio. The walls of the captain's cabin were lined with mirrors, and above the bed another large mirror had been installed. The head had everything from a bidet to a frilly shower cap, and its cabinets were stocked with whatever a modern young woman might find at her corner pharmacy.

It might have been the perfumed aura of *La Zaca* that got the sailing off to a rather tense start. Rita noticed Aly ogling a pretty girl sunbathing on the deck of a yacht moored alongside. She stamped below and there, surrounded by Flynn's mirrors and geegaws, they had angry words.

Rita didn't like boating much, but she and Vidor talked a lot about Hollywood. When he got back to Hollywood, Vidor announced that Rita would definitely return to pictures as soon as Columbia found a story for her.

Aly took the news graciously. All he asked was that Rita first accompany him on a tour of the Ismaili communities in Africa. In preparation, he requested Columbia Studios not to distribute any new pin-up photos. Interest in Rita's movies had taken a sudden spurt wherever Ismailis lived. One young Ismaili woman recalled later how all of her highly religious family, from her seven-year-old sister to her seventy-eight-year-old grandmother, who had never seen a movie before, solemnly filed into a Bombay theatre to see one of Rita's pictures, which was being shown with great fanfare the week after Rita and Aly were married. Aly's marriage to an American actress was being stoutly defended by most Ismailis. The same young woman recalls: "If a Hindu teased us we would say, 'Your god Krishna married many dancing girls.' To the Moslems we said, 'Don't forget that one of the Prophet Mohammed's wives was a wrestler.' "

Africa was a plunge into terra incognita (except for movie sets) that Rita viewed with misgivings: "I'm frightened of the idea, but Aly is anxious for us to go." To make the trip more palatable to Rita, Aly invited two of her Hollywood friends, Lola and Jackson Leighter, to join them.

Aly, never more agreeable, even fell in with Leighter's proposal that he make a movie of the trip. Thenceforth, Leighter's camera recorded everything, including the slow downward descent of their marriage. The Leighters joined them in Cairo, where Aly had the time of his life in his old wartime haunts. He seemed to know everyone. Rita could never be sure whether the charming woman she had just met was an old girl friend of Aly's or—come to think of it—a current one.

They were in Cairo over New Year's Eve. Sybilla Szczeniowska gave a party. "Everybody was dancing," she recalls. "You know how it is on New Year's Eve. Very dark, all candlelight. I think half the people didn't realize Rita Hayworth was there. She was sitting alone at a table. Nobody was dancing with her. Aly was busy with several other people, all of them at once, as usual. I looked at her once or twice to see how she was getting along. She was getting grimmer by the minute. At a certain moment, she got up from her chair. 'I am going—right now,' she said. She whisked out without saying good-bye. Aly left behind her, looking rather unhappy."

Rita's apprehensions about the trip increased as *The Avenger* came down in Nairobi. Long flights in small planes unsettled her, anyway. Crowds terrified her, and Eastleigh Airport was a swarm of gesticulating hands popping cameras in her face, handing her bouquets, and draping garlands around her neck. "I really wasn't prepared for as much as I saw," she says. "But it was one of my functions as Aly's wife."

She trailed along behind Aly like the trouper she was. They visited *jamat-khanas*, ate cakes baked by domestic science classes at the Aga Khan Girls' School, asked for encores from a percussion band made up of eight-year-olds. Aly dashed off to lay cornerstones and perform marriage ceremonies. Rita handed out the prizes in a baby show that had no less than seventy winners, congratulating every mother. She went to reception after reception where Ismaili women, dark-skinned, smiling, pressed around her to stare, say a few words in stilted English, and vanish into a thicket of saris where they discussed her among themselves in rapid Gujarati. She wanted very much to go swimming but Ismaili leaders begged her not to. She sat around the Aga's bungalow with the leaders' wives—invitations from Europeans were noticeably lacking in color-conscious Nairobi—while Aly disappeared for hours or even days at a time.

Aly had changed the moment he arrived among his followers. There was a new authority in his manner and a crispness in his voice that Rita found hard to identify with the charmer of the Chateau. She glimpsed him with the community's elders and for the first time got some idea of the scope and power of the Ismaili organization. But he seemed to be avoiding her and, after a busy round of religious duties, settled down, not with Rita, but at a bridge table—he had brought along a quartet of Egyptian cronies as partners.

In Nairobi, Rita told an interviewer that she was through making movies, that she hoped never again to "work from five o'clock in the morning until six or seven at night, as much as ten to fifteen months, on one picture."

Aly went out of his way to correct that impression in an interview he gave in Zanzibar later in their tour. It would be, he said, "a grievous waste of the Princess's wonderful talents" if she didn't go back to the screen when the right story came along. Both he and the Aga favored it, he made it clear.

That done, Aly returned to his bridge game.

In Dar-es-Salaam, he gave a lecture on "The Middle East," arriving late with Rita because, as he put it, of "a last-minute tangle." He was trying to do too much. His valet, Tutti, rigged up an extra-long cord on an electric razor so that Aly could shave while Tutti undressed him and slipped on his evening clothes. It gave him a few more moments for other things.

And there was still the safari to face. It meant a flight in a plane smaller than *The Avenger*. At the last moment Rita pleaded illness. Lola Leighter stayed behind with her. Aly flew up to Telek with Leighter, and joined the safari party he had ordered up from Ker and Downey Safaris, Limited. Every comfort was laid on—four white hunters, two Land Rovers, hot baths, and cold champagne. (He paid his bill a year later.) Aly got a buffalo which, he said later, "was coming straight for us. Just brought it down in time." He also grew a mustache. The white hunters reported that "he spent most of his time playing bridge, not hunting."

He was still gloating over the buffalo when Lola Leighter arrived in camp by the shuttle plane with a note from Rita. Aly read it impassively. Two hours later the Leighters left with all of their camera equipment. The letter had informed Aly that Rita was leaving for Europe immediately.


2


Aly flew back to Nairobi that night. Later the newspapers would say that Rita had departed without his knowledge, but the fact was that he spent an entire day with her before she left. He made no effort to keep her from going; he understood perfectly; she was tired and missed the children. He nodded as she told Ismaili leaders who thronged into the bungalow to say good-bye. "Four months is a long time. My children will have changed so much I'll hardly know them." He went to the airport with her and the Leighters. There was a coolness between them, but it could all be attributed to Rita's indisposition and the pace he had set. He would see her back in Cannes.

He doggedly went on with his schedule—Uganda, the Belgian Congo, and Ethiopia, where he was the guest of the Crown Prince. He stopped off in Cairo on his way home.

Rita had been brooding at the Chateau over her experiences

in Africa. Life with Aly was no less fatiguing than making movies in Hollywood. Life with Aly was a contest, and she suddenly began worrying that if the contest became fierce, Yasmin might be the prize. She knew how much the Aga loved Yasmin. She knew he was a powerful man. As the Aga wrote in his autobiography later: "Miss Hayworth somehow got it into her head that either Aly or I myself might try to take her daughter away from her, indeed, kidnap the child." Ismaili law would not have allowed that, the Aga wrote, but he did not mention French law, which often does award custody of children to the father. The Aga never got over the fact that on the very night he and the Begum returned from Pakistan, Rita, her children, and a nurse slipped out of the Chateau and boarded a sleeper for Paris. With the aid of the Leighters, they moved furtively behind a blanket of evasive action, aliases, and other ruses to reach the French liner *De Grasse* at Le Havre. Their names did not appear on the passenger list and Rita stayed in her cabin most of the trip.

News of Rita's departure caught up with Aly in Cairo. He tried to toss it off with typical Aly casualness. There was nothing strange about his wife's departure, he insisted. "We're traveling people." He might go to the United States soon himself. But not now, with the European racing season just beginning. A London newspaper commented: "It is good to see a man who puts first things first."

Aly didn't really think Rita was walking out on him permanently. A bracelet, some roses, a double helping of charm, would win her back. He was, after all, Aly Khan.

Twice Aly spoke to Rita on the telephone. For a month she lingered in New York. It was plain she wanted to be pursued. But Aly didn't move in her direction. Finally Rita told her attorney, Bartley C. Crum, a distinguished New York and California lawyer, to start proceedings for a legal separation. She headed for Reno with the Leighters.

When she finally heard from Aly, it was in the form of a long, reproachful letter, sent from l'Horizon on April 29, 1951. Aly was "terribly sad," he wrote, "for two reasons: First, your decision, and secondly, your want of confidence in me and the

way you have carried it out." He asked her to give up the idea
of a legal separation and be satisfied instead with a "friendly" one.
He assured her that Yasmin would be well taken care of financially and that should she, Rita, wish to remarry at some future
date, he would give her a divorce.

Not until the final paragraph did Aly strike a romantic note
and then one that was more flat than blue. "If in time your
thoughts ever turn to me and the love I have always had and have
for you, my arms are then open."

As soon as she had read the letter, Rita phoned Crum to
forget about a legal settlement. She wanted a divorce.

She also wanted a trust fund of three million dollars for
Yasmin.

Poetry might have won the day but there was no stargazing
in Aly's letter; it was a thinly veiled appeal to avoid a public
scandal.

Aly was in serious trouble, more than even Rita suspected.
One of his girl friends and her husband, taking advantage of his
vulnerability, were threatening him with a new scandal, unless
Aly soothed the husband's injured pride with an application of
£50,000 ($140,000). Aly was short of cash, as usual. He finally
had to go to the Aga for help. His father paid the black-
mail, but insisted that Aly win Rita back and save the family's
good name.

Aly girded himself for an arduous campaign. Everything he
knew about winning a woman's heart would have to be deployed
against Rita's. She was furious with him; the six weeks' Nevada
residence she needed to get a divorce was almost up. He had to
gain time. He had to get her to postpone everything. He sent his
attorney, Charles Torem, of the Paris office of the Franco-
American law firm of Coudert Brothers, across the Atlantic to
talk to Rita. He asked Crum to come to Paris to meet with him.
A desperate Aly promised that if Rita gave him a six-month delay
he would eventually co-operate in a Nevada divorce—if Rita still
wanted one.

Rita returned to Hollywood. She had come back from
Europe broke. She had borrowed twenty-five thousand from the

William Morris Agency to keep her going. Now she was in a hurry to get back to work and worried about what kind of a reception she would get. She hurriedly signed a new contract with Columbia which she was to regret bitterly later. "Columbia caught me at a weak moment," she later told Art Buchwald, the columnist. "I was scared and I signed a contract that didn't give me any script approval or any say on my pictures. They told me I had been away from movies for three years and they didn't know if the public would accept me. I had no idea if they were right or not and I needed money. I had to do what they said."

She walked into a highly charged atmosphere at Columbia. Cohn was still furious at her. One close associate of those days said: "Cohn was maniacal about Rita. He was determined to show her who was boss. She thought she was a princess? Well, he would show her what is a princess." Cohn immediately put her into *Affair in Trinidad*, a movie that called for long, rigorous dance routines, something that Rita, now past thirty, hadn't done in some time. Valerie Bettis, the choreographer of the film, recalls that "I never had anyone at any time work harder than Rita." Another associate recalls that Rita was her old obliging self, "just trying to keep out of trouble, trying to say the right thing, doing a good job." But Cohn continued to needle her. One day Rita came to publicity director Lou Smith.

"I just can't stand Harry Cohn any more," she said. "He always picks and argues."

"He's annoyed because he can't make you jump through a hoop," Smith replied. "Why don't you go and see him, make him feel like a big man. Tell him you are going out to a party and can't decide what to wear; ask his advice."

Rita agreed to try this strategy. Later she came back to Smith's office to report: "All Cohn said was, 'What in hell are you going to that party for?' And started arguing about that."

Rita had been away from Rebecca and Yasmin so much while traveling with Aly that she now was anxious to spend more time with them. Rebecca was lively and imaginative; she made up long stories as dramatic as her father's movie plots; she worried about her mother when Rita seemed unhappy. Yasmin was daintier, small-boned, olive-skinned—already something of a cutup, she later was doing hilarious imitations of her mother in her film, *Gilda*.

On their second wedding anniversary, Aly sent Rita two-dozen American Beauty roses with the message: "Remember me?" When the time was ripe, he was sure he could convince her of the absurdity of what she was doing.

## 3

As usual when Aly was frustrated in one direction, he shored up his self-confidence with even more frantic activities in another. All that summer and fall he operated at top speed. Even on the way back from Africa, while Rita was on her way to New York, Beirut newspapers reported he had invited the eighteen-year-old daughter of a White Russian bar proprietor to pay him a visit.

In Paris, Aly escorted actress Joan Fontaine to one of Elsa Maxwell's dinners. At Deauville, he took advantage of all of the facilities including the companionship of the resort's beautiful mistress of ceremonies, a former Schiaparelli model. Aly also got a black eye at Deauville—by accident, from his athletic coach, he said,—although others swore they'd seen an irate French businessman swing in his direction after Aly spent an evening flirting with the Frenchman's wife. Aly dated French stage star Dany Dauberson and squired twenty-two-year-old Lorraine Dubonnet, daughter of his old friend, André Dubonnet of apéritif fame, whom he had known since she was a child. Aly was always a favorite of his friends' children; he paid them the kind of gallant serious attention they seldom got from adults, a formula which often worked equally well when they grew up and, Peter Pan-like, this continued into the next generation. Lorraine Dubonnet, now Mme. Gerard Bonnet, says that *her* children, too, were crazy about Aly.

One evening Aly was invited to a costume party at the home of couturier Jacques Fath. Rushed, as usual, he had no time to get a costume. When he arrived in dinner clothes, Fath took him upstairs to a wardrobe full of old costumes—perhaps every couturier has one—and hauled out a wig and a long black cloak. Thus garbed, Aly danced away the evening with another good friend, Pamela Churchill, the red-haired former wife of Randolph Churchill, Winston Churchill's son. He was, he explained to anyone who bothered to ask, supposed to be Robespierre, the French revolutionary leader. But hardly anyone asked. Such was Aly's reputation they took it for granted he had come as Casanova.

In June, Aly gave his annual Grand Prix party following the famous horse race at Longchamps. It was held, as usual, at the Pré Catalan restaurant in the Bois de Boulogne. The party brought out 180 guests who speculated which of the women guests was Aly's romance of the moment. It was hard to tell, he was so attentive to so many. But as the early morning hours approached, one after another of the young ladies bid their host good-bye. Lise Bourdin, a blue-eyed brunette, daughter of a Vichy hotel keeper who had come to Paris to study interior decorating and had switched to acting and modeling, remained. At 4:44 A. M. Lise and Aly disappeared into the fresh air of the Bois de Boulogne.

Aly had met Lise Bourdin in Cairo where she was touring with a company of French actors. He immediately began to include her in his wholesale invitations to visit him at the Chateau, in Paris, to take trips to Ireland, to India, to South America. Lise didn't accept many of these. "I wasn't quite free. I was in love with a Frenchman," she explains in her charmingly accented English. "But my friend was married and so sometimes I was mad and I would go. Aly was very nice. When he was seeing that I was sad, he was always inviting me. For three years I went to the South of France for Christmas at the Chateau."

Aly and Lise drifted into a friendship which was to last for several years. At one time, when she had broken with her French lover, it became serious enough for them to have "some big conversations about being together. He said, 'You will have a wonderful life with me. We will travel around the world. You will have everything. You will be amused.'" Lise refused. By that time she had a good idea of what life with Aly would be like. "I have visited him often at the Chateau because I have a house at St. Tropez," she recalls. "I met so many girls there. American girls and English girls, women from Italy and from South America. So many, I don't even remember. All beautiful strangers. They were girls passing through France to have a good time, single or married, actresses some of them. And all of them, they were interested in Aly. You know, for a lot of women, a man who is well known to have success with women, already he is the winner."

Would Lise have married Aly? "I suppose, yes, because if you are married to a man you are always protected, socially, and for everything, and so you can accept many things. But we were not speaking about marriage and so I told him, 'No, I am very jealous, I couldn't stand it, to see you all the time with all those other women.'"

Despite her doubts and her other attachment, Lise met Aly in South America in the winter of 1951. Aly stopped first at Rio de Janeiro and lingered on for nearly a month, selling horses, visiting Ismailis and giving parties, including a big one for Lise's birthday on November 30. As the party continued into the early hours of the next morning, December 1, Lise noticed that Aly was not eating or drinking anything. She asked him why. "It is the anniversary of my mother's death," he explained. "I always fast, every year."

The Brazilian idyll was rudely interrupted when some Rio newspapers published stories about their romance. Lise flew home to her angry French friend. Aly tried to salvage the rest of his trip but ran into difficulties again in Buenos Aires where the press reported on a gay party at a nightclub where Aly's guests drank champagne spiked with cognac. The Argentine Ismailis were aghast. So was the Aga, when he read about it. He began to question seriously Aly's fitness to succeed him as Imam.

## Chapter XXIII

*"I have studied the matter a great deal and, so far as I can find out, the leadership normally passes from father to eldest son."*

—SADRUDDIN AGA KHAN

Confined more and more to his bed or his wheel-chair at Yakimour, his great head sunk on his chest, hands folded across his massive belly, the Aga's thoughts about the future must have turned to Sadruddin, now eighteen and starting Harvard after finishing his studies with tutors in Switzerland.

Many tales have been repeated about the supposedly immutable laws governing the succession to the Imamate. One of the most frequently cited is that the succession can pass only through the elder son. While this has been the tradition, Ismaili history is studded with exceptions, and, in any case, as the Aga was wont to remind people, the Imam's word superseded all law. The succession was wide open, so that newspapers were not wrong in speculating that Sadruddin, rather than Aly, might be the choice of their father.

The Aga always considered Sadruddin the most like himself of his two sons and two grandsons. He is big physically, and, like the Aga, tends to stoutness. "Even when he was ten years old he had to watch his weight," one long-time friend recalls. "We used to kid him and say we hoped he would become Aga because he would get a lot of gold when he was weighed." Sadri was a serious and methodical youngster and a good athlete. He had won the Swiss gold medal for skiing by the time he was ten. But he didn't like to take part in competitions. "I don't think he wanted to risk losing," a former schoolmate has observed. At Harvard he majored in Middle Eastern history, founded the Harvard Islamic Association, was a member of the *Lampoon* staff, the Hasty Pudding Club, and a top man on the varsity swimming team. He mingled with an intellectual crowd of young men of good family who hoped to write someday; eventually some of them founded the literary *Paris Review* and Sadruddin became its publisher and one of its principal backers. He was shy with girls. "He was self-conscious about his weight and he never seemed to have the self-confidence to put his best foot forward," one friend recalls. "One always felt that Aly had a real attraction for women quite aside from who he was. With Sadri the women were interested because he was the son of the Aga Khan." Sadri himself seemed to feel that something a little more spectacular was expected of him—a son of the Aga Khan and a brother of Aly. Once when Eartha Kitt was singing at the Mayflower Hotel in Boston, he reserved a place for every performance and ostentatiously showed up nightly at a ringside table. But his Harvard classmates doubted that he was really interested in the Negro singer. Said one: "He just seemed to feel he had to make a splash."

Aly was twenty-one when Sadruddin was born and the brothers saw very little of one another. Sadri, as he grew older, regarded Aly with a wonder tinged with envy. One friend recalls: "Aly used to come and go in a flurry of excitement. He was like the king. Everyone knew him, every head waiter. Sadri looked at him like at a bird."

Sadri had neither the Aga's force nor Aly's flair and suffered by comparison in either direction. Nonetheless, he was showing a seriousness of purpose. As Aly made headlines, Sadri was making steady progress with his studies at Harvard. In 1954 he received his B.A. and started work on a Ph.D. The old Aga couldn't help musing that perhaps the future of the Imamate, after all, lay with him.

Ill and dispirited, disheartened by Aly and disenchanted with the overzealous Begum ("She's the only woman who can make me cry," he confided to one friend), the Aga's thoughts harked back to an earlier, less complicated time. He had been spending part of every day at the quiet, peaceful Villa Jane-Andrée on the Cap d'Antibes which he had built twenty years before for his third wife. Andrée was not there, she was living in Switzerland, but the few intimates who knew about the Aga's visits to the house thought they might presage a reconciliation. "Something might have come of it," one of them has said, "if Aly and Rita hadn't split up. When that happened, the Aga knew he could not change his life. One divorce at a time in the family was enough." Aly's behavior obsessed him. "My life is not going to be a Hollywood plot," he declared. He poured out his grievances: Aly's conduct, his gambling debts, his love affairs, the bad impression these made on the Ismailis. The Begum would soothe him, agree with him, advise him, emphasize her own loyalty toward him. Her importance to the Aga grew in the wreckage of Aly's reputation.

Early in 1951 the Aga and Begum made a nostalgic trip to Iran, the home of the Aga's forefathers. The occasion was the marriage of Shah Reza Pahlevi to a young German-Iranian beauty named Soraya Esfandiary.

Relations between the Shah and the Aga had been growing warmer for a number of years. The Aga, tossed from pillar to post in his search for a country he could call his own—Britain had never seemed the same to him after the war; Pakistan and India were cool to him—had asked the Shah to permit him to "readopt" Iranian citizenship. The Shah had not only agreed but had given the title of "Royal Highness" to the Aga and his sons.

The Aga received the usual hysterical welcome from his followers in Iran. He advised them to educate their children and start a co-operative bank; he bestowed names on scores of babies —Suhra, Fatima, Sakina, or Saainab if they were girls; Mohammed or Ali if they were boys. Smiling and bowing beside him was the

Begum, more regal and self-assured than ever. She had come to Iran with thirty-five trunks of clothing and jewelry. An awed Iranian observer reported that "she could not open several of these as not enough wardrobes and hangers were available. . . . Since her arrival she has not worn the same jewelry twice; one ruby is as big as a hen's egg—the picture of a flower is carved on it." (Soraya later reported in her autobiography that *she* had had to borrow the jewels she wore to her wedding; they belonged to the state, not her husband, and were jealously guarded by the government.) By now, the Begum was not to be outdone in any sphere. She not only shared the Aga's public appearances, but, since he was ailing, got around even more than he did. She attended Friday prayers at a mosque in Isfahan wearing the black *burka* (hooded cloak) of the devout Moslem woman, a tiny attention to detail that only a woman with thirty-five trunks would be likely to undertake.

Early in 1952 the Aga felt well enough to undertake his annual trip to the East. In India, however, he suffered a heart attack and was rushed home by chartered plane. Aly was hurriedly hauled out of the family doghouse to take the Aga's place for the rest of the tour. In everyone's mind was the possibility that *Kismet* might intervene and give him the job permanently.

After the fiasco of his South American trip with Lise Bourdin, Aly was anxious to prove his seriousness. He buckled down to a grueling schedule, conscientiously attending meetings, visiting the homes and businesses of the faithful, consulting with leaders about their budgets and programs. His trip was going well, Madras and Nagpur were awaiting his arrival, when he abruptly left for Europe in a flurry of canceled appearances. His entourage whispered that the Aga's condition had taken a turn for the worse. Another explanation seems more likely: Aly had heard from his lawyers that Rita might now be amenable to a reconciliation. This, Aly knew, would be the most triumphant get-well present he could set before the Aga.

Rita was ready to listen, it seems, but where? A studio spokesman explained: "Rita has two weeks of work on her current picture, then she has several weeks of still photography. Her next picture starts in a month. I don't think she can do much junketing around the world in that time." Mohammed's descendant would have to come to the Hollywood hills. Aly was willing; with Tutti he sailed on the *Queen Elizabeth*, stopped off en route to Hollywood to attend the yearling sales at Saratoga Springs where he sold twenty yearlings at record prices—a whopping total of $173,500, almost double what the experts had agreed they were worth—then flew on to Hollywood.

Rita didn't meet him at the airport. Charles Vidor drove him and 175 pounds of excess baggage, including five sacks of toys for Yasmin, to Vidor's home where he was to stay and later to Rita's home in Beverly Hills. It was nearly midnight. At 3 A.M. Aly emerged, minus his jaunty walk, his hands stuffed into his trousers pockets and a disappointed look on his face. He came back again the next afternoon and left three hours later looking more cheerful. Reporters, who had quickly gathered around the house, begged Rita for some news. She sent out word: "If you'll go away, we'll pose for pictures tomorrow." The reporters left and missed the next, near-tragic event. Three-year-old Yasmin was discovered asleep on the floor with an empty bottle of sleeping pills near her hand. "It was horrifying," Rita still recalls with a shudder. "We didn't know whether she had taken one or taken the bottleful. There was nothing to do but rush her to the hospital—fast."

A distraught Rita telephoned Aly. They met at Santa Monica Hospital and paced the corridor hand in hand while doctors pumped out Yasmin's stomach. Aly left Hollywood a few days later confident that he had convinced Rita to give their marriage another chance. A month later, Rita sailed for France. At Le Havre, she wearily told reporters she was tired from making two films, and looked around for Aly. His car was there, but Tutti, not Aly, was in it. They drove to Paris, to the house on Boulevard Maurice Barrès which Aly had so triumphantly bought for her a year before. It was, as usual, full of people—Mrs. Mary Elizabeth Whitney Person, the American horsewoman better known as Liz Whitney; Carlos de Campos, a Brazilian polo player, and his wife. But Aly wasn't among them; he was at the Chateau de l'Horizon. He arrived the next evening, announcing that he had driven up at breakneck speed.

He was delighted to see Rita, solicitous and attentive. But something new had been added: he was unusually friendly to the reporters and photographers who stood vigil outside the door. Sometimes it seemed as if he were courting them rather than Rita. The morning after their reunion, he went out in the rain to let the press know that he and "my wife" had spent the night under the same roof. The next day Rita dutifully made an appearance with him and acknowledged that she had no immediate plans for going ahead with her divorce suit. Aly did most of the talking: "My wife came here for her vacation. She is staying with me in my house. She is my wife. We're not divorced." He grinned. Obviously, he felt the trouble was over. It was a *fait accompli* and now everything would be fine. Never a man to concentrate for too long on one problem, he already was thinking ahead to a future that, in his euphoria after a difficult job well done, he envisioned as not much different from the past: "As far as I am concerned, we have no intention of breaking up. She has her job that takes her to various places, and I have mine. A wife does not interfere with her husband's business and he does not interfere with hers."

In a mellow mood, Aly took Rita to lunch at a picturesque restaurant in the Bois. As usual, photographers and reporters pounced on them as they emerged. Aly, the new co-operative Aly, stopped to chat but Rita surged on ahead, got into his Mercedes convertible, and, as Aly's grin faded, slammed the door and drove off. A week later Rita moved out of the house and into the Lancaster Hotel. The reconciliation, she felt, had been no more than a stunt by Aly to appease the Aga and public opinion. She issued a statement through her Paris attorney, Mme. Suzanne Blum, disclaiming any responsibility for "conclusions which may have heretofore been assumed. The whole affair was organized by my husband without consulting me. I am bored with my husband's entourage and see no chance of a reconciliation with him." A second statement detailed her immediate grievances: "I love Aly very much. He is very nice. But he doesn't understand family life. He thinks only of gambling, horse racing, and big-game hunting. Almost as soon as I arrived in Paris, Aly announced he was planning another big-game hunt in Africa. He is a playboy, while I work all around the year in Hollywood. When I come to Paris, it is not to live in a house where there are eighty friends of all kinds coming and going, and it is not to dine at Maxim's. What's more, Aly spends too much, while I have to work for the two of us."

One of Aly's Paris lawyers, Roger Palmieri, promptly counterattacked. Rita, said Palmieri, was a "wet blanket." Furthermore, she was a "homebody." Then, rising to the very heights of disparagement in the International Set: "At eight o'clock at night the only thing she is interested in is putting on slippers and sitting by the fire. She ignores nightlife and is not interested in social life."

Rita cabled Bartley Crum: "Reconciliation attempt has not worked out. Proceed with divorce."

## 2

Some people react to problems and disappointment with brooding moodiness, they withdraw from other people, they can't seem to get interested in anything. Not Aly. He met all setbacks with redoubled activity elsewhere, especially in the sphere that interested him most. He never was busier than that summer and fall when he was trying, unsuccessfully, to win back Rita. Newspapers alternated reports of the reconciliation with speculation about other women.

In May, Aly went south for the Cannes Film Festival, that annual seaside circus in which starlets, rather than seals, perform. Aly gave a party at the Chateau which brought out dozens of celebrities including such beauties as Yvonne de Carlo and Gloria DeHaven from Hollywood, Gina Lollobrigida from Italy, and Irene Papas, an intense, dark-eyed Greek actress. It was sultry Miss Papas's name which was most persistently linked with Aly's by the end of the Festival. Unknown until then, Miss Papas's photograph and life story appeared in newspapers around the world. It was the kind of publicity for which most aspiring actresses make the dangerous pilgrimage to Cannes. But Miss Papas was a more serious type. "That meeting with Aly Khan set me back ten years," she recently declared. "I thought, what is this, four years of work in pictures, four years in drama school, to play the tramp in the newspapers?" By the time she made this candid appraisal Miss Papas was again in Cannes, again receiving a lot of attention, but this time for reasons that suited her better: *Electra*, the Greek film in which she starred, had won one of the 1952 Festival's awards.

There were other passing fancies that busy year of 1952. A seventeen-year-old stenographer in Milan announced her "engagement" to Aly after he had invited her to visit the Chateau. "No doubt she believes they still make miracles in Milan," wryly commented one Italian newspaper. Nicole Largille, a twenty-year-old Parisian, revealed she had dodged luncheon dates at Deauville with nineteen-year-old Sadruddin to meet Aly; when Sadri angrily asked what she saw in his brother, Nicole delicately refrained from telling him but later tried to explain it to all the readers of *France Dimanche*, a popular weekly newspaper: she and Aly had picnicked in Normandy on stolen apples, she confided; Aly had carried her suitcase on his shoulder to her tiny attic room on the fifth floor of a Paris walk-up. "With Aly women feel so at ease, so gay, so confident," she said. And there was Zsa Zsa Gabor, in Paris to play in the movie *Moulin Rouge*; years later she would say: "The secret of Aly's success was his concentration. He knew how to give a woman the idea that he would die if she did not give in to him. He was after me for years, the sweet thing. I used to tell him, 'No, no.' He never gave up."

At the Lido night club in Paris, Mistinguett, that indestructible star of the Folies Bergère, got up from her table when she heard that Aly Khan had arrived. Standing on tiptoe on her still-lovely legs, she peered around, demanding in a loud, clear voice: "Where is he? Show me this guy who has such a way with the girls." She was restrained by her son.

As the year ended, Aly gave another party, a New Year's Eve celebration at a Cannes night club. The Aga and the Begum came. It was one of the Aga's first nights out in a long time. But nothing about the party pleased him. For one thing, Aly was paying obvious court to still another actress, Hollywood star Gene Tierney, whom he had met a few weeks previously in South America. The low point of the evening, the Aga felt, came when waiters distributed green cotton balls which the guests were supposed to soak in champagne and fling at one another. For a man who had dined with Queen Victoria and enjoyed the sophisticated gaiety of La Belle Epoque, this child's game was outrageous. He said so, loudly, from within the shelter of his upraised arms as he warded off the pelting he was getting, particularly from Aly. At midnight, the lights went out; Aly took Miss Tierney in his arms and gave her a long, lingering kiss. The Aga looked on darkly with the premonition that he was living through the Rita Hayworth episode all over again.

# Chapter XXIV

*"If I feel very close to a man, I must know that he is as much in love with me as I am with him."*

—GENE TIERNEY

Gene Tierney's world was closer to Aly Khan's than Rita Hayworth's had been. She is often described as a member of New York "society." While not exactly that, Gene Alisa Taylor Tierney spent her early life within commuting distance in fashionable Fairfield County, Connecticut.

At fifteen, she was packed off to a Swiss boarding school to get her away from the boys who had started calling for dates. "Father was very old-fashioned," Gene recalled recently. She learned French, acted in school plays and developed into a green-eyed beauty who, on her return to the United States, was offered a screen test during a trip to California.

Gene's father, an insurance broker whose own business affairs had not been going well, insisted she try Broadway first: "If you go to Hollywood from Broadway, you go the right way with a good job and good parts." He personally made the rounds of Broadway casting offices with Gene, arranging for introductions to several producers whom he knew. George Abbott gave her her first walk-on part in *What a Life*. Just as Tierney had predicted, a Warner Brothers executive, Robert Taplinger, invited Gene and her parents to lunch to discuss a possible movie contract. He has since described the luncheon as "unnerving and physically wearing. Gene never got a word in edgewise. Her father and mother did all the talking and considerable bickering. Every time one of them thought the other was saying the wrong thing, someone got kicked under the table—frequently me."

A year later, Twentieth Century-Fox gave Gene a contract for $750 a week. Mrs. Tierney accompanied her to Hollywood. In June, 1941, without taking it up in family council, Gene eloped to Las Vegas with Oleg Cassini, an elegant and ambitious designer with a pencil-thin mustache and the Polish title of Count which he said he had inherited through his mother. Family quarrels led to a suit for fifty thousand dollars, Gene's parents charging that her career was a family business in which they should share. They lost. A baby girl, born after Gene had been exposed to German measles while entertaining troops at the Hollywood Canteen, failed to develop normally. She now lives in a small private home for retarded children. The effect on Gene, always high-strung, made itself known in many small ways to her friends. She developed the habit of slowly putting on a pair of gloves, painstakingly smoothing each finger into place, and then just as slowly and carefully, removing them. She and Cassini separated, reconciled, had a second daughter, Christine, born in 1949, and finally separated for good in 1951. Cassini meanwhile had opened a New York salon and made a name for himself as a top designer; he eventually became Mrs. Jacqueline Kennedy's couturier. Gene had emerged as one of Hollywood's top stars in the era of Lana Turner, Linda Darnell, Maureen O'Hara, and, of course, Rita Hayworth. She was in Argentina late in 1952 making *The Way of the Gaucho* when she met Aly Khan. According to one story, she came over to meet Aly at a night club, explaining that she brought him greetings from one of his female fans. "He immediately asked her for a date," a friend recalls. "That is the way he operated; the panzer approach." Elsa Max-

well, hearing that Gene had been seen with Aly, gave her a
warning: "Take care, my child, and don't take him seriously.
Only I can love him because I am now seventy and he cannot
hurt me." (In her autobiography, Miss Maxwell confessed that
she had never had a sexual experience and never wanted any;
only two men ever attracted her: "Cole Porter for his wit and
musical genius and Aly Khan for his masculine appeal" but she
met them when she was "much too old.") "My advice to Gene
was wasted," Elsa realized. "Arriving in Paris the following
spring, I found her desperately in love."

By then the New Year's Eve kiss had led to others—in, of
course, many different parts of the world.

In Monte Carlo, Gene accompanied Aly to one of the
private rooms of the Casino where he played hour after hour,
losing stacks of chips each worth $285. Gene went to England to
make a movie and Aly commuted there by plane on week ends,
faithfully picking her up at the studio after Friday's work. They
spent a holiday in Ireland, and in April flew to Milan, where Aly
planned to enter the Mille Miglia, the biggest of Italian automobile races with its hazardous seven thousand curves. Among
the 570 drivers was Roberto Rossellini, the Italian movie director,
whose affair with Ingrid Bergman had caused even more astonishment than Aly's with Rita Hayworth. The race might have become an epochal showdown between two great Continental
lovers except that the Aga laid down the law, and "for family
and sentimental reasons" Aly's Alfa-Romeo was withdrawn.

Gene and Aly spent part of the summer in Deauville, then
went back to England for the Oaks race at Epsom and the Coronation in London. Aly spent money lavishly—$14,000 on a
buffet supper for fifty friends in a suite of the Piccadilly Hotel
that overlooked the Coronation route. At that year's Grand Prix
party in the Bois de Boulogne, Gene was the last to leave.
Always one of the world's best-dressed women, she wore a gown
of pale blue and silver and outshone such dazzlers as Merle
Oberon, the Countess de la Falaise and the Maharanee of Jaipur.
It was a pretty heady life, even for a glamorous movie star. Aly's
magic carpet had never been more richly embroidered. To Gene,

as to Rita Hayworth, and so many others before her, Aly seemed to be offering a de luxe one-way ticket away from her problems.

Gene took an interest in everything Aly did. She loved gaiety and gladly stayed up late with him. She liked horses and handled ably the grey filly he selected for her at his Gilltown Stud in Ireland. They played tennis at the Carlton courts in Cannes where Tommy Burke, who always took the long view, decided "she was about the best of them all." Gene spoke French and entered eagerly into Aly's world of international society. She even took an interest in his households. Observed one French friend of Aly's: "She was very much a *'femme d'interieur.'* She was an orderly person, interested in organizing a house, giving receptions, even seeing to the way Aly managed his money." Most of Aly's friends found her an admirable influence. "She kept Aly quieter than usual," one recalls. "She kept him from doing silly things."

When Gene visited l'Horizon in the fall, Lise Bourdin was a guest there too. She viewed Gene with the special perspective of a passenger on an outbound ship, looking over the passengers of another vessel just heading into port.

"I must say," observed Lise, "that with Gene around, Aly did not, let us say, have much to do with the others. He was not exactly what you would call faithful but he was—restrained. I think he knew that Gene's temperament wouldn't stand for it. We would all go to the casinos together. But she would stay with Aly, watching him gamble, while the others danced down-stairs."

Gene's imperious orders to servants sometimes made Aly wince. She betrayed an underlying nervous strain in her compulsive gestures and occasional spells of depression. But these, after all, might be the moods of any lovesick girl; they seemed to draw her and Aly closer together. "Let us say," Gene responded to one enquiry about their romance, "that we have both known a lot of unhappiness." It should have been relatively smooth sailing on their magic carpet, but just around the next cloud lurked two formidable obstacles: Gene's mother and Aly's father.

Aly had heard of "the American mother," but Belle Tierney was the first one he had seen close up. She was omnipresent, as much a part of Gene's household as Gene's four-year-old daughter, Tina.

Aly soon found that he was not only the ardent suitor of a beautiful woman, but part of an American family constellation. In the fall, Gene and Mrs. Tierney rented a house in Paris and started Tina in school there. Aly was invited for Thanksgiving dinner. Some cousins of the Tierneys were in town too, and Mrs. Tierney busily supervised preparations for a big family holiday. Aly, as usual, arrived late, after the turkey had been carved. He grimaced when prevailed upon to try some cranberry sauce and, as one guest recalled, "bolted down this strange meal having no idea what a big occasion it was to Americans." Still, Mrs. Tierney said she liked Aly; she often told friends how much she admired him. And Aly enjoyed charming women, all women, of any age.

The Aga was something else again. He had taken an instant dislike to Gene at the New Year's party in Cannes. He found her too independent, a touch pretentious, too possessive of Aly. He criticized her appearance and her striding American walk. But most of all he objected to her occupation. He was horrified at the thought of Aly having another highly publicized romance with an actress and he was dead set against Aly marrying her. He made no secret of his views. One day he heard that Elsa Maxwell was going to dine with Aly in Paris. He asked her to meet him for a confidential chat at the Ritz Hotel. Elsa recalled: "He wanted me to take a message to Aly. 'I can't talk to Aly,' the Aga said. 'I want you to talk for me. You must tell him that if he marries Gene Tierney, my door will be closed to them both. He must respect his responsibilities to the Ismaili people. I have told him repeatedly I will not permit him to destroy our family heritage with indiscriminate marriages.'" When Elsa relayed this message to Aly, "he was furious, was livid."

Both Aly and Gene frequently had denied reports that they were going to marry. But before Gene sailed for the United States in December, she announced that Aly had proposed. "It happened nearly eight months ago," she said, which would have placed it about the time of their trip to Ireland. "I have been considering it ever since." When she got back to Hollywood, she made it plain that the option still was hers: "I haven't made up my mind yet. Aly has been telephoning me two or three times a week from Europe and Africa. He is coming here as soon as he has finished some business in Paris." She was, it seems, as anxious as the Aga that no odious parallels be drawn between her romance with Aly and his earlier frenetic travels with Rita Hayworth. Not only had she been chaperoned every inch of the way by her mother, but the gentleman had proposed, right at the outset.

Aly knew well that shadowy no man's land between the acknowledgment of love and the definite decision of two people to marry. It was an area women felt more impelled to explore than men. It was booby-trapped and dangerous; journalists, especially, were likely to convert a man's carefully side-stepping answers into a time bomb which exploded later in print. So Aly said nothing. If Gene wished to issue statements, there was nothing he could do about it.

Aly and Gene met again in late March at Rosario Beach, a rundown one-hotel resort seventeen miles south of the border in Mexico's Baja California. It wasn't chosen for its glamour; it was close enough to Hollywood for Gene, who was making another picture, *The Egyptian*, but safely outside of United States territory for Aly, who was afraid of being served with papers in Rita's suit for a settlement for Yasmin. It also seemed sufficiently obscure to be overlooked by the press. But it wasn't.

Mrs. Tierney arrived with Gene and the reporters brought up the rear. Gene and Aly received them beside the swimming pool. Again, Gene did all the talking. Yes, she was "very much in love" with Aly. The diamond ring she wore on her left hand was a gift from him but it was only a "friendship ring." She was still considering his proposal of marriage. "I'm going to think about it very thoroughly before I marry again." If she married Aly, Gene said, it would be in about six months, in Paris, with a honeymoon in Paris or Naples; if the marriage took place she didn't think religious differences would be a problem although she intended to remain an Episcopalian; if she became Aly's wife, she would want to be known simply as "a housewife." She had all of the answers but the crucial one, like a girl whose hope chest is filled but who is still waiting for Mr. Right to set the date. Newspapers divided just about fifty-fifty in their accounts of this equivocal interview; half seeing it as an announcement, half as a denial. The reports were dated April 1, 1954, and there was an element of April Fool about the whole affair. Aly had long since confided to friends: "Don't worry. I'm not marrying again."

Having reached a "gentleman's agreement" with Rita's lawyers that he would not be served with a subpoena, Aly drove to Los Angeles with Gene. They went straight to the Farmer's Market below Hollywood; Aly loved its gooey desserts and novelty shops. Then they went to the studio. Gene was two hours late and the publicity men were wringing their hands. Thirty photographers had assembled to photograph her taking an archery lesson. And Hedda Hopper wanted her to call.

Aly spent a month in Hollywood and left, still evading questions about Miss Tierney. Would she follow him to Europe? "Ask her," he suggested.

The next people heard of him, he was in Paris at his annual Grand Prix ball. As usual, the matchmakers studied Aly's dancing partners to see in which direction his romantic interest had turned. There was his old flame of prewar days, Margaret Whigham, but she was with her Scottish husband, the Duke of Argyll. There was Zsa Zsa Gabor, but she was with Porfirio Rubirosa, a diplomat of parts. There was also Olga Deterding, the daughter of Sir Henry Deterding, the English oil oligarch, whose mother had just given a ball for her on the grounds of Versailles to rival those of Marie Antoinette. Aly danced with one and all. At Deauville that season, he was seen with a strawberry-blonde Canadian singer named Lois Maxwell. He turned up a little later in Munich to visit Yvonne de Carlo, the sultry American movie actress who was making a movie there. He got to a number of parties given by Mrs. Lorelle Hearst, the former wife of William Randolph Hearst, Jr., who was seeing Europe in the knowledgeable company of Mrs. Clark Gable, the former London model, Sylvia Ashley. It was as if the earth had opened up and swallowed Gene Tierney. And in one sense, it had.

Her depressions had become uncontrollable. She spent much of the next six years under psychiatric treatment.

# Chapter XXV

*"Yasmin bounces—like Aly."*
—Rita Hayworth

.

In April, 1954, just before Aly made his anticlimactic exit from Hollywood and the troubled life of Gene Tierney, he and Rita Hayworth were again in the news, this time in a context bizarrely improbable for two wealthy and prominent people. The Society for the Prevention of Cruelty to Children—the very name has a Dickensian ring hard to connect with the sun-bronzed dwellers of the Chateau de l'Horizon—had hailed Rita into court in the sedate New York suburb of White Plains. Her children, the Society charged, had been discovered to be "neglected" in the home of a White Plains antique dealer named Dorothy Chambers. Rita and her fourth husband, the singer Dick Haymes, whom she had married six months previously, had left the girls with Mrs. Chambers, a friend of Haymes's mother, while they vacationed in Florida.

A two-hour closed hearing produced the rather enigmatic decision that Rita was "a loving and devoted mother," but nevertheless the girls had been "neglected." Aly had flown East for the hearing, gallantly instructing his attorneys that "Rita and

I will be together on this." But the net effect of the incident was to make Yasmin once again the fulcrum of their legal seesawings. These had been going on for three years and would continue for several more; they would involve courts of law in three countries on two continents and some of the highest-priced legal talent in the world (not all of which was paid—Mme. Blum, Rita's Paris lawyer, says Aly never did settle her bill). The stakes were high, both human and monetary, and the emotions aroused were intense and diverse. The issues ran an explosive gamut: money, religion, politics, and personal pride. And not only a clash between Aly and Rita was involved—the Aga also was very much affected. This was, he felt, just one more thing that Aly had bungled.

The divorce itself had been easy, routine. Rita had obtained it in Reno in seventeen minutes on January 26, 1953. She neither asked for nor received alimony. The sticky issue was the support and custody of Yasmin and that was postponed, to be followed by an endless series of court orders, suits, and countersuits. The question of a financial settlement was complicated by the fact that no one knew—or was telling—exactly how much money Aly had. Rita's lawyer, Bartley Crum, at times speculated that Aly might not be very rich himself, that it was the Aga who controlled the purse strings.

Rita, too, was having her financial difficulties. She was in debt for income taxes dating back to her marriage to Orson Welles. Her current husband, the Argentine crooner, Dick Haymes, who was fighting a deportation order from the United States, had heavy alimony and child support payments to make to his ex-wives, actress Joanne Dru and Nora Eddington Flynn, the latter the former wife of Errol Flynn, on whose yacht, *La Zaca*, Rita and Aly had taken that unforgettable Mediterranean cruise. Rita's studio had loaned her fifty thousand dollars to straighten out Haymes's financial affairs and ease her mind enough to work. The whole financial tangle was so well-known that *The New Yorker* magazine ran a cartoon which showed two turbaned men chatting in a bazaar. One was saying: "What I object to is that I pay my taxes to the Aga Khan. He gives the money to Aly, who gives it to Rita, who gives it to Dick, who gives it to a woman called Nora Eddington Flynn."

The issue of a settlement for Yasmin bounced in and out of court and from one legal office to another as Rita sued for child support and her lawyers pressed for a trust fund while Aly countered with demands that touched all of the other sensitive chords: He wanted Yasmin to be reared in the Moslem faith; he wanted at least part of her education to be in Europe; he wanted her to visit him for several weeks each year in Europe.

Innocent sounding requests, but every one of them made Rita bristle.

"All the money in the world can't buy my child's right to be raised as an American," she exploded. As for religion, while she respected the Moslem faith and all faiths, she said: "Yasmin is now being reared as a normal Christian American child and will continue to be." She would stick by her guns, Rita declared, "whether there is a settlement or not."

The question of Yasmin's religion was especially delicate for Aly and the Aga. Not only was it inconceivable to them and their followers that a member of their family, a direct descendant of the Prophet, be raised outside the Moslem faith, but there was the special circumstance that she was a girl. Crum had several times hinted that the reason Rita and Yasmin were being treated so cavalierly was that Moslems don't really care about their female children. Karim and Amyn, Crum pointed out, had been provided for amply and promptly, but not Yasmin. The charge made the Aga squirm. It was an extremely unflattering picture to have set before Western public opinion, just the sort of sinister view of Moslems as people who buried unwanted girl babies alive that he had spent his life combating. It wouldn't set too well with Ismaili women either.

Crum also had dropped the observation that considering the position of women in the Moslem world Yasmin would be infinitely better off drinking ice-cream sodas in America. He also took a dim view of her prospects among her father's crowd in Europe. When Aly, at one point, went to court on the question of custody, Crum promptly announced: "We shall show the court what kind of home life Aly Khan has, and no doubt shall also subpoena his current girl friends, including some of Hollywood's most famous stars." (It was right after this that Aly paid a soothing visit to Gene Tierney, who was ill in Connecticut.)

The most ticklish question of all was that of Yasmin's vacation visits to Aly in Europe. Rita still was terrified that she would never get Yasmin back if she let her outside the jurisdiction of United States courts. The entire settlement, when it finally was reached in 1954, hinged on this one point. Instead of a lump sum settlement, Aly agreed to deposit $100,000 with the Guaranty Trust Company of New York before each of Yasmin's annual visits. The money would be used for any expenses incurred in "recapturing" Yasmin in the event Aly failed to return her on schedule. Any money not spent for that purpose would remain in trust for Yasmin until she was twenty-five.

But even this cash guarantee of good faith didn't satisfy Rita; she also demanded, and got, a personal letter from the Aga Khan assuring her that Yasmin would be returned on schedule. To backstop even that, Crum declared: "Before I would permit her to take the baby to Europe the agreement must be filed for legality in the French courts. Then, to put it in American parlance, if Aly should snatch the kid in Paris, Rita could call the French cops."

The terms of the agreement were humiliating to Aly and the Aga. They had never been brought to heel like this. The Aga fumed helplessly. He announced that he planned to sell off a large part of his stables, a move which was not carried out but was clearly directed against Aly. He also asked Joan to send both Karim and Amyn to Pakistan for a visit. "I have no idea what is in my father-in-law's mind," Joan said, adding, perhaps hopefully: "Both my sons were brought up in the Moslem faith."

## 2

Finally, all of the details of Yasmin's custody were worked out and Rita left in the fall of 1955 for Europe, taking along Rebecca and Yasmin. Everyone made a show of cordiality and family solidarity as Rita docked in France. She was thin, tense, and exhausted, preparing to divorce Haymes. Torem met her with a personal message of greeting from Aly. The next day the Aga and Begum arrived with a giant teddy bear for Yasmin.

At five, Princess Yasmin Aga Khan was a winsome little girl, accustomed to seeing adults come and go: her father, her step-father, her governesses. Rita tried to spend time with her but, as one friend put it: "Rita seldom relaxed with Yasmin and Rebecca; she was either working too hard or had some emotional crisis. She wanted them to be brought up properly. She was always looking for a governess who was 'very refined,' and seeing that they dressed well. She was very proud of them both."

As Rita herself explains it: "I've had to be mother and father —and working besides." She supported both girls. Only recently did she begin getting partial support for Yasmin.

Both girls tried hard to please their mother, to draw her out of her extraordinary reserve, to make her react to them. One friend remembers: "Yasmin never said, 'I want this' or 'I won't do that.' She always would ask, 'Do you think my Mummy would want me to do that?' "

Physically, Yasmin resembled her father; she had his brown eyes and broad brow. She also had his restlessness. Ted de Bry, who got to know her well later on when he was secretary to Rita's fifth husband, movie producer James Hill, describes her as "the type of child who couldn't wait to get started if you suggested doing something." She adored going along with de Bry at Christmas time when he "played Santa Claus" to a number of poor families in Los Angeles. She was generous and unspoiled, "mature beyond her years," de Bry observed, "with an extraordinary understanding and perception of things." But like Aly she had a mischievous streak. Once she was having lunch in a restaurant with her mother, Hill, and de Bry. "Suddenly we discovered she was flipping elastics under the table and hitting the legs of people in other parts of the restaurant."

Yasmin's rediscovery of her father was a singular event in her young life. She was used to luxury, to big houses, cars, chauffeurs, servants. She took them for granted as most children do, even those who have not had them before. But at five, Yasmin already knew a good deal about people, and Aly was a different order of adult. He always had been a Pied Piper to his friends' children. He knew how to enter into their special child's world. "When he came to stay with us," recalled Daphne Fielding, the former Lady Weymouth, who had known Aly since he was sixteen, "he spent hours playing Red Indians with my children. He gave them wonderful Red Indian equipment—costumes, a wigwam, bows and arrows and peace pipes. He was their prime favorite of all the visiting grownups." Gordon Grand, Aly's friend from wartime days with the American army, has a snapshot of Aly in a bathing suit balancing a glass of water on his head for the amusement of Grand's five children. "They all adored him." Aly was always in a great rush before Christmas, Grand recalls. "He would say, 'What does little Gordie want?' [Aly was Gordie's honorary godfather.] I would say, 'Now, Aly, you can't spend time on that.' But he would reply, 'One of my basic principles is never disappoint a child.' He never did. He never forgot Gordie's birthday. Come hell or high water, he did remember. He was fantastic."

Aly took Yasmin to the circus and to the zoo. He took her to the Le Tremblay track near Paris to watch him race in the Prix Greffülhe, known as the "Grand Prix for gentlemen riders." The Aga and Begum came too, for the race was the climax of an exciting contest between Aly and Group Captain Peter Townsend, the former equerry to Queen Elizabeth, whose name, at the time, was linked with that of Princess Margaret. This was the third meeting between the two gentlemen jockeys. Townsend had placed ahead of Aly in the first; Aly had outraced Townsend in the second. Yasmin sat on Tutti's lap to watch this third, decisive race. She clapped and cheered as Aly came in second, Townsend fifth. Later that year in Deauville Aly taught her to ride and got her a pony so that they could ride together along the wide beach where Aly himself had first discovered horses so many years before. In the late afternoon, they could be seen, side by side, Aly reining in his horse to keep pace with Yasmin's pony, their elongated shadows loping beside them on the sand.

Yasmin told a friend about it when she returned to California. "Weren't you afraid that the horses would fall on the wet sand?" asked the friend. "Of course not," answered Yasmin with the certitude children have when adults demonstrate their ignorance. "It makes the horses' hoofs strong to ride in the sand." She paused and added the weight of authority. "Daddy told me that."

Yasmin visited Aly almost every summer after that. Between visits, Aly sometimes came to California to see her. A former classmate in the Beverly Hills public school which she attended recalls that even at school, "Yasmin always was being called away to the telephone; her father was phoning from some exotic place."

Just opposite Aly's bed at the Chateau, he kept a water color of Yasmin by his friend, the painter Constantin Terechkovitch. He loved to talk about her, boasting of her impish charm and speculating about her future as a horsewoman. She was the only one of his three children who liked horses.

But for all Aly's genuine adoration of Yasmin, his life was no more geared to being a father than to being a husband. He would have hated the parallel, but his visits to Yasmin were in many ways reminiscent of the Aga's childhood visits to him.

"Aly was like Santa Claus," Rita recalled. "Whenever Yassy saw him, she'd see him for a day or two and he'd bring her a lot of presents and then leave. He really loved her but . . ." Her voice trailed off.

# Chapter XXVI

*"The Aga always brushed aside Aly's comments about politics, current events or Ismaili affairs. Once, only once, did I discuss politics with the Aga when Aly was present and taking part. Afterward, Aly said to me: 'If you hadn't been here, he would have turned the conversation to horses.' I had the same trouble with my father. You're either too frivolous or you're trying to jump into the old man's boots. You can't do anything right."*

—Viscount Astor

The seventy-seven-year-old Aga had been expected to name his successor at the climactic moment of his Platinum Jubilee observance in Karachi in February, 1954. It was another lavish celebration with sixty thousand Ismailis gathered to watch him weighed on a specially built electric scale that tipped fourteen of his 215 pounds for every ounce of platinum set on its other side. As a revolving platform slowly turned to give everyone a good view, the Aga announced that the 2,600,000 rupees ($764,-

700) collected by the community for this event would be used to set up a Platinum Jubilee Finance Corporation in Pakistan. It was a good show but the ceremony came and went without any official word on the matter of the succession.

Aly, with Viscount Astor, had gone out to Pakistan in advance to make preparations, but once the festivities started, Aly was shoved into the background. The Aga, concentrating all of his remaining vitality on the project, relied on his cane and the Begum and made his way alone through a strenuous schedule that would have exhausted a much younger man. Astor was shocked one day to hear some of the Ismaili leaders speculating that Aly would not succeed his father as Imam. He mentioned the conversation to Aly, who just scoffed.

Nevertheless, it was obvious that the Aga was not letting Aly play too important a role. When someone asked the Begum about the succession, she snapped: "We will talk about that twenty years from now. The Aga expects to live to be a hundred." Inspiring as this may have been to older members of the community, there were those who wondered what was really going on in the Imam's mind. The community, as so often happens when the reign of a strong man draws toward its conclusion, was restive.

For years it had been taken for granted that Aly would succeed his father. Ismaili Boy Scouts learned to chant the names of all the Imams ending with: "the present Aga Khan is the forty-eighth, Prince Aly *Waliahad* will be the forty-ninth, and young Aga Karim the fiftieth." But the Aga's behavior now strengthened contrary rumors and doubts.

The affairs of the community were run by an old guard whose positions were as much assured by their wealth as by their piety. To them, Aly's selection would mean continuity—some felt their power might even increase, for they doubted that Aly would give community affairs the concentrated attention and iron leadership of his father, but others were inclined to distrust Aly. They often were shocked by his personal life but their uneasiness went beyond that. He was impetuous and irreverent; he didn't have the proper respect for the established order. They recalled how at public meetings he might jump the ropes stretched out to mark his path to drape a garland of flowers on the humblest in the crowd. He had established nursery schools with the avowed purpose of making Ismaili women even more independent. He spent hours with the youngsters of the community, and very little time praying with the *wazirs* in the *jamat-khana*.

The more far-sighted saw in Aly's barnstorming the touch of a master politician who could hold the allegiance of the community's burgeoning young bourgeoisie. They felt his talent for charming people everywhere and for effecting human compromises could help Ismailis to operate amidst the touchy new nationalisms of India, Pakistan, and Africa. But all of this was uncharted territory and the more conservative were fearful of leaving its exploration and their own fortunes in Aly's unpredictable hands.

A few put their hopes in Sadruddin, inspired to dreams of glory by a rumor that the Aga planned to marry him to the daughter of the Shah of Iran, a plump fifteen-year-old named Shahnaz. The Shah had divorced Shahnaz's mother, Fawzia, sister of King Farouk, because she had produced no male heir. His new wife Soraya was still childless (and eventually went the way of Fawzia). If the Shah were to die without male issue, leaving the throne of Darius heirless, might not someone close to it, of impeccable family and religious background, be elevated by an advantageous palace sleight of hand?

Even the Aga's grandsons, Karim and Amyn, had their supporters who pointed significantly to a statement which the Aga had once angrily made, declaring that *any* male of his direct line might succeed him and there were, therefore, four possible candidates.

The Aga kept aloof from these speculations but he listened, and when he pressed his tired old ear close to the ground, he heard an even more dangerous kind of ground swell. It was not *for* anybody. It was against *him*.

A new barrage of attacks on "Agakhanism," was under way, especially in East Africa. In pamphlets and letters to newspapers the critics called upon the Aga, and Aly, too, as *Waliahad*, to renounce their claims to godship and to abdicate their leadership of the Ismailis. They berated them for their absences from the community, their luxurious mode of living, and Aly's romantic adventures in Europe and Hollywood.

No one knew the authors or the origin of the propaganda. The Aga's agents checked printing plants and watched post offices, but to no avail. It was rumored the pamphlets had been printed elsewhere and smuggled into Africa. The Khoja Reformers were suspected. Or were there other unknown and therefore even more insidious dissenters within the community itself? Some of the pamphlets indicated an intimate knowledge of community affairs.

In angry frustration, the Ismaili leaders of East Africa requested Britain's Colonial Secretary, Oliver Lyttleton, to investigate "the campaign of vilification" against the Aga and Aly. The newspaper *Ismaili* of Bombay published editorials protesting the attacks and also the space being given to the charges in other newspapers. The Ismaili community of Nairobi endorsed a resolution which decried the "surreptitious and libellous statements," and advised everyone to "keep calm against all provocations."

By telephone and by telegram, the ailing Aga mobilized his forces. Ismaili leaders were called to France to consult with the Aga on strategy; it was decided to ask all Ismailis in Africa to sign a declaration of loyalty to the Aga or risk expulsion from the community. The family would do its part too. The indefatigable Begum set out on a pilgrimage to Mecca. Piously clad in the long white cotton robe of the pilgrims, she made the exhausting, scorching trip in midsummer. Karim and Amyn were hurriedly summoned for a tour of East Africa where seventeen-year-old Karim reminded followers that the 104 Aga Khan schools there were maintained by grants from the Imam. Plans were pushed for a second even more gala celebration of the Aga's Platinum Jubilee to be held in East Africa the following February.

The Aga seemed to be storing up strength for the occasion.

Early in 1955 he retired to his island home at Aswan in the middle of the Nile while speculation swirled about him like the river's muddy waters. The Aga loved the warmth of Aswan for even the mild winters of the Riviera now racked his frame. And he loved the privacy. He no longer liked to be seen off guard in his moments of weakness or pain. The island at Aswan was his own small world, where no one intruded except by invitation. He still enjoyed having guests, like his old friend Somerset Maugham, who visited him there, but he put them up at the Cataract Hotel on the bank of the Nile, furnishing them with a car and a boat but seeing them only at specified times when he could shine with his old brilliance.

The Begum was content, or seemed to be, in this lonely existence. She had few friends of her own except for her women secretaries, with whom she formed devoted attachments. Her life was given over to the Aga's care, increasingly complex, often physically and emotionally wearing, as he became less and less able to take care of himself. He read the London *Times*, wrote letters, prayed, ate as much as his nurses would allow him, telephoned friends for gossip, pondered the past, and ran through the possibilities of a future in which he might or might not be involved.

2

Everything was in readiness for another weighing-against. The special electric scales were en route to Kampala, Uganda, where the ceremony was to take place in a new three-story *jamat-khana*, which oddly resembled a county courthouse in the American Deep South.

A few weeks before the ceremony word came from Aswan —the Aga was ill. At first it was described as gout, later as influenza. Aly flew in from London and found the Cataract Hotel already buzzing with people and rumors.

David Burk, the Middle East correspondent for the powerful London *Daily Express*, was pulled out of Greece to cover what the correspondents privately called "the Aga Khan circus." The Aga's party was always "large, comprehensive, self-sufficient and generated as much excitement as a circus whenever it pulled in somewhere for a stay," Burk recalls. He knew it well and had covered it often. It would have been a routine assignment except for the aching question of the Aga's successor. Burk decided to try it on Aly, who readily agreed to an exclusive interview and suggested a meeting in the lobby of the hotel. There, on a brocaded couch, his blue sports shirt unbuttoned to the midriff, he rambled on in response to Burk's questions: He didn't see why there should be any question about the succession. "There has never been the slightest disagreement between Father and me on this or any other subject. I know there are rumors, but someone must have dreamed them up. Perhaps it's because I have been married twice. So what? My father had four wives." As for the talk that he was a playboy—"Every time I am seen with a pretty woman it it automatically assumed I am going to marry her—or worse," he grinned. "I know many pretty women. Anyone who gets around as much as I do is bound to. Why shouldn't I talk to them?"

Aly told Burk how he had been "groomed" to be his father's successor since the age of eleven. "And this," he said, "is a point often overlooked in the Western world; a leader of Ismaili Moslems is not expected to assume the mantle of a priest. I am a devout Moslem, as is Father. But even more important is the worldly facet of the job. Without the experience of life my father collected in his earlier years, it would have been impossible for him to give wise judgments, gainful advice, and therefore to gain the respect of his people."

Aly seemed nervous, defensive; he babbled on loquaciously for forty minutes. As soon as he finished, Burk dashed to his room, dictated his story by telephone to a colleague in Cairo who cabled it "urgent" to London, beginning: "Aly Khan . . . felt able tonight to dispel rumors about his future."

The next morning, when Burk arrived in the lobby of the Cataract Hotel he found Aly waiting for him, obviously agitated. He invited Burk to have coffee on the terrace, overlooking the famous cataract of the Nile river. He said he hoped Burk had written nothing about the interview of the day before. Burk replied that he had and Aly begged him to cable the *Express* and ask them not to print the story. Burk told him: "Even if I were willing to agree, it is much too late; either the story is already on the *Express* front page [it was] or it will never be printed at all." Aly was incredulous; he talked on and on, urging Burk to cable or phone London at his expense. "I don't think I ever convinced him, that day, that it was too late," says Burk.

Aly left the table, pale and distraught. Burk, his journalistic curiosity piqued, sought out some of his friends among the Aga's entourage, to find out what had happened. He discovered that earlier that morning, the Aga, feeling a trifle better, had invited Aly to join him in a drive around the Aswan golf course. During the drive, Aly had mentioned his interview with the "nice young man from the *Daily Express*" who had wanted to know about the succession.

The Aga had been furious. No one, he said, had any right to discuss a successor during the Aga's lifetime except the Aga himself. It was presumptuous, outrageous, that Aly had done so. He ordered him to make certain the story did not get into print.

When Aly's frantic efforts to do this failed, he chartered a plane and flew first to Cairo, then to Ceylon and Pakistan, denying in press conferences at each place that he had made any comments or predictions about the succession. The very notion shocked him. "As a faithful son I would not dream of talking about such a delicate matter, especially when Father is ill."

While Aly dashed about, trying to rectify his blunder, Burk remained at Aswan. Despite the interview, he was not ostracized. On the contrary, the Begum, for instance, was as cordial as ever. She took tea with him twice and even posed for a photograph engaged in her new hobby, sculpting; she was modeling a bust of the Aga. Even the Aga granted Burk an interview in which he seemed to blame Aly for the whole mess. The Aga's health gradually improved and in February the entire entourage moved to the Semiramis Hotel in Cairo where Aly, back from his travels, joined them.

He was somewhat chastened by his indiscretion and its aftermath, but he felt he had made amends and was soon as jaunty as ever. As usual, he was not traveling alone; a pretty Belgian woman was with him. On the night of February 11 he took her and his aide, Geoffrey Cross, to the newly opened

Inchass night club near the Pyramids where Juliette Greco was singing. When another party arrived, led by an attractive young woman whom Aly had not seen before, he looked her up and down and let out a low wolf whistle. Then he saw Burk, accompanied by Merioneth Whitaker, the Aga's secretary, and Walter Hamilton, the Aga's doctor, bringing up the rear of the party. Aly scowled and turned away. But Burk, who had not exchanged a word with Aly since his hurried departure from Aswan the previous month, decided to capitalize on the situation. On one of his calling cards he wrote: "Prince Aly, I utterly forbid you to whistle at my wife." Aly, never one to nurse a grudge, and feeling the crisis had passed anyway, replied on one of his own cards: "All is forgiven—come home." Burk and Aly grinned and waved at one another and Aly shifted his attention to Juliette Greco, who had just come on stage in her beatnik garb and long flowing hair. He recently had met her and tonight obviously found her more alluring than the young Belgian woman at his side. His friends settled back to watch another Aly conquest, but by the time Miss Greco had finished singing and the lights had been turned back on, Aly, Dr. Hamilton, and Miss Whitaker had vanished. A telephone call had summoned them to the hotel. The Aga had had a heart attack.

Ismaili leaders from Kampala, Mombasa, Nairobi and Dar-es-Salaam clustered, as if for comfort, in the Semiramis's lounges and clogged the corridor outside the Aga's suite. The Aga sent word to them that he was feeling better and would go to Kampala as scheduled.

He felt so much better one day, that, according to a story published in the French picture magazine, *Paris-Match*, he escaped the vigilance of his nurses and, shuffling around his apartment, found a complete dinner for six which had been sent up by room service for some of the people attending him. The Aga had been living on yogurt for weeks; this savory temptation was too much. One nibble then led to another until the entire serving— six portions each of roast quail, rice pilaf and *poires Hélène*—had disappeared. It was a spectacular burst of gourmandizing even for the Aga and it put him back in bed. A new heart attack brought an ultimatum from the doctors: there would be no going to Kampala, no triumphal tour of other African cities, no pageant, no fireworks. The Aga was widely reported to be on his death-bed, the Begum sat by his side day after day. Yet the old man's vigor was astonishing. He held on, as if challenging Aly's ill-timed words. His rage seemed to give him strength. He and he alone would dispose of the prize that was his to give. And in his own good time.

A week later he was well enough to participate in a boiled-down, displaced version of his Jubilee in the lounge of the hotel. The Begum sat on his right; Aly on his left. Aly winced notice-ably when asked about the seating arrangement. However, he had learned a powerful lesson in tact. "Her place," he said, "is not only on my father's right but in the hearts of all his followers, including me." Aly read a short speech of gratitude for his father. Otherwise, there was no sign that he was *Waliahad* and only a faltering heartbeat away from the throne. The difference between father and son had never been so underlined. Aly never had been able to meet his father on equal terms; the lesson of the Aga's superior strength had been driven home in childhood and had never been relaxed. He was dwarfed by even this weary wasted man beside him now in Cairo.

A friend of Aly's, the French writer and painter, Betty Bouthoul, once made the discerning comment: "How many kings have killed their sons? Is it jealousy? Are they afraid, finally, of losing out to their sons? Perhaps Aly would have been content to remain the best friend and confidant of his father. He was fas-cinated by his father, but he was never given the chance."

Elsa Maxwell, who knew both the Aga and Aly well, had her own explanation: "No one was a greater *coureur* (woman chaser) than the Aga Khan. He had thousands of mistresses. He made love to so many women, important women in England, great big names. In his failing powers, he saw himself renewed only in his son. Aly had taken over. Aly had all the women. So the Aga had this strange jealousy."

The Aga complained about Aly to his friend Lord Carnarvon, begging him to use his influence to curb Aly's scandalous behavior. "I have given him every chance; he is a stupid boy and I won't have any more scandal."

The pursuit of sex can be viewed objectively only when it is in the past. Looking back, the Aga minimized the part it had played in his own life and in time came to believe that it hadn't really been important. There was no one to remind him that he too had sowed his wild oats long past the regular season and that Aly's conduct, while exceptional, might be said to have been inspired by his own. No one would have dared describe Aly to him as a chip off the old block and, as a matter of fact, no one in the Aga's intimate circle at this time had any urge to. The Begum felt, as any fourth wife would, that the Aga's life had reached a crescendo, after years of muddling around on the keys, only with her arrival on the scene. And the Aga's view of his past was formed by his old man's urge to rewrite history. He was keeping a journal in a green leather notebook and he had just written, with the aid of Miss Whitaker and a British writer named John Connell, his autobiography, *World Enough and Time*. Before embarking on that project he had asked Somerset Maugham how he should treat the subject of womankind. Maugham, who is startlingly candid about himself, urged the Aga to tell all. Had the Aga taken his advice, he surely would have written a much longer book—perhaps a couple of volumes —and a more popular one. He wrote instead an apologia which left unsaid more than it revealed. The record thus officially set straight, the Aga sat feebly on his borrowed throne in Cairo and regarded Aly with the innocent eyes of old age.

## 3

In Paris that spring, the Aga saw his attorneys and looked over his will. Then the will was redeposited in the vaults of Lloyds Bank in London. It was done quietly, quickly, and routinely.

The next time Aly saw his father, the Aga was in high spirits. His health was better, his mood benign; he positively beamed at Aly. He stretched out his arms from his wheelchair and took his eldest son in his arms. Aly was able to report that negotiations with Rita were progressing and that his father would soon see Yasmin. In celebration of his father's remarkable recovery, Aly asked him to be guest of honor at his annual Grand Prix ball.

"I'm looking forward to Aly's party," the Aga assured a British reporter. "It should be the best for years. There are going to be plenty of Rothschilds, ambassadors from all over the place, French generals, and some of your nice ladies and gentlemen. Sir Gladwyn Jebb, the Duchess of Devonshire, the Duke of Argyll, the Duchess of Argyll. . . . Then there's Prince Alexander of Yugoslavia and that pretty little thing he married a while ago . . . you know, Umberto's daughter, Princess Maria Pia. Oh, everybody's coming."

And at the dinner, the Aga tapped his cane in time with the music. Anyone seeing him realized his gloom had passed. The Begum and Aly exchanged knowing glances; they had never felt so warm toward one another. And why shouldn't everyone relax? It had been a long hard winter.

# 4

The art of the seducer can be practiced anywhere, at any time, and on anyone. Sex may have nothing to do with it, either as means or end. It is valuable in politics, in society, and in business. But it has one danger for even its most expert practitioner—he may run up against a seducer even more expert than he. Then it becomes a question of who is seducing whom? He or she? Buyer or seller? Aga or Aly?

## Chapter XXVII

*"Usually a woman falls in love with an extraordinary man and then immediately sets about trying to change him, to make him like everyone else. Bettina was that rare woman who accepts a man as he is."*

—BETTY BOUTHOUL

Aly never alighted any place long enough to become part of its society. He was always the visiting fireman, just in from Bombay, just leaving for New York. No sooner did he arrive in Karachi, London, or Buenos Aires than his telephone was ringing with invitations—from a hostess who felt his presence would brighten her dinner party, from a friend who had a horse to sell or a new girl for him to meet. People loved to introduce him to women just to see the sparks fly. When Soraya showed up on the Riviera after her melancholy separation from the Shah of Iran, whom did Princess Andrée think of first as a possible escort to cheer her up? Aly, of course. The peripatetic Aly brought a fresh breath of excitement to any party. Famous people, from whom the words sound downright ironic, said seriously that they always loved seeing Aly because he "met so many interesting people."

His status in any given society never had to be defined and probably everyone felt more comfortable with this hit-and-run arrangement—including Aly, who had more than one reason for keeping on the move.

Only in France did he become part of a social group, one that was worldly, cosmopolitan, and peculiarly suited to receive and reward him—it was that fluid, glittering amalgam of the rich, the lovely, the celebrated, the sometimes notorious, known as *Tout Paris*. Literally translated it means All Paris; what it really means is all of Paris that counts—the Paris that attends the first nights, starts the literary fads, sets the styles in fashions. There are no guided tours of *Tout Paris*; American Express cannot show it to tourists either by day or by night. It is a sharp-edged, brittle society that moves by its own calendar, lives by its own rules, and makes its own cool appraisal of who is in and who is out. Wealth does not guarantee one a place in its ranks nor does aristocratic birth. Talent in the arts scores high but it must be financially successful talent—one cannot be more *avant garde* than one's bank account. To be born into *Tout Paris* is no guarantee of ultimate acceptance; one must make one's own way or, not having a firm foothold, slip out of sight into the abyss of just plain Paris. On the other hand, its ranks are constantly filled by new recruits, especially by beautiful girls, who scale the heights of *Tout Paris* in bevies. One of their favorite routes is via the Paris fashion houses. A girl from the provinces with a bewitching tilt to her chin, the small breasts, pert buttocks, and tiny wrists and ankles the French admire, may be transformed overnight into the cynosure of the autumn collections.

In 1945 a twenty-year-old, freckled-faced redhead carrying a straw satchel and $25 worth of francs arrived in Paris from Elbeuf, a small and dreary textile-manufacturing town in Normandy. She was Simone Bodin, born in Brittany, the second daughter of a railroad freight agent who had decamped when she was a baby. To get away from the gossip of the neighbors, her mother had moved to Elbeuf with Simone and her elder daughter, Catherine. A brisk and personable woman, she got a job teaching kindergarten—she sometimes had as many as one hundred three- to five-year-olds in her charge, she recalls ruefully. It was tough going. Her salary was only nine hundred francs (eighteen dollars) a month. The war came; food, clothing, all the necessities of life were scarce. A snapshot of Simone in those days shows her wearing wooden clogs and an oversized dress.

Both Simone and Catherine had red hair and lots of freckles, a heritage of seafaring Celtic ancestors who had settled along the Brittany coast. "The other children made jokes about us," Simone recalled years later. "We also had another handicap. We had no father and our playmates sometimes acted as if we never had had. But mother had big ideas for us."

Simone's best subject at school was art; her mother still has a water color, painted when Simone was twelve years old, hanging in the living room of the small Elbeuf apartment where she now lives in retirement. Simone was a dreamy girl, considered something of an eccentric at school. She was the protégé of another Elbeuf oddity, an American ballet dancer named Joan Roberts who had married and then divorced a local industrialist. Jacques Talbot, a classmate, now Elbeuf correspondent of a Rouen newspaper, remembers Simone dancing "The Fire Dance" in a school show, to the wonder and astonishment of her friends.

Elbeuf still had the social structure of a nineteenth century industrial town. There were only two classes: the wealthy factory owners who lived behind high walls in ugly massive stone houses, and the workers who huddled in dismal little apartments along grey, treeless streets.

It was the kind of a town that any youngster with ambition left. Simone dreamed of getting away, of going—of course—to Paris. Her mother encouraged her. "It was dangerous to send a young girl to Paris but there was nothing for her to do here. She was not the kind to spend her life behind a *guichet*." Simone's sister, Catherine, made the trek first. After a few discouraging months she came back to Elbeuf, married the local pharmacist, and settled down to bear and raise six children.

That didn't daunt Simone. Shortly after the Americans

landed in Normandy, swept east, and liberated Paris, she left too. Besides the same straw satchel that Catherine had carried to Paris and back again, Simone took with her a nylon slip which had appeared on the black market in the wake of Allied parachutists—it was her pride and joy; she washed it every night before going to bed and put it on, fresh and dry, every morning—and the name and address of one of Catherine's friends in Paris, a model at the small *haute couture* house of Jacques Costet.

Simone's fresh, rather Anglo-Saxon looks were unusual and struck the right note in postliberation Paris, still glowing with Allied solidarity and struggling to re-establish its pre-eminence as fashion capital with British and American clients. Costet hired her as a mannequin.

The other models showed her how to walk, in slow even strides, body swaying gracefully. But Simone, nervous and confused, walked too fast; her body didn't sway, it wiggled, at least one part of it did. Her first appearances were greeted with amusement by the women and admiring gasps by the men. Almost overnight, her "switch walk" singled her out from the rest of the mannequins. A witness of one of her early appearances recalls: "She went back and forth, turned, and she seemed to be saying: 'You don't exist. I am just a girl taking a walk in the woods.' It was so good, so refreshing that the audience burst into applause."

But it was at the famous establishment of Jacques Fath, where Simone went to work next, that she came to the attention of *Tout Paris*. Fath, the blond young man who had become the reigning prince of the Paris fashion world, liked to rename his models. His new girl reminded Fath of the red-haired character in the operetta, *La Mascotte*. Three weeks later a Paris newspaper observed:

"There is a new sensational model at Fath, her name is Bettina. . . ."

2

It is hard to pinpoint when Bettina and Aly Khan met because she was aware of him long before he noticed her. One of Bettina's modeling jobs at Jacques Fath was to show bridal gowns to Rita Hayworth. Aly was there but "he never once looked at me," Bettina has recalled. "He kept looking at her." Rita and Aly were quickly caught up in their own tumultuous destiny; Bettina went on to hers.

The *haute couture* of postwar Paris was changing; its market was no longer a handful of rich women who could afford to go to the Paris salons, but women all over the world who studied the Paris styles and then bought the copies and adaptations which were mass-produced and sold off the rack in their local department stores. The small, select world of the Paris *haute couture* was suddenly concerned with getting its message beyond its own exclusive portals to the cash customers in San Francisco and Dallas. The influential mannequins no longer were those who paraded patiently in the salons but those who appeared on the covers of the fashion magazines.

Bettina by 1950 was the leading "cover girl" in Paris. Photographers found her high cheekbones, green, almond-shaped eyes, elfin expressions, and vivid coloring were especially photogenic. Not only that, she had the patience to hold a pose for minutes on end, to spend hours under hot lamps, to climb over statues and under bridges to provide fresh backgrounds for otherwise hackneyed photos. She had intelligence enough to understand what the photographers wanted and persistence enough to work until they got it. Other models might tire easily or be late or satisfy themselves with short-range ambitions. Not the redhead from Elbeuf. She was patient, compliant, and persevering, qualities which one day would stand her in good stead in quite another sphere.

Her career went on; a brief marriage to a young journalist named Gilbert (Benno) Graziani, did not. But there were other companions. For several years her name was linked with that of Guy Schoeller, a handsome, elegant man about town, heir to a publishing business, who subsequently, in 1958, at the age of forty-five, married France's literary *enfant terrible*, Françoise Sagan, then twenty-two. Bettina had a romance with Peter Viertel, an American screen writer whose mother, Salka, had been the grey eminence of Greta Garbo's life. She moved in the more intellectual echelons of *Tout Paris*. She always had been bright;

Paris gave her polish and laid before her the books to read, the painters to admire, the political intrigues to puzzle over and the most knowledgeable people with which to discuss them. When Jacques Fath died, Bettina moved on to Givenchy, where she was not only a top mannequin but also a designer and a minor executive charged with furthering the house's public relations. There, she one day modeled the collection for Aly and Gene Tierney. This time Aly noticed her and, by her account, slipped away from Gene Tierney to try and make a date. In the behind-the-scenes confusion of Givenchy's, they missed one another—Bettina says she fled—but Aly had been alerted to her charms. They were introduced again at a ball, in the summer of 1955. "But, of course, I know Bettina," Aly said with his most winning smile.

Aly once said that what first drew him to Bettina was the way she wore a raincoat as though it were a mink. People turned their heads when Aly entered a room with Bettina; columnists took note and friends were envious. But Aly soon found that the intelligent thirty-year-old model was more than another handsome trophy to display in the Paris night clubs or introduce to the rites of life at the Chateau de l'Horizon. Bettina put him at his ease in a way no other woman had. She didn't expect him to be witty; she wasn't herself. Brilliant conversation was not required; Bettina even enjoyed silences. If he wanted to shine, she wouldn't compete. But he didn't have to be always at his best; Bettina was sympathetic to his problems and as understanding of his weaknesses as she was dazzled by his wealth and charm. She had become sophisticated during her years in Paris, but never cynical or blasé. A certain humility had never left her. She was warm, unpretentious, sympathetic; the kind of young woman who would burst into tears reading a book on the Nazi atrocities against the Jews. When she smiled, it wasn't a dazzling smile; it was a slightly questioning, faintly sad smile.

By the time Rita Hayworth arrived in France for Yasmin's long postponed visit, it was Bettina who reigned at the house by the Bois de Boulogne. No one except a few journalists still talked of a reconciliation between Rita and Aly. "That's an old story," Rita told them wearily and implied it was best forgotten. Assured that Yasmin was safe and would be returned to her as promised, Rita returned alone to the United States while Yasmin and Rebecca went to the Riviera for a gay Christmas with Aly and Bettina. Bettina was tender with Yasmin; perhaps she saw in her the child she too might one day have by Aly. Speculation was mounting that Aly would marry Bettina as soon as his divorce from Rita was recognized in France. The Aga was reported to favor the match. He liked Bettina's quiet manner, her feline grace, and, above all, her tremendous discretion. Two of his wives, Andrée and Yvette, had come, like Bettina, from the French *petit bourgeoisie* and he had found them tolerant and admirable helpmates. Even the Begum, for once, approved of Aly's choice, perhaps because she could see so much of herself in the young woman from Normandy whose father, too, had been a railway worker. There was something almost schoolgirlish in the Begum's friendship with Bettina. She expanded in Bettina's receptive presence; she laughed heartily and teased coyly. At a party that Aly gave in Monte Carlo, the Begum bombarded Bettina with colored confetti balls, to the wonderment of the other guests.

It was a happy Christmas for Aly that year at the Chateau de l'Horizon. Yasmin was there. Bettina, in tapered slacks and shaggy mohair sweaters, her red hair falling simply in a shoulder-length pageboy, sped about the Riviera with him, visiting his favorite haunts, entertaining his friends, many of whom also were hers. They played golf at Mougins where the Aga, trailed by his favorite nineteen-year-old girl caddy, was a familiar figure; they played tennis at the Carlton in Cannes with Tommy Burke. For Christmas Aly gave Bettina a Dior mink coat and a small gold ring imprinted with the Ismaili signet. Bettina's face was radiant and Aly had not looked so contented in years.

# Chapter XXVIII

> *"I'm rather fond of this one, and I'm very, very fond of that one, and I must confess I rather love the one over there, so to keep them all happy, it is no great problem."*
>
> —ALY KHAN

One evening in Deauville, Bettina and Aly went out to dinner with a friend of Aly's, the Baroness Michèle de Posson, an elegant, long-striding young woman who, although she was in her early thirties and the mother of two, looked and acted like an American coed. The wealthy, twice-married daughter of a Belgian steel and coal family, she and Aly shared an interest in horses, fast cars, and carefree hilarity. Aly had invited Michèle to spend a week at the Villa Gorizia. Bettina would be delighted, he assured her. At dinner, they got into a discussion about the pedigree of a yearling in which they both were interested. Bettina took no part, she didn't really care for horses. Aly, who prided himself on being able to spiel off ancestry, attributes, and racing records the way American youngsters recite batting averages, was piqued that Michèle did not take his word on the horse. When they got back to the Villa Gorizia at 4 A.M. Michèle went to her room to get a book which would prove her point. Returning to the salon, she found that Bettina had gone to bed, leaving Aly there alone. She and Aly pored over the book, sitting together in the half-lit room. When they had finished their discussion, Michèle excused herself, insisting: "I'm very sorry, Aly, I'm going to bed, it's finished." Aly shrugged and went up to his room.

The next day, Bettina took Michèle aside.

"I never thought, Michèle," she said, "when I left Aly downstairs, that I would see him coming up so soon."

Aly's life had changed since his meeting with Bettina—but not radically and not quite as predicted.

All through 1956 the newspapers continued to print reports that they would wed but the couple had settled down to another sort of domesticity. Bettina had given up her career at Aly's insistence. She traveled with him—when he wanted her to. She stayed behind, if that was his wish. She was always there, waiting, smiling, sympathetic.

Once in Ireland, Aly suddenly flew off to London, pleading business, leaving it to Bettina to bring to Paris several large framed paintings he had purchased. Bettina did a good deal of the packing herself, for Aly's households had a tendency to melt into lethargy the moment the master was out of sight. She had to get the paintings through Irish customs and onto the coach plane. Aly had gone off without leaving her enough money so she had to borrow some. On the plane she glanced at a London tabloid; in it was an item about Aly, night-clubbing with the leading debutante of the day.

For all her warm and eager compliance with whatever were Aly's demands—on the dance floor, in the casinos, at the race tracks, the tennis courts, or any playing field—Bettina could no more keep him by her side than had Joan, Rita, Gene Tierney, or any of dozens of other women.

Where Bettina differed from the others—and, in a way, succeeded where they had failed—is that she didn't try.

Julien Duclos, presiding over the Casino at Cannes, observed: "She always stayed in the background, very reserved. She let Aly do whatever he liked, she never said anything, and so he has kept her. The others, they revolted, and so they didn't last."

Aly may have talked to Bettina about marriage, but he confided to Tommy Burke: "I married Rita and it caused too much trouble and cost too much money. I like Bettina and she is my companion but there is no question of marrying."

Bettina didn't insist.

"Bettina is a woman who in a way likes to suffer," explained one friend. "She had a very hard time with other men before Aly. Guy Schoeller, for instance; she was much more unhappy with him. She really loved Aly. And she was made for him. She is like a true Oriental woman, passive, a little fatalistic, ready to accept everything. She always arranged things to accommodate Aly's moods, including disappearing when she saw that his attention was elsewhere."

Aly never allowed Bettina to dance with anyone else. Yet she was expected to sit quietly by while he waltzed away the evening with others. One night, seeing Bettina alone, Lord Carnarvon invited her to dance. "I couldn't," she replied. "You know it upsets Aly." "I didn't think he would count me," muttered Lord Carnarvon, who was twenty years Aly's senior, as he walked away. Another evening at a London hotel, when Bettina could no longer stand the sight of Aly's ardent attentions to a young Hollywood starlet, she retired to the lobby. Baroness Bentinck, Aly's old friend from Cairo days who was now living in London where her husband was Dutch ambassador, kept Bettina company until 5 A.M. when Aly, finally, was ready to go home.

It would be inaccurate to say that Bettina's life with Aly was unhappy. Even for her, the league in which he traveled was exciting. She enjoyed spending the evening—sometimes without Aly—dining with Jean Cocteau or discussing poetry with Jacques Prevert. The financial security was a relief; she hadn't forgotten the little girl in the wooden clogs from Elbeuf. But most important, she was passionately in love with Aly. In a certain bemused way, she even enjoyed the special role she played. "Are you going out *again*?" a friend would exclaim as she dressed to accompany Aly on one of his impulsive excursions. She would shrug with one of her silent you-know-Aly smiles. "What can I do? I'm in love with a crazy man," she once said. She felt she understood Aly and accepted with silent dignity the slights and humiliations so frequently imposed upon her. If a new rival was sparkling triumphantly on Aly's right at a dinner party, perhaps she comforted herself with the thought that she would be there when the rival had gone.

"To live with Aly, a woman had to have a level head," Bettina's mother observed. "He was charming, but difficult. Bettina did everything he wanted. No recriminations. She took all. She always did. Even when she was a child, she used to say to me, 'Don't cry, everything comes out in life.' But Aly was very kind, you know, and he valued Bettina very much."

Aly did appreciate Bettina's devotion; he confided to Juliette Greco that she tried so hard to please him. Michèle de Posson noticed that "Aly was always much nicer with Bettina in private than in public. He was sweet to her, kissing her, taking her hand. But never outside. I think it was important to him not to pay too much attention to the woman known through all the world as his mistress. For one thing, other women would not so much run after him."

Students of Aly's pace noted no slackening as they observed his encounter with Kim Novak, the platinum-haired American movie star who seems to see life through a purple haze. And no wonder. Purple is her favorite color. Her home, her car, and her well-filled sweaters are done in shades of purple. Even her hair has a touch of lavender. An aspiring Chicago model, she came to Hollywood as a traveling demonstrator of household appliances—of which she, obviously, was the one most worth having. Through one agency and another, she came to the attention of Harry Cohn, who needed a glamour girl to fall back upon in case Rita Hayworth followed through with her threats to desert her contract and marry Aly Khan. Was it fate, then—the inevitable linking of their destinies—that brought Kim and Aly together on the Riviera in 1956? Actually, it was the Cannes Film Festival. In that lavender setting—the purple haze along the Esterel at dusk, the purple smoke rising from producers' cigars in the Carlton Hotel bar, the purple prose of half the world's press agents—Miss Novak met Aly under unique circumstances which she has described in a *Ladies' Home Journal* article by George Christy. She was visiting the Aga Khan and Begum at their villa, Miss Novak says, when:

> After the photographers finished their picture-taking of the Aga Khan, the Begum and me, Aly came in from the garden. He wore faded Levis and a soiled shirt. His hands were grimy from working in the earth, and I couldn't take my eyes off them. They were strong, powerful, muddy from working in the rose garden. When we shook hands, he apologized for the dirt, and I told him I loved the earth. He smiled and asked if I wanted to see his garden. We walked around and around the garden, and he asked if I liked horses. We made our first date to go horseback riding.

This portrait of Aly as a gangling, blue-jeaned adolescent, dropping in from the rose garden at Yakimour to see who was visiting Mom and Dad, is a priceless example of Miss Novak's gift. Just what Aly was doing tending roses at Yakimour, a house to which he came only by invitation, might puzzle less romantic types, who always thought that Aly's roses were ordered from his favorite florist in Cannes. Miss Novak continues, as Aly leads her down the garden path:

> I loved the quick brisk way he walked. I had to run to keep up with him, but I didn't mind. I liked it. He took deep breaths of air, and I had the feeling of a man enjoying every minute of life, who wasn't going to waste one precious second of it. Whenever I was with Aly, I felt sorry for all the people around us who seemed half alive.

Aly's schedule was often skin-tight. Once, dashing back to a hotel in Paris to change for a dinner date, he began undressing in the elevator. Jean Fayard, who was with him, started laughing.

"I do it all the time," Aly said, grinning. "I did it once in a taxi in New York. Then the taxi almost had an accident. I would have had to get out naked."

And there is the recollection of a London chauffeur who was told to drive slowly through Hyde Park one evening while his employer and a lady friend, whom we shall identify for the purpose of this anecdote as No. 1, dallied in the tonneau of the Rolls. There is nothing so remarkable in that crowded conjunction except its context. As the awed chauffeur later recalled, Aly was en route at the time between one lady's flat (No. 2) and another's (No. 3).

As Aly raced down hotel corridors and across countries, his reputation as a global Lothario skipped oceans and continents with him.

Gianni Agnelli noted that Aly "now seemed to court publicity. I don't know whether he liked the publicity for its own sake or because it attracted more girls. It is a wonderful technique to get to know a lot of girls. Word spreads, you know."

In Cairo Aly bumped into Juliette Greco again. He asked her to dance.

"You have too bad a reputation," she replied. "We're going to sit very much apart."

"What are you doing tomorrow?" he insisted.

"Tomorrow I take a plane to Beirut."

When she boarded the plane, Aly was already on it, grinning at her surprise.

He also met an American model in Cairo named Clara Margherita Kelly, who later committed suicide in Buenos Aires, leaving behind several notes which never were made public. Across the world in Hollywood, a movie producer sued his actress wife, Virginia Lang, for divorce, charging misconduct with Aly; while in Dusseldorf, Germany, Aly had only to show up for a race to bring out a screaming, pushing mob of women who had to be restrained by the police.

Or, as Juliette Greco put it recently:

"I don't know who didn't have an affair with Aly."

Dressed in tight black leather slacks and a black sweater she stretched languorously in an armchair of her Paris house and observed:

"They say I am a dangerous woman. Well, Aly was a dangerous man. He was charming in a very special way. There is a kind of man who is very clever with women. He takes you out to a restaurant and if the most beautiful woman comes in, he doesn't look at her. He makes you feel you are a queen. Of course, I understood it. I didn't believe it. I would laugh and point out the beautiful woman. But that is me. Aly and I were pals, like two boys out for a good time.

"Most women are made very happy by that kind of attention. It's pure vanity. She thinks: 'I'll be the one and the others will leave.'

"Of course, his love-making had a lot to do with it. I can only repeat what all his friends knew about it. It was a matter of timing, plenty of time, time without end.

"It always made me feel sad. Here is a man who cannot bring things to an end for himself. I don't think it was a matter of choice; it was the way he was. I felt it because I am a giving woman as well as a receiving one. But another woman, perhaps, was attracted by a man who took so much time. It flattered her. He was thinking only of her. Too many men only think of themselves. Or maybe, she was helped in a way she had never been helped before. With another, it could be a challenge: 'I'll be the one who makes him do it.'

"With Aly, how the woman felt was most important. What interested her? He used to talk to me about paintings; he loved Dufy, so did I. Sometimes he would telephone me at 2 A.M. 'What are you doing, sleeping? I am alone. Come down to l'Horizon. I've got to talk to you.' He would send me a ticket. What could I do?"

Miss Greco visited the Chateau twice.

"The second time it was summer and it was a madhouse. Women crying and slamming doors. Putting the girls together at night. The American girls drinking a lot. They would wake up and decide they had been drunk and foolish the night before, so they would take a little drink in the morning. Aly was every-

where. He was a great charmer, a great seducer. He made you
feel fine and that everything was easy. No problems. Nothing
to worry about. Or regret. It was always, 'What can I do for
you? What do you need?' Airplane tickets, cars, boats; you felt
you were on a pink cloud."

## 2

The reasons behind Aly's behavior might be as simple as
one friend's "Aly just liked women," or as darkly Freudian as
the suspicion that he was a latent homosexual who repressed his
tendency in epic fashion.

Certainly there was a connection between his headlong
pursuit of pleasure and his feelings about his father. The question
of the succession still hung over them, like an ominous shadow.
Aly, of course, never asked it. But reporters did and the only
reply they got was an enigmatic chuckle. The Aga was enjoying
their perplexity. And doubtless Aly's too. Aly had spent most
of his life with his father in just this position—not sure of where
he stood. So he bested his father with every new feminine conquest—and reassured himself that he was man enough and more.

He still was obsessed by his mother, too. The first night he
met Juliette Greco, she recalls: "He didn't stop talking about
his mother. It all came out so fast, as if he had never discussed
her with anybody before."

A psychiatrist might say that Aly was seeking his mother,
whom he lost so early in life, in every woman he pursued. Or, he
might go even deeper, and explain that a young boy's feelings
about his parents can be devious indeed. Young Aly had adored
his mother, longed for her with every fiber of his being. But
she belonged, after all, to his father, that powerful and awesome
man. And so, in a way, Aly hated her too—for her betrayal in
not being exclusively his, for letting his father send him away
from her to England, and even for dying and leaving him behind,
alone. In a way, the psychiatrist would say, Aly hated all women
—and was getting his revenge on each and every one.

Aly, of course, would have snorted at such complex explanations. He scoffed at psychiatrists. He never patronized one or took their theories seriously. And he never looked behind him if he could help it. Why think of Oedipus when Venus awaited? He lived for the day and each day brought its own excitements. If the past haunted and the future perplexed, they stayed in some recess of his mind which he left unexplored and carefully hidden from the view of others.

# Chapter XXIX

*"Nobody, including Sadri and Aly, will
know who is my heir until I die. I have made
up my mind which of them it shall be, and I
have written out the necessary instructions. But
just as I have to wait and see about their marriages, so they will have to wait and see about
their inheritances."*

—AGA KHAN III, on November 25, 1956

Aly chortled when Sadruddin, the quiet, scholarly
Sadri, fell in love with precisely the kind of woman the Aga had
so often berated Aly for choosing. She was Nina Dyer, a sleek
and feline young woman who looked like every man's dream of
a jungle princess. She kept a leopard and a panther as pets. Born
in Ceylon, the daughter of an English tea planter, and educated
in South Africa, she had left the veldt to become a mannequin in
London and Paris. She had married and divorced Baron Henry
Thyssen of the German industrial family, an art collector and
the brother of Aly's friend, Baroness Gaby Bentinck.

Sadri met her in the summer of 1956 while he was home

from Harvard. It was not without precedent as summer romances go—a college boy in love with a glamorous divorcée, three years older than himself. But Sadri was a serious sort and when he fell in love, it was serious too. He returned to Harvard but bombarded Nina with cabled flowers and, in one burst of enthusiasm, flew the Atlantic to spend a week end with her. His friends couldn't get over it. "Nina was attractive," commented one of them, "but none of us dreamed he could be serious about her."

Aly's eyebrows jiggled over the turn of events. In many ways, not the least of which was the unusual slant of her eyes, Nina was Aly's type of woman. But he was not a man to cry over one fish escaped from his net. Somewhat condescendingly, he admired Sadri's taste, commented on the younger man's ability to handle so large a catch, and predicted that their father would be furious.

He was right; the Aga's comments were acerbic: "Aly has got himself thoroughly into the hands of the lawyers over his affairs and I have no doubt Sadruddin will do the same before he has finished."

It was a new experience for Sadri, being likened to Aly. But nothing his father or mother might say could get Sadri back in the groove he had so conscientiously followed the first twenty-four years of his life. In the end, it was the Aga who gave in. Sadri summoned reporters and photographers to his mother's villa and posed for pictures, hand in hand with Nina. The wedding, he said, would be July the fifteenth.

Karim left Harvard early that semester to be with his grandfather. He didn't stay with his father at l'Horizon, but took a place of his own and spent nearly every day at Yakimour. He was, after all, the eldest son of the eldest son and would someday be Imam. He read through the Aga's files and helped the two secretaries—Mlle. Gaetane Beguel, a Frenchwoman, and the American Miss Whitaker, with their voluminous correspondence with the community. For the first time he got an idea of the complexities, the cross-breeding of religion, politics, and finance his grandfather ordered with an iron hand.

The Aga's health varied from day to day. He would be up

one day, sunning himself in his wheelchair, lunching with Karim and the Begum. The next day he would take to his bed again. When Cannes Film Festival time came around, the Aga, who so loved meeting the starlets, could not go. Only one vicarious pleasure remained. Whenever he possibly could, he bundled up in a blanket and, with a nurse beside him, went down the hill in his Rolls-Royce for a slow and stately circuit of Cannes, down along the Croisette, and up to the door of the Carlton, where Jules, the bar manager, would come rushing out with a cold glass of Vichy water and the latest gossip. The Aga still wanted to see and hear everything.

The Begum marveled. "He is not eating. He has a persistent fever. Yet he wants to read the newspapers. We have to read them to him."

The Aga knew all about Aly's debts. The newspapers reported the baccarat sessions with Darryl Zanuck and Jack Warner. Sometimes, casino directors, bookmakers, and restaurant owners became impatient dunning Aly and sent his bills to the Aga. "When Aly won at a casino, he would ask one of his friends to cash in his chips for him," Baroness Bentinck says. "He owed money at every casino." He was as broke, or as nearly broke, as a millionaire could be. For years, he had lived on unlimited credit, investing any capital he got in more horses, larger bets, lavish living, on the strength of his potential fortune as the heir of "the richest man in the world." Now his creditors were getting worried. They read the newspapers, too. What if Aly did not become Imam? They detected the same anxiety in Aly and pressed him for payment.

Joking that he had to "buy better oats for my horses," he reluctantly put his paintings up for sale at the Galerie Charpentier in Paris. Mike Todd and his wife, Elizabeth Taylor, were in town and Todd, anticipating profits from *Around the World in Eighty Days*, was buying everything in sight. Aly sat sadly and quietly in the first row with Bettina, studying the catalogue, watching his beloved Dufys and Utrillos, his Degas self-portrait, his Renoir, and his Boudin go on the block, while the crowd hailed a new hero, Todd, who paid out $71,000 for three of them. The collection of fifty-two drawings, water colors, and paintings brought in a total of $235,000. A lot of it went into new bets.

Things always had worked out. This would too. His confidence was returning. His problems with Rita seemed to be at an end. The Aga had asked again to see Yasmin and this time Aly had been able to assure him she would come, a vibrant flesh-and-blood symbol of their reconciliation. A Swiss court had recognized Rita's Reno divorce and, thus reassured that her custody of Yasmin would be respected in Europe, Rita had agreed to the trip. The only question was: would Yasmin get there in time?

On the night that Yasmin sailed from New York, Todd took over the Battersea amusement park outside London for a memorable party to advertise the London premiere of *Around the World in Eighty Days*. Aly and Bettina were there, riding a merry-go-round. From the Aga's villa in Switzerland came a communique: "Only the Aga's tremendous interest in what is happening in the world is keeping him alive. He refuses to let go of life."

## 2

The Aga had been flown to Geneva and then taken by ambulance to his Villa Barakat in Versoix, a Geneva suburb. As much as he loved Yakimour, the Aga was too practical a man to die anywhere but in Switzerland. Barakat was his legal residence—a square, two-story house of beige stucco, lying between the lake and the highway. Dr. Arnold Naef, a tall white-haired physician who had his offices a few doors down the highway, had been treating the Aga for three or four years. When he saw him this time, he was shocked. The Aga had gone down from two hundred and forty-two pounds to one hundred and fifty-four.

Naef, and other doctors, stayed on call. Nurses never left the old man's side. The Begum worried that he was starving himself to death: "He doesn't want to eat anything." Years of gourmandizing had damaged the Aga's liver and kidneys. But he remained alert and indomitable.

He decided to cheer up the Begum by planning a gigantic reception in honor of his eightieth birthday. It would be celebrated that fall—in New York. He instructed the Begum to make steamship reservations and to engage a ballroom of the Waldorf-Astoria Hotel. She, humoring him as much as he was humoring her, fell in with the plan. When some American friends, Dr. and Mrs. Milton Berliner (he is a prominent New York eye specialist, while his wife, Constance Hope, is a public relations woman) called from Paris to suggest canceling a planned visit in view of the Aga's condition, the Begum urged them to come. "The Aga wants Constance to advise him about his eightieth birthday party," she explained. "It will encourage him so much to have you here." But to another friend the Begum confided: "I am only afraid that it will never happen." Whatever the Aga thought of his chances, he kept the Begum by his bedside for hours as, out of his prodigious memory, they drew up the guest list.

And then Yasmin arrived. She came on the *Ile de France*, occupying a suite with her nurse, Marie Walla. Aly met them at the dock in Le Havre and sped them off to Le Bourget airport outside Paris. Yasmin threw her arms around Bettina, who was waiting there, and they all took off by plane for Geneva. A car met them and whisked them to Versoix; there was no time to lose.

The driveway was lined with cars. A Swiss detective stood guard at the gate. The little girl, still in the blue dress and grey coat she had worn when she got off the ship, held her father's hand as they went into the dimly-lit room where the Aga lay amidst whispering figures. The Aga recognized Yasmin as she leaned close, grinning down at him; he managed a grin in reply. They whispered together for two minutes. Aly told the reporters at the gate: "They were both tremendously happy to see each other again. Yasmin is the best medicine in the world for my father, but it was very brief, for my father can speak only a very little."

Then he delivered his exhausted little daughter into the arms of her nurse at the Hotel Beau Rivage. In other hotels around the city were Sadruddin and Nina Dyer and Ismaili leaders. Karim was in London with his mother but was expected soon; Amyn was still at Harvard.

There was some visiting back and forth, whispered consultations, hesitant speculation. Everyone was in the dark. Perhaps the Begum knew the answer to their questions but she sat immovable, weeping beside the Aga's bed. She never left his side. Her final vigil was to last forty-eight hours.

## 3

At 2 A.M. on the morning of July 11, phone calls from Barakat summoned Aly and Sadruddin to the house by the lake. They drove out, in separate cars, at top speed. The Aga's heart had noticeably weakened. It was a matter of hours, one of the doctors said. At seven they returned to their hotels to shower and change. At nine they were back at the villa again.

The driveway was jammed with cars now. When Bettina arrived in a taxi at 10:15 she found it difficult to make her way up to the door. The Begum and Bettina took a walk around the house. Nina Dyer, her wedding scheduled for four days hence, went for a drive. Yasmin and her nurse took a walk in Geneva. At midmorning, a servant came out and locked the villa gates. The plainclothes man was unobtrusively reinforced by a police car.

At 12:40, the Aga's heart stopped.

"I was talking on the telephone to the Swiss ambassador," Miss Whitaker recalls, "and Suleiman, the Aga's valet, came by and shouted 'He's gone. He's gone.' I hung up immediately and went into the room and there he was. The Begum sat on a chair by the bed. Aly was weeping. It was terrible, the realization of it."

Miss Whitaker and one of the Aga's former secretaries, an Englishwoman named Frieda Blain, who had volunteered to help, went down to the gate. "Everyone was just milling around. We were shaking but we went down to the gate and announced that 'His Highness has died.' "

Dr. Naef wrote the death certificate: heart failure complicated by cancer and jaundice. The Ismailis arrived at the villa. One of them was admitted to the death chamber. He bowed before the body and recited a long prayer. With him he had

a long white shroud in which the Aga's body would be clothed
for burial. Only his face would show. Soon after the Ismailis
left, a white-coated embalmer drove up in a taxi and lugged into
the house the utensils of his trade: a carboy of chemicals, several
trays, and a pump. The process of embalming was not finished
until Friday morning, twenty-four hours after the Aga's death.
The body of the Aga was to lie in state, for Ismailis were coming
from as far away as Burma to pay him homage.

Aly's face was grey with fatigue as he drove back to his
hotel. His hands shook with tension. No one had ever seen him
so exhausted. All of the vitality and sparkle for which he was
known had drained out of him. He took Yasmin in his arms:
"Grandpa has gone away from us." Yasmin burst into tears.

The same question that reporters kept firing at him dominated his own thoughts as, with Karim in shirt sleeves at the
wheel, he drove about Geneva the next day seeing to the myriad
details that attend a death, particularly the demise of a giant.
He and Sadruddin conferred with André Ardoin, the Aga's business manager. They talked about the complex legal procedure
that lay ahead, settling the Aga's estate, his vast world-wide
financial and religious empire. They discussed Swiss law and
English law and Moslem law in tired husky voices. But their
minds, obviously, were elsewhere. Someone telephoned Lloyds
Bank and the reply came that the will would be taken out of the
London vaults and flown to Geneva the following morning.

# Chapter XXX

*"I SULTAN SIR MAHOMED SHAH
AGA KHAN C.C.I.E., G.C.S.I., born on the
Second day of November One thousand eight
hundred and seventy seven at Karachi tem-
porarily residing at the Hotel Ritz London
HEREBY REVOKE all Wills and other testa-
mentary dispositions heretofore made by me
AND DECLARE THIS TO BE MY LAST
WILL. . . ."*

Aly spent the morning with Merioneth Whitaker,
answering some of the messages of condolence that had poured in
from all over the world. She found him "so intelligent, regardless of how scatterbrained he might have seemed at times. He
put some wonderful touches into the notes he dictated. They
were gems, absolute gems."

Then he went to Lloyds Bank and learned that an officer
of the bank had arrived from London, carrying the Aga's will

in his briefcase. Otto Giesen, a solicitor with the firm of Slaughter and May, also had flown in from London. It was all set for the afternoon. Aly conferred with the bank manager and with Ardoin, the family business manager. The heat in Geneva added to his tension. He strode out, face haggard and puffy behind sunglasses, coat off and slung over his shoulder, a sheaf of telegrams in his hand. His shirt was unbuttoned nearly to the waist.

This was Aly during the most severe ordeal of his life. Since boyhood he had schooled himself to keep cool, to laugh off defeats, to show a smiling face to the world. His mother's quixotic moods, the Aga's sudden arrivals and departures, the rebuffs of his early years in England, the sudden searing death of his mother, all had taught him it was safer to be unconcerned. Aly never allowed himself, if it was at all possible, to be shocked, to be taken by surprise. His passion for living he expended on the trivial: fast drives, late nights, another flirtation. From the deeper commitments of life, he drew back. They could be too painful. If one didn't care, one couldn't be hurt. This coolness had made him successful in the boudoir and on the race course. It had failed only with his father. There he had met an equal coolness. There he had sought a commitment, hungered for it, but never achieved it. The Aga, he felt, had played with his feelings and withdrawn, led him on and withdrawn. And now, with his father's death, he faced a possible final rejection, a judgment that no woman, no horse, no columnist could countermand. Had his father finally recognized him?

He soon would know. The telegrams of sympathy, the solemn handshakes from ambassadors, the staccato questions from reporters—these came to him because he was assumed to be his father's heir. His life had pointed toward this moment. For thirty years he had been cloaked in the adulation of the Ismailis for their *Waliahad* and in the glamour with which the West invested his role as the future leader of a Moslem sect. Reporters, suspecting that he had just seen the contents of the will, cornered him outside Lloyds Bank. "I cannot tell you anything yet," he said. "I am still too broken-hearted to make an announcement but I may be able to tell you this afternoon." He and Bettina lunched with Sadri and Nina on a hotel terrace.

At 2 P.M. he drove up to the Villa Barakat with Karim. His face sagged at the sight. Around the entrance to the villa, locked and guarded by five Swiss policemen, a carnival had sprung up. The highway was clogged with parked cars and by others that slowed down as they passed the gate so that their occupants could peer, point, and snap pictures. There were women carrying squalling babies, fanning themselves with newspapers, some of them in shorts, their sunburned legs hanging obscenely out of the open doors of their cars. The men were wet from the heat, their heads covered with knotted handkerchiefs or fore-and-aft caps of folded newspapers. Youngsters dashed back and forth between the cars and a nearby café. Everyone seemed to be munching or chewing or drinking.

The photographers and reporters held the vantage points in the shady spots under the trees along the fence. Like snipers, they pointed their cameras toward the house at every rustle of activity. Aly grimaced as he recognized his old enemies whose telephoto lens had poked into his life so many times before; their scribbles—"Wait, don't write yet," he used to say—committing his every pleasantry to paper and posterity. And now they were massed, waiting for him, to glorify him if he succeeded, to bury him with the ignoble mementos of his past, if he failed.

Inside the gate about twenty Ismailis, the men in Western suits, the women in saris, sat on the lawn and chatted patiently, a council of dignitaries awaiting the news, wanting to be the first to know and to pass on the word to their brethren around the world.

Aly and Karim went into the house. The Aga's body had been moved upstairs; the embalmer was still at work. The shutters had been closed so that there was a faint smell of formaldehyde as the family gathered in the sitting room off the entrance and took seats on its flowered cretonne chairs. Giesen, the solicitor from London, cleared his throat and, speaking with the trace of a German accent, began to read the will:

I SULTAN SIR MAHOMED SHAH AGA KHAN . . .
HEREBY REVOKE all Wills and other testamentary disposi-
tions heretofore made by me AND DECLARE THIS TO BE
MY LAST WILL which I make this Twenty fifth day of May
One thousand nine hundred and fifty five. . . .

The date quivered in more than one mind. That had been
only four months after his illness at Aswan.

I DECLARE that I have made my permanent home. . . .

The Aga's domicile was Geneva; he had complied with Swiss law
in declaring that "my estate be governed by Shia Moslem law
which is my personal law in force for all the members of the
Shia Moslem Ismailian Community in my country of origin Pakistan." He appointed Lloyds Bank (Foreign) of London as
executors and trustees.

And then he reviewed his marriages: Shahzadi Begum, married 1897, divorced December 8, 1926, "in accordance with the
requirements of Shia Moslem law." Cleope Teresa Magliano
married 1908, "according to the Muta form of marriage as recognized by Shia law. The period and dowry were fixed at fifty years
and ten thousand francs [about $2,000] respectively." Married
again, according to "the permanent form of marriage," January
23, 1923.

The divorce from Shahzadi had not taken place until December 8, 1926, one week after Teresa had died.

The names, the language, the technicalities unrolled softly
in the silent room. For some of the people present, it was the
first time they had glimpsed the tangled underbrush of the Aga's
romantic life. For the first time, they understood certain em-
barrassments and evasions, certain sensitivities—of Aly's, for
example. The Aga, even in his will, felt it necessary to mention
by name the witnesses to his "permanent form of marriage" to
Teresa in 1923—two British knights and two of his male relatives
—a detail which was omitted in reference to his other marriages.

Giesen read on: Andrée Josephine Marie Louise Carron,
married December 7, 1929; divorced in Geneva December, 1943.
The Aga asked that his bank honor "conventions made at

Geneva" between Andrée and himself "as a debt contracted by me." And Yve Blanche Labrousse, married October 9, 1944. "Previously to this I had married her according to Moslem law at Geneva in the presence of several Moslem witnesses and of a Notary Public. . . .

> UNDER Shia Moslem law my only heirs are my two sons ALY SALOMONE KHAN and SADRUDDIN AGA KHAN and my said wife YVETTE called YVE BLANCHE LABROUSSE and none others.

Giesen paused for a moment at the end of another technical paragraph. He was on the fourth of thirteen pages, each initialed at the bottom with the Aga's shaky "SMSAK." Each new paragraph began with a capitalized word:

> EVER since the time of my ancester ALI the first Imam that is to say over a period of some thirteen hundred years it has always been the tradition of our family that each Imam chooses his successor at his absolute and unfettered discretion from amongst any of his descendants whether they be sons or remoter male issue (notwithstanding that under Shia Moslem law the issue of a son is not an heir if there be a son alive) and in these circumstances and in view of the fundamentally altered conditions in the world in very recent years due to the great changes which have taken place including the discoveries of atomic science, I am convinced that it is in the best interests of the Shia Moslem Ismailian Community that I should be succeeded by a young man who has been brought up ...

The room was silent, eyes riveted on Giesen's mouth.

> ... and developed during recent years and in the midst of the new age and who brings a new outlook on life to his office as Imam. For these reasons and although he is not now one of my heirs I APPOINT my grandson KARIM the son of my son ALY SALOMONE KHAN to succeed to the title of AGA KHAN and to be the Imam and Pir of all my Shia Ismailian followers ...

There was a slight rustle in the room. The solicitor looked up briefly, then his eyes returned to the paper and went on.

... and should my said grandson KARIM predecease me then I appoint his brother AMYN MAHOMED the second son of my son ALY SALOMONE KHAN as my successor to the Imamate. I DESIRE that my successor shall during the first seven years of his Imamate be ...

He paused to turn the page.

... guided on questions of general Imamate policy by my said wife YVETTE called YVE BLANCHE LABROUSSE the Begum Aga Khan who has been familiar for many years with the problems facing my followers and in whose wise judgment I place the greatest confidence. ...

The voice went on in the dark, cool, carpeted room with its smell of formaldehyde and its arc of white, haggard faces. There were eight more pages to go. The Aga had specified how he wanted to be buried (The Begum would be in charge), the disposition of his horses (Aly got first option to buy those they owned in partnership), the disposition of his other property. Aside from a few bequests like £10,000 ($28,000) for Halldis Poppe who had faithfully nursed him through his final illnesses, his estate would be divided among the Begum, who would get one eighth, and his two sons, Aly and Sadruddin, who would equally share the remaining seven eighths.

On page eleven there was a codicil which had been added less than one month before, on June 18, 1957. Giesen began to read it:

THIS is a Codicil to the last Will and Testament of me SULTAN SIR MAHOMED SHAH AGA KHAN. ..."

Aly, ashen-faced, strained almost imperceptibly forward.

I confirm the declaration made in Clause 1. ...

The legalistic language droned on. It was merely a change occasioned by the death of a relative. There were also some increases in bequests: all of the Aga's employees would receive their wages for two years after his death instead of the eighteen months provided in the original will; the sum allocated to the Begum for the Aga's funeral, and the mausoleum, was increased from £25,000 to £50,000; the Begum was to have the furnishings of the Villa Barakat as well as those in her own home, Yakimour, which always had been in her name ever since its construction in 1938, six years before her marriage to the Aga. The lawyer read on through six paragraphs to the seventh and final paragraph: "In all other respects I confirm my said WILL. . . ." But the brief technical clause fell on deaf ears.

Aly was no longer listening. The important thing was that Karim had gotten it. Twenty-year-old Karim was the new Imam. Notwithstanding Shiah Moslem Law which said he was not even an heir. Notwithstanding Aly's thirty-year apprenticeship. Notwithstanding Sadruddin. At last, the Aga had spoken. And it was not Aly. It was Karim.

2

Dusk had fallen as Sadruddin drove down to the gate. It was shut and the police were preoccupied with the mob outside. Ignored, Sadri honked his horn. A policeman came out of the gate house, swung the gate open, and Sadri slowly drove out into a massed line of photographers. Grimacing, he inched forward, honking his horn, forcing them to give way. The photographers stood their ground as long as they dared, snapping their shutters, catching his face twisted with impatience and anger so that, ironically, Sadri, who had never liked to compete, who had never stood much of a chance, was the one whose face showed up in newspapers all over the world the next day looking bitterly disappointed.

Aly went out next, not saying a word, smiling, and many of the reporters dashed off to trail his car into Geneva. The Ismailis who had waited so patiently on the lawn were led into the house, where the Begum greeted them and left them with Karim. He told them he would meet with them again the following day, and they left quickly for they were anxious that their communities learn the news from them instead of from the newspapers. By the time Karim got to his hotel, Miss Whitaker was there and, acting on instructions, had read the journalists that part of the Aga's will pertaining to the succession. Aly and Karim spoke briefly to the press and posed for a photograph, side by side. Karim seemed dazed as he faced their questions. What had he done first on hearing the news? He had telephoned his mother in London. Yes, she was thrilled. Yes, he hoped to be able to finish his studies at Harvard. Yes, he would like to continue rooming with John Fell Stevenson, son of Adlai Stevenson. Aly, the usually ebullient Aly, was silent. When asked what his own role would be now that his son was Imam, he shook his head and referred the question to Karim, who replied: "I am sure you understand, there are certain questions I prefer not to answer." As for the Begum: "My grandfather willed it that I should be guided when necessary by Her Highness." The reporters had many more questions but neither man was ready to answer them. Aly only smiled. The same smile would cross his face whenever, on subsequent occasions, the subject of why he had lost the succession came up. He remained silent, and smiled. Only those few who understood him—out of the hundreds who knew him—guessed how tightly stretched that smile was.

Karim was suspicious of the press. He'd had little experience with reporters himself and what he'd heard about them from Aly terrified him. The Begum suggested he talk with her house guest, Constance Hope, the New York publicist who had guided many a celebrity through a sticky encounter with the press. Driving into Geneva with Miss Hope to do some errands, Karim told her about his suspicions. Reporters, he felt, were only interested in scandal and sensation; look what they had done to his father. "If there is one thing I do not want to be known as," he declared heatedly, "it is as a playboy."

"You have the wrong attitude," disagreed Miss Hope. "Most reporters are serious; they are more intelligent than average but they have a job to do. If you will give them a chance to do their job, they will do it well. Talk to them candidly. Look them in the eye." She advised him not to leave the reporters floundering among their rumors but to call a press conference of the top journalists in Geneva, give them a prepared statement "so that they will get all the names and spellings correctly," and attempt to answer their questions. "If they ask you something you don't want to discuss, simply tell them so."

Following her formula, Karim held a news conference on the lawn of the villa. The reporters were impressed by the charm and poise of the young man and by his maturity and candor. One of them began his story: "I met Prince Charming today. . . ." Gratified and encouraged, Karim faced the other public duties awaiting him.

"My religious responsibilities begin as of today," he told an assemblage of Ismailis who had gathered on Barakat's lawn for an informal enthronement ceremony. Sitting on a makeshift throne, a Louis XVI armchair from Barakat's salon, Karim looked solemn, scrubbed, and very young. He wore an American blue flannel suit, the only one he had brought with him in his hurry to reach the Aga's bedside, and shoes which the European journalists agreed among themselves were "violet" (they were cordovan, the plum-colored leather shoes favored by American college students).

Aly was not present. It was the Begum who led Karim out onto the lawn and said gravely to the swarthy men in Western suits and their sari-clad wives: "I present to you the new Imam." Then she hurried back into the house, a tall figure shrouded in a grey sari who watched the rest of the ceremony through the draperies of an upstairs window.

Everyone was falling into his role gracefully. Sadruddin had announced the postponement of his marriage to Nina Dyer until after the forty-day prescribed period of mourning. Bettina and Nina Dyer were keeping discreetly out of sight. Princess Andrée had come to Geneva to pay her last respects. Even Yasmin made one brief appearance on the terrace of her hotel at a reception for Ismaili women. As the women pressed toward her to pay their respects, the little girl, showing the careful training of her Beverly Hills governesses, curtsied and offered her hand to each of them. Aly's secretary stood near her whispering: "Smile, smile. Keep saying 'cheese.'"

The Aga's body, clothed in a white satin shroud, surrounded by red roses except for one giant bouquet of white flowers at his feet, was lying in state on a white satin divan at the Villa Barakat. Illness had wasted him away; only the shrunken frame remained of a man whose corpulence had been worth its weight in gold, diamonds, and platinum. The press was permitted to view the body first, after promising that no photographs would be taken. But some pictures of the embalmed Aga appeared in the Cairo press, where they brought severe criticism from the Sunnis. Dignitaries like the French consul-general and the Egyptian ambassador came to pay their last respects. And then came a shoving, shirt-sleeved, sweating line of Swiss, English, German, American, and French tourists. To the family's horror, the Aga's remains had become one more sightseeing attraction. After more than three hundred persons had filed through, the doors of the villa were ordered shut.

The Aga's body was placed in an oak coffin covered in white satin and loaded into a hearse behind which a convoy of thirty cars formed. Karim and the Begum rode in the first limousine, Aly followed in the second. A motorcycle escort led the cortege down the Avenue de la Paix, past the old League of Nations Building where the Aga had achieved his zenith as an international statesman. At Cointrin Airport, a crowd of several hundred waited. The hearse went out to the plane, a DC6-B chartered from Swissair, where a freight elevator lifted the coffin into a forward compartment. The limousines, cars, and taxis pulled up to the airport restaurant to wait until the plane was ready. Aly, Karim, and the Begum would ride in it. Sadruddin, Amyn, and twelve of the Ismaili leaders would leave later on a regular Swissair flight. All were bound for Cairo, for the Aga had asked to be buried not in Persia, land of his forefathers, not in Pakistan, where he was born, not in India where he grew up, not in any of the countries of Europe which he had so loved, but in Egypt, beside his villa at Aswan. He had confided to the Begum that he had a horror of being buried in mud and wished to be in a dry place where his body would be preserved, like those of the Pharaohs, for centuries. Shortly before midnight, the Begum, tired, drawn, still weeping; Karim, whose boyish face showed the strain of the past several days; and Aly, his coat open, wearing tan suede shoes, hurrying slightly behind the Begum and Karim, walked out to the plane. Three berths had been arranged in the rear compartment, separated from the coffin by a partition.

But Aly, for one, did not sleep. His mind was whirling with a tantalizing bulletin from Syria whose Ismailis, upon hearing of the Aga's death, had immediately proclaimed their own beloved *Waliahad*, Aly, as the new Imam.

# Chapter XXXI

*"I will have to see them and talk with them. There have been similar cases in the history of Islam."*

—ALY KHAN

The funeral was a nightmare. Aly's mind and body ached with fatigue. Syria hovered in the background like a tormenting mirage. The traveling seemed endless. First to Cairo, where, blinking in the morning sun, surrounded by confusion, the family and the yellow oaken coffin in its white satin draperies were shifted to a smaller plane for the flight to Aswan, five hundred miles south.

From the moment the plane landed at Aswan's dusty airport, disorder took over. Since the event promised a profuse sowing of baksheesh, a crowd of helpers, mostly offering their services in a managerial capacity, collected to share the harvest. The sun, hanging overhead like a molten wrecker's ball, dulled minds and slowed footsteps. A dozen policemen in khaki berets and stained uniforms struggled to transfer the coffin from the plane to a bright red fire engine, the only vehicle in Aswan seemingly available for so important a procession. Then, with police jeeps clearing the way, and the family, photographers, journalists, volunteer managers, and sightseers following, the cortege drove off. A swirl of dust and the screams of children, attracted by the fire engine and the shiny cars, followed it to the river bank.

There a barge, lashed to a canopied motor launch, was moored. The Aga had requested that his body be transported across the Nile in an oared barge, as had been the remains of the ancient Pharaohs buried nearby. The Begum took one look at the barge that awaited them and collapsed in sobs. Not only would it have to be pulled by a motor launch instead of being rowed in stately pomp, but its decks were caked with dust, its usual function being to carry granite for building projects. The managers milled around, conferred, and announced that no other barge was available. The sun was overhead and the Nile threatened to turn to steam. Donning a pith helmet to avoid sunstroke, the Begum relented. The Aga's coffin, stripped of its draperies for easier leverage, was loaded aboard the barge. The launch tugged it into the stream; behind it chugged another motor launch in which, on a sofa rented for the occasion, Karim sat, while weeping Ismailis knelt before him, kissing his hands. Next to him was the Begum in a black sari, her face buried in her hands.

With posthumous irony, the Aga's love of impressive ceremonies had caught him in a final state of ludicrousness.

Upstream and across the Nile, the convoy went to dock at the Aga's wharf. His blue dhow lay there, its sails sadly curled. A dull glare reflected from the white, dome-roofed villa. The reluctant policemen shouldered the coffin again and ascended the path. Most of the men had stripped off their coats and opened their collars. Aly, Sadri, and Amyn kept their coats on, their faces set in grim lines. The Begum and Karim retreated to private quarters in the house, whose main salon had been converted into a mosque for the occasion. In the courtyard, workmen had just finished plastering a shallow grave and into this the Aga's coffin was lowered. It would be only a temporary resting place, until the mausoleum the Aga had ordered built on a promontory above the house was completed. As the coffin disappeared, so did the last shred of propriety. Everyone tried to crowd into the courtyard: photographers, sightseers, Ismailis, and volunteer managers. They elbowed one another for vantage positions around the grave. The policemen at first tried to sort out the dignitaries in Egyptian fashion, using rifle butts. Then they slammed the gates shut while a wreath from President Nasser was laid on the grave. The family and Ismailis retired indoors for funeral prayers, after which they angrily announced that a public memorial service planned for the following day would be canceled.

## 2

Right after the funeral services, Aly took off for Syria. The plane left Cairo and headed north across the Mediterranean. Out of a starboard window, Aly could see the jagged profile of the continental land bridge stretching toward the horizon. Islam had been born on that causeway, as had Christianity and Judaism. For centuries man had crossed that bridge or sent across his ideas and caravans or disputed the rights of others to cross. Even today it was being contested, for the plane's strict northward heading was dictated by the pilot's orders to keep clear of Israeli air space.

The stewardess came past and smiled at him; he allowed himself a slight jiggling of the eyebrows in response. Tutti, his man of all chores, slumped in the adjoining seat, still limp from Aswan's heat and turmoil. Aly leafed through the newspaper restlessly and then folded it in his lap. It didn't contain what he was looking for. He wanted to know more about what was happening in Syria. And in Pakistan, too. In Cairo he had heard that some leaflets had appeared among the Ismailis of Karachi which supported him as the new Imam. Their authors were anonymous; the tone was militant. One leaflet insisted that the Aga's will was illegal, that he could not pass the Imamate on to his grandson as long as a son existed. Another insisted that part of the will had been concealed.

Aly had often thought of himself as Imam. He knew how pleasant the roar of the Syrian crowds would sound in his ears. Dazed with fatigue and still stunned by the events of the past

week, he leaned back in his seat and thought of the last time
he had visited Salamiya, the remote town which had been the
secret refuge of persecuted Ismailis back in the ninth century
and which had lapsed into obscurity until Aly himself had
come and brought the Syrian Ismailis back into the mainstream of history. Aly was their hero. The children, playing in
Salamiya's dusty streets chanted:

> *Ali Shah, hāmina,*
> *Fi sēf wa martina,*
> *Wa illi ma bihubbū*
> *Mnisruf bi saramina.*
> (Aly Shah, our leader,
> With sword and rifle girt,
> We will crush beneath our feet
> Whoever loves him not.)

Approaching Salamiya on one occasion with an escort of
three Syrian police jeeps, Aly had been swamped by the crowds;
so many people had tried to hop aboard that the three jeeps had
collapsed. For twenty miles, men, women, and children had lined
the roads. Finally, Aly had leaped out of his car and joyously
ridden the last several miles on horseback. He couldn't help
dreaming of what life might have been like had he been born
in another, more heroic era, whose pulse was closer to his own,
or, in another part of the world where his passions would have
been better understood.

Aly always had wanted to equal his father and now the
possibility lay open. Schisms were not new to Islam, nor to the
Ismailis. But the Aga had preached unity and in thirty years of
traveling among his countryless and disparate people as his
father's deputy, Aly had done his part too. Unable to share
his father's mysticism about the religion, he had considered it his
primary job to preach unity and to bring to isolated communities—like the Syrians—the assurance that they were not alone.
Out of this unity had been forged a golden cornucopia that
poured out schools, banks, hospitals, housing co-operatives, and
the highest standard of living in the East for the Ismaili people;
and for the Aga Khan and his family, wealth, status, and power.

Smashed into shards, it would yield nothing, neither for the community nor for the family, neither for Aly nor for Karim. Any split, whether ultimately successful or not, could result only in arguments, excommunications and lawsuits that would tear the community apart. The Aga had passed Aly by but at that moment, the future of the community and the family rested squarely with him and nobody else—it was up to Aly.

The Aga, in his will, had named the Begum as Karim's adviser. If Aly now felt betrayed, it was not by his father but by the Begum. Years later he would claim that in the final months of his father's life, he had never seen him alone—the Begum was always present. Friends, like Gaffié, observed that the Begum "was not—how shall we say it—pro-Aly; certainly she never insisted to the Aga that he name Aly as his successor." Elsa Maxwell warned him: "Be nice to her. She is your father's wife and she makes him very happy." Shortly before her death in 1963, Miss Maxwell said: "I think Aly felt he might be passed over but he didn't believe the signs until the last moment. Then he thought, 'I don't care; I still won't make up to that woman.'"

The Begum, more than a year before the Aga's death, confided to a friend that she thought the Aga had changed his will to name Karim rather than Aly as his successor. She always denied influencing the Aga on the succession and surely so strong-minded a man made his own final decision. Yet her influence was assumed by such diverse people as an intense and ascetic Ismaili homeopath, Dr. Aziz Ali, in the small upcountry Pakistani city of Chiniot, and Sadri's old nurse, Halldis Poppe, an intimate of the family for twenty-five years, who was at the Aga's bedside, nursing him through his final illnesses. Dr. Aziz, who still is not reconciled to the choice of Karim and leads a small splinter group, insists that a conspiracy existed against Aly which included the Begum and "those big personalities of the Community who . . . were sure that the installation of Prince Aly as Imam would mean the end of their regime; they dreaded that Prince Aly would deal with all corrupt workers with a firm hand." Miss Poppe says: "The Begum thought if Aly was Imam, she would have nothing more to do with the Ismailis but thought

Karim, being so young, would let her give him advice for many years."

In Aly's mind, the Begum became the villain of the piece. He had been undone by a woman, the one woman he had never charmed. His father emerged blameless, sanctified by death. Karim became the son whom he must help.

With Karim, at least, the Begum would not have her way.

Aly's decision required no change in his goals—he really believed in the unity of the community—and no drastic revision of his way of life. He liked pleasing people; he liked moving in and out of situations quickly, assuaging his ego without staying on to become involved; his most tender moments contained that contradiction, passion without engagement.

Even had he been so inclined, he was not the man to lead a rebellion. His need was to be liked; he flinched from stirring up antagonisms. He empathized with others too much to be ruthless. To sacrifice his personal pleasures for power was contrary to his nature. As one of Aly's closest friends observed: "Do you think, after all, that the Aga was so wrong? Aly was not made to be an Imam."

# 3

From Beirut, where the plane landed, Aly drove to the Syrian border. Often, on previous visits, he had donned *keffiya* and burnoose but today he wore the standard costume of visiting Westerners, khaki bush jacket and slacks. On the Syrian side of the border, carloads of Ismaili dignitaries awaited him and the cavalcade barreled across the countryside toward Salamiya. The village people were out, as usual, and Aly's car slowed down and stopped so they could see him and touch him. He went straight to his house where the *emirs* of the community had assembled, expectant and anxious. Aly talked to them quietly, nervously. He spoke of the unity of the Ismailis and the prosperity and prestige it had brought to the community. He praised Karim and quoted Karim's words: "I dedicate my life to the well-being and uplift of Ismailis all over the world." He promised to remain the Syrians' spokesman in community affairs but told them firmly: "The succession has passed from my father to my son."

If Aly was the odd man out, there was still a moment of glory awaiting him. In the late afternoon he stepped out onto a balcony and addressed a crowd of thousands that had been waiting for hours to see him. Grinning, spreading his hands in a gesture of benediction, Aly looked down on the tightly packed mass of shouting, cheering people, whose dark faces and white headdresses strained toward him. Had he asked them to storm Yakimour, they would have headed straight in that direction. As it was, they barely could be restrained. So many persons crowded onto another balcony to cheer Aly that the railing gave way and one of the dignitaries who had come to greet him, the Syrian minister of agriculture, Emir Mustafa Mirza, was precipitated into the mob. Gesturing for quiet, Aly promised that Karim would visit Syria (he came two years later) and that he himself would come again and often. As he tried to leave the building, the crowd surged around him, tearing at his clothing, stretching to touch him. Finally he pushed his way through, climbed into his car and left. Salamiya had been won—for Karim.

In one afternoon, Aly had gone from heir apparent to elder statesman.

# Chapter XXXII

"*When he died my grandfather left me enormous responsibilities. Everything he did not have time to do in his lifetime, I now have to do. Even if I didn't want to be serious, I'd have to be from now on.*"

—KARIM AGA KHAN

When Karim set out on the tour of the community that was to see his formal enthronement as Imam, Aly was with him. So was Joan—a rousing demonstration of family unity from which the Begum was notably excluded.

Apart from soft brown eyes, a quick smile, and a tendency toward baldness, there was little physical resemblance between Aly and the tall, slender son who had inherited the title of Aga Khan IV, 49th Imam, Mowlana Hazar Imam. Karim stood an inch below six feet tall and walked with a long awkward stride, while Aly, shorter, paunchier, and swaybacked with the years, loped along with his rolling jockey's walk. They were both athletic but Aly was a "natural" who liked feats of derring-do like horse racing. Karim was dogged, training himself to a sharp edge in skiing, his favorite sport, despite one sports-writer's comment that "he is not blessed with more than average talent." Karim's movements were stiff, Aly's were fluid, and the same disparity appeared in their personalities. Aly's personality was Latin, Eastern, as instinctive and flowing as the sinuous motions of a belly-dancer and often as exasperating; Karim's was methodical, rigid, often self-conscious. He spoke French fluently but with a slight English accent and English with an upper-class British accent, bracketing the Americanisms he had picked up in rather condescending parenthetical inflections. Some Ismailis described him as "typically English" and anyone looking for family resemblances would find the closer traits in his mother's line—although only time will tell how many of Aly's more fascinating genes have been lost in transit.

Certainly father and son were brought up differently. From the moment Karim was born, it was taken for granted that he would one day become Imam, and, unlike Aly, he was educated for the job from the beginning. When he was only seven years old, living in Nairobi, he was dressed in a tiny uniform and taken to the *jamat-khana* to chant: "We are the direct descendant of the Prophet Mohammed, may peace of God be on him." When, at the end of the war, he returned to Europe to attend school in Switzerland, an Ismaili scholar came to live nearby to give him lessons in Moslem history and Arabic. In the solicitous and steadying atmosphere of Le Rosey, where he remained until he graduated at seventeen, Karim developed from a lonely eight-year-old, afraid of the dark and miserable over the breakup of his parents—he had arrived at a good idea of the cause, as children do—into a six-letter athlete and passable scholar. He vacationed with one or another of his parents or with the Aga and they visited him in turn at school. Aly was apt to arrive late and at top speed, his apologies punctuating his expostulations of joy. He often arrived in a new car—or with a new companion. Mlle. Helen Schaub, Le Rosey's headmistress reported: "We're often asked how the boys respond when a king or a prince visits the school. Well, they don't respond at all, beyond mild curiosity. But I must confess that when Karim's and Amyn's stepmother came here—Rita Hayworth—the boys were distinctly agitated."

Karim met and was courteous to all of the important women in Aly's life. But the publicity and notoriety that attended the romances embarrassed and embittered both him and his brother.

When Karim became Aga, he was on leave from his junior year at Harvard, which had been recommended to Aly by his wartime friends, Harvard graduates Henry Cabot Lodge and Chandler Bigelow. Karim wanted to major in engineering and he would have preferred M.I.T., but in his freshman year he did poorly in chemistry and mathematics so he switched to Middle Eastern history. He studied industriously and methodically, and lived quietly, always a little aloof from the other boys. He didn't own a car, claiming: "I don't need one." His roommate was astonished to discover that he had only two suits and one pair of shoes in his closet. Aly was forgetful about sending his allowance, and although the Aga often had slipped him money, Karim never knew whether it was going to be a few coins or a hundred pounds.

Winters he skied at Stowe, Vermont. Three or four times a year he went to New York for a night out. But he seldom dated. Occasionally he accompanied his roommate, John Fell Stevenson, home to Libertyville, Illinois, where at parties he was introduced as "Mr. Khan, a friend of John Fell's from Harvard." He met John Fell's father, Adlai Stevenson, and greatly admired him.

During Karim's early years at Harvard, one of his classmates recalls: "He was best known for being vaguely related to Rita Hayworth." But after he became Imam, the boys found "an air of Oriental mysticism about him."

Some of Karim's Ismaili advisers urged him to forget about Harvard after his enthronement and give his full attention to his work as Imam. Aly vehemently disagreed. He regretted his own scanty education. One of the few things on which he held

strong views and made the effort to take a position was the
education of his sons. It was he who had insisted they go to
Le Rosey and to Harvard. Now he talked earnestly to Karim.
"He encouraged me to go back to Harvard, to go on with my
Oriental studies, to stick to the serious things," Karim recalls.
Aly's counsel prevailed.

But try as he might to remain just one more Harvard man,
Karim had become a celebrity. One day he received a large
package in the mail; a passing student wisecracked: "Ah, money
from home!" Another student hoped for the day when he could
induce the teetotaling young Aga to step out for a beer. "I want
to say, 'Have a lager, Aga.' " The bulletin board in the lobby
of Leverett House was hung with photographs of all its residents.
Some of the boys, including Karim, did not put up their photos
and their spaces were sometimes filled with humorous drawings;
in Karim's had been hung a cartoon of a tramp puffing on a cigar.

Karim was on the varsity soccer team and the hockey team
and had just missed making the crew because he was too light.
But he had little time for athletics now. He had brought back
with him to Cambridge one of his grandfather's former secretaries, Mlle. Beguel, to help handle the flood of correspondence
that came to him from the Ismaili community, and a London
journalist, Michael Curtis, as his personal aide. Under Curtis's
guidance Karim accepted invitations to TV panels and gave interviews that gradually sculpted an image that was a denial of
everything Aly was known for. He was not a playboy, Karim
reiterated, and had no ambitions along that line. He didn't enjoy
horse racing nor had he any immediate plans to get married. He
steadfastly refused to answer questions about his personal life.
He insisted he was too busy for romance—a consideration that
never would have occurred to Aly—and too young to marry.
"There is one thing I know," he told reporters, "an unhappy
marriage is the worst thing in the world." He would first "bring
order into my job and into my life."

Karim acknowledged Aly's human qualities: "He wasn't a
father in the old-fashioned sense," he once said. "You didn't have
to kowtow to him. He didn't like that. He taught me how to

enjoy skiing and tennis and swimming." But Karim seemed to be searching for kind things to say and he didn't intend to be anything like him.

In June, 1959, Karim graduated with honors. Both Aly and Joan were there. Then he turned his full attention to his new duties as Imam. Aly never considered the Imamate a full time job and felt Karim should have another career as well, but perhaps he underestimated its complexity and its challenge. Karim immediately began traveling extensively among the community. Despite his training, he pulled some boyish blunders. In London one day, he was presented with a plate of chocolates to bless; he cheerfully helped himself instead of uttering the solemn incantations.

The Aga's will had asked Karim to be guided by the Begum's advice; this provision he continued to ignore, causing the Begum to observe plaintively that, personally, she considered a will "a sacred document." Nor did he rely on his parents. For a time, Joan spent a lot of time with him, chaperoning his social life and issuing denials that he was engaged. A friend observed that she still spends "as much time as Karim will let her" with him but that it has become less and less.

Aly, of course, went his own way, looking for other compensations for the humiliation he felt. As usual, he tried to conceal his real feelings. His uncle Mario had observed that even as a child "Aly never wanted to abase himself by showing weakness, by showing that anything hurt him." But an Ismaili leader thinks he got a glimpse of Aly's hurt one day in Karachi. Karim had arrived for a visit. A gold throne had been prepared for him, surrounded by red and green Ismaili flags, in the *jamat-khana*. Shortly before Karim was to arrive, Aly telephoned that he had just flown in and would come to the *jamat-khana* too. By the time he got there, Karim was sitting on his throne in the middle of the platform, a gold turban on his head. Aly hurried in wearing a business suit and took his place in a chair to one side. "Karim was very quiet, he hardly knew anyone," observed the Ismaili. "Aly greeted everyone, for he knew us all well." Then the ceremony began. Karim made a short speech and called up people to be blessed. "Aly sat there, a sad expression on his face. He just sat and watched."

Karim quickly learned his job. If there was something anachronistic about it—a young man of three-quarters European ancestry, Harvard '59, wearing a golden turban on a golden throne in the religious halls of a small Moslem sect in the East— he never acknowledged it. The West might find it faintly ridiculous. Certain younger Ismailis might even question its relevance in this day and age. But it was the job Karim had inherited and he plunged into it, juggling a dual life of European sportsman and Eastern religious leader, almost as agilely as his grandfather had.

He carried two passports, British and Iranian, using the one that seemed most politic for the occasion—and the country.

He had two titles: the hereditary "Prince" which the Shah had bestowed upon his grandfather, and a lifetime title of "His Highness" conferred upon him by Queen Elizabeth II. He traveled several months a year in the East but his home was Switzerland, which had the same tax advantages for him that it had had for his father and grandfather. He built a chalet, named Darannoor (House of Light), in Gstaad which had the skiing he loved (in 1963 he participated in the Winter Olympics as a member of the Iranian ski team) and the friends he had grown up with —a fun-loving international set of young people who congregated in Switzerland for the winter sports, and on the Riviera in the summer.

The press, recalling the wide furrow Aly had plowed through the world's boudoirs, was merciless in its reportage of Karim's romantic life. "Wherever I go," Karim complained, "I find myself faced by lenses as big as cannons and even more menacing." His rages and run-ins with cameramen became legendary. French television recently devoted part of a documentary on news photographers to shots of Karim fleeing from them in various parts of the world. True to his word, Karim has not provided much grist for their romantic mills. There was a brief flirtation with Sylvia Casablancas, the blonde daughter of a wealthy Mexican rancher whom he met while she was at school in Switzerland;

there were occasional dinner dates with Patricia Rawlings, daughter of a British textile manufacturer, Tracy Pelissier, stepdaughter of Sir Carol Reed, the film director, and Bunny Esterhazy, stepdaughter of a Riviera millionaire named Arpad Plesch. But since 1959 Karim has had only one serious romantic attachment—Annouchka Meks, a baby-faced blonde. Annouchka, although she is sometimes described as a baroness and given an aristocratic "von" before her name, does not come from Karim's glittering world. Her German-born father is a manufacturer of cocktail and evening gowns—"Créations Elite," in Paris's garment district. She lives with her parents in a middle-class neighborhood; one enters their apartment house between a horse butcher's shop and a hardware store. Karim first met her when he asked her to dance at a night club in St. Tropez. She is supposed to have burst into laughter when she asked his name and he replied: "The Aga Khan." She was only seventeen.

Rumors that Karim and Annouchka were engaged were countered by the usual denials from Joan. Annouchka disappeared behind the wall of reticence maintained by Karim—a wall sometimes reinforced by hired detectives who threatened bodily harm to anyone carrying a camera in the vicinity. When a photographer finally succeeded in getting a picture of Karim and Annouchka relaxing at the Chateau de l'Horizon, Karim asleep, his torso bare, his head pillowed on Annouchka's bare legs, it was considered so newsworthy that *Paris-Match*, France's most important picture magazine, spread it over two pages and it was carried in newspapers from London to Karachi.

As the years passed, the romance flourished and Annouchka matured into a bouffant-haired, stunningly dressed beauty, a certified celebrity in *Tout Paris*. But the question asked in Europe's still avid press was less often—Is Karim going to marry her? It became—Why hasn't he? One offered explanation: Annouchka's Jewish ancestry might make her unacceptable to the many Ismailis living in Arab countries.

Another aspect of Karim's personal life—and that of the rest of the family—continued to interest the press. The Aga's will had given Karim, as the new Imam, title to all of the community property used for religious purposes, but specifically excluded from this provision "buildings belonging to me and used for secular purposes such as clubs, flats, shops, schools, etc., used by my followers for which they pay nominal rents." These, along with the Aga's personal fortune, were left to Aly, Sadruddin, and the Begum. However, the Aga's wealth was scattered around the world, hidden in the matted jungle of legalities, corporate fronts, and tax havens. Attorneys, sleuths, and estate agents combed records and consulted maps, while safe-deposit boxes were hunted down and their contents evaluated—one report had eight private detectives roaming Europe, the United States, Asia, and Africa. It was said there were other detectives working secretly for individual heirs.

Like his grandfather, Karim has interested himself in a variety of personal business enterprises, advised and aided by the family business manager, André Ardoin. One of his favorites is a vast vacation resort, a complex of villages, hotels, and yacht harbors called the Costa Smeralda, on the island of Sardinia, which offers escape to those who can afford it from the traffic jams, billboards and campers of the Riviera. The project was greeted with enthusiasm by the Ismailis who, still dreaming of a homeland of their own, reacted with great joy to the garbled news that their Imam now owned an island. (Sadruddin also has invested in resorts; among others, a restaurant in Gstaad. Divorced by Nina Dyer, he also embarked on a diplomatic career as Deputy High Commissioner for Refugees of the United Nations. Amyn, a silent partner in some of these enterprises, stayed on at Harvard as a graduate student and teaching fellow in Romance languages..

Aly had his own special financial problems, since he wanted to keep the stables going. Stiff English and French death taxes fell heavily on the stables and stud farms, which couldn't be hidden. To raise money he sold about two hundred horses. The performance of the stables dropped, but only temporarily; the best years still were ahead.

While attorneys worked to settle the estate and the family waited in enforced truce, Karim steadily took over the multifarious affairs of the Imamate. The college-boy wonderment with which Karim had greeted his succession as Imam in 1957 vanished and in its place appeared a careful dignity. "Karim now weighs everything he says," remarked one old friend. He is reserved and does not encourage familiarity in others. He is a poor listener and when he becomes angry, his jaws tense and his voice becomes petulant. Perhaps a certain arrogance is understandable. Karim has fallen heir to all the prerogatives which his grandfather, that master diplomat and propagandist, won for the leader of a heretofore insignificant Moslem sect. When Karim travels by air, for instance, the airlines see to it that he gets on and off the plane first. Among the passengers who waited on one flight, while Karim was shepherded off, was Lady Clementine Churchill, wife of Sir Winston.

Karim also is the recipient of the intense adoration the Ismailis focus on their Imam. He is pursued, indeed besieged, by his followers, who patiently wait weeks and even months for an appointment with him. He receives hundreds of letters a week beseeching his advice—a textile merchant in Bombay wants to know whether to expand his business; an ambitious youngster in Karachi asks which Western university he should attend; an Ismaili community in Uganda wonders if it should move out en masse in view of the upsurge of African nationalistic feeling against Asians; an excommunicated Ismaili in Khartoum appeals a decision of the supreme council.

Karim tries to answer them all conscientiously—except appeals to which his answer is negative; these go unanswered and after three months the applicants are to consider them denied. His concern for the community is genuine. Shortly after his first trip to the East as Imam he enthused: "Do you know what thrills me—what *really* thrills me? Well, I believe the community's secondary schools in Dar-es-Salaam and Kampala had the highest pass rate in school certificates of any Asian school in East Africa."

Being the Ismailis' "God" he finds more difficult. Their belief in his divinity embarrasses him, especially in the West, and he takes great pains to deny it. So do the more recent official publications of the Ismailis, which couple their denials with learned and complicated treatises on why it is still, nevertheless, a "paramount sin" to disobey the Imam.

But abstract religious doctrine is not as satisfying as a flesh-and-blood God, especially to the simpler people of the towns and villages. Not long ago a French journalist was driving with Karim in Pakistan. Noting the "white forms prostrate on the road," the "enormous feverish eyes glued to the windows of the car," and an old woman who rushed forward, "her face transformed into a terrifying apparition" at sight of Karim, the Frenchman turned to Karim:

"But you *are* their God."

"No, no, no!" Karim replied. "I am not a God."

The journalist concluded: "Theologically speaking this was strictly true but it was belied at every moment of our journey by the eyes, hands, and mystical trembling of his followers."

Karim has taken steps to streamline the religion—shortening daily prayers, eliminating some of the Hindu dichotomies—but he does not go as far as some young Ismailis who feel their future lies in merging entirely with the Moslem mainstream. Karim enjoins them to hold tight to their religion and warns them not to marry outside the community without the express permission of their local council.

Tithing and tribute continue as before. At a recent meeting in London, Ismailis paid five pounds apiece for a chance to see and chat with their young Aga. Not long ago Karim was recounting to an acquaintance how one of his followers in India had managed to turn the Hindu veneration of cows into a profitable business: when the sacred cows finally drop dead, he collects them and makes a bone meal which he sells in America and Germany for use in making glue. "Well, now," Karim suddenly reminded himself, "I shall have to check on whether his contribution to the community is proportionate to his gains." The Khoja Reformers' doughty spokesman, Karim Goolimali, now in his sixties, emerged from several years of silence to address open letters to Karim which complained about Ismaili religious practices and the "huge amounts of money being poured into your coffers." Karim, like his grandfather, ignored him.

Karim has pushed welfare ventures even more energetically than Aga Khan III. But by far his most challenging problems have been in the political sphere, particularly in Africa where as one country after another has become independent, the nationalistic fervor and xenophobia of the blacks were turned against not only their former white colonial masters but also against the Asians settled there.

"The Africans may try to break the Asians in Africa but I hope that will not happen," Karim said, not long after becoming Imam. To try to prevent it, he travels frequently to Africa, seeking out its new leaders, offering investments by his "East African Industrial Promotion Service," a German corporation in which he is the principal shareholder, pointing out that black Africans too benefit from Ismaili institutions, like the secondary schools and the Platinum Jubilee Hospital in Nairobi, which are open to all races. He is constantly in search of new business opportunities for the Ismailis. He does not believe they can survive as small retail merchants and exhorts the young people to go into the professions and industry, where their talents will not be resented, at least for a while. Some observers believe the best he can do is buy time. There are rumors that he already has made plans to fly out his followers if violence comes. Meanwhile he looks for support wherever he can find it. He conferred with Vice-President Richard Nixon in 1959 and with President Kennedy in 1961, reminding reporters as he left, that Kennedy "knew my father very well." In 1961 he also flew to Morocco to see King Hassan II. Since there are few Ismailis in Morocco, there was speculation that Karim was looking for opportunities for the future. Brazil is also said to interest him as a possible home for his stateless flock.

In late 1960 he made what must have been a satisfying journey to the one country in the world where Ismailis are in the majority—a remote, semi-independent state in a valley amidst the Himalayas called Hunza. It is only nine miles from the Soviet border and shares a frontier with China's Sinkiang province. Completely cut off in the winter and reachable in summer only by donkey or jeep, Hunza has a Shangri-La quality: many modern diseases are unknown, longevity is common, and men still father children when well past eighty. Eighty per cent of its twenty-five thousand inhabitants are Ismailis, like its hereditary ruler, Mir Mohammed Jamal Khan, a blue-eyed, light-skinned gentleman who came out to welcome Karim when he arrived. As Karim entered the drawing room of the Mir's palace his eyes wandered to the far wall. There he saw, smiling down at him, two autographed photos—of Rita Hayworth and Gene Tierney.

# Chapter XXXIII

> *"We are delighted to see Aly Khan appointed as Ambassador to the United Nations from Pakistan. What could be more fitting than to name to the world organization the world's most prominent man of the world?*
>
> *"And we have no doubt that this realistic and experienced gentleman will bring some wisdom to the UN. He knows that some of mankind's problems, at the very least, are the same the world over no matter what language the lady speaks."*
>
> —*The Wall Street Journal*, February 13, 1958

Aly was exhilarated by his tour of Africa with Karim, by the enthronement ceremonies, by his triumph over the Begum. But, as usual, the letdown was quick in coming. Karim was on his own now. Aly needed something to do, something exciting and important to occupy his attention and repair his self-esteem and prestige.

In November, 1957, four months after his father's death and

Karim's succession, he saw President Iskander Mirza of Pakistan in Paris. In the course of their chat, Mirza offered Aly a post as Pakistan's "roving ambassador." The inspiration for it was not hard to find. Aly had been impressed by the appointment of his wartime friend and commanding officer, Henry Cabot Lodge, as United States ambassador to the United Nations in 1953. His friendship with Lodge and other influential people all over the world, the reputation of his father as an East-West mediator and as president of the League of Nations in 1937, were well known in Pakistan, which was at odds with India, struggling with the problems of a new independent state, and in need of a spokesman who could get attention for her case. Furthermore, Aly possessed that traditional ambassadorial prerequisite: he could pay his own way. Next time he saw Lodge, Aly told him there was a possibility he might be appointed Pakistan's permanent representative to the UN. "He consulted with me as to whether he should take the job or not," Lodge later recalled. "He said he didn't want to make a mess of it and he had no training. What did I think?

"I said, 'If you surround yourself with some very competent advisers you could be very useful and it would be an interesting and valuable experience for you.' He asked me if I would help him, and I said I would. I told him he would have some very fine men in the Pakistan mission in New York. And then there was a friend of mine who had been a member of the United States delegation, John C. Ross, and Aly arranged to take him on as adviser."

On February 6, 1958, a fortnight after Karim's formal enthronement ceremony in Karachi, the Pakistan government made public Aly's appointment.

The announcement clattered through Pakistan and into the United Nations Headquarters in New York with the same gathering velocity as a lady's string of pearls coming undone on a ballroom staircase.

The first bead dropped the following day in Lahore, the ancient Sikh capital in western Pakistan, which is close to, and therefore emotionally concerned with, the Kashmir issue over which India and Pakistan had been locked in dispute since partition. A speaker at a political meeting proposed that with Aly representing Pakistan in the UN, "we should delegate Marilyn Monroe, Ava Gardner, and Gina Lollobrigida to handle the Kashmir issue and effect a quick settlement." Lahore newspapers picked that up, and Urdu and English-language dailies in Karachi added their voices to the outcry. The English-language *Pakistan Times* asked its United Nations correspondent, Marcelle Hitschmann, for a reaction piece and got a dispatch which began: "Consternation is the right way to describe reaction in United Nations circles to the news . . . [they] still hope it was all a mistake." In an editorial headed "Fantastic Choice," the *Times* complained that Pakistan's diplomatic corps had never been "very satisfactory," that "far too often diplomatic assignments have been regarded as sinecures that could, without any great disadvantage, be distributed among favoured officials, friends and relations. . . . Even so, it will not be easy to think of anything more fantastic" than Aly's appointment. It pointed out, as the other newspapers were doing, that Aly was not even a citizen of Pakistan.

The *Times* followed up its editorial with a cartoon depicting "Aly" arriving at the United Nations in baby rompers, sucking a pacifier, clutching a female doll under one arm, and dragging a toy horse with the other.

Through all the tumult, Aly was in Karachi, the house guest of Oxford-educated Prime Minister Malik Firoz Khan Noon, who did the talking for him: "Prince Aly has tact, polish, and charm; he should make an ideal diplomat." The Foreign Office let out a reminder that its new ambassador would accept a salary of only one rupee (twenty cents) a month.

In one of his few public appearances between briefings at the Foreign Office, Aly went to the airport to greet Cabot Lodge, who fortuitously had come on an official visit. Aly wore the uniform of a Pakistan army colonel, for he recently had been named honorary commandant of the Fourth Cavalry regiment. Beneath his gold-braided cap, set squarely on his head for once, there looked out an unsmiling, tight-lipped Aly, jaw squared to meet all exigencies, shoulders back as if to display his two rows of campaign ribbons, the very picture of patriotic responsibility.

This new self-portrait of Aly was slow in getting to New York. There, excitement rose as the delegates—and press—awaited his arrival. The sedate Secretary-General, Dag Hammarskjöld, reacted to such frivolity by forbidding his press officers to announce exactly when Aly would present his credentials. Instead, rumors—and jokes ("When would Aly make his *maiden* speech?")—circulated in the delegates' lounge. As Aly could have told Hammarskjöld, he had learned back in the Rita Hayworth days that nothing interests the press so much as a routine event suddenly cloaked in secrecy. On the March morning that Aly arrived at the UN Secretariat, extra police were needed to curb the reporters, photographers, radio men, and television crews. Unsmiling, wearing morning clothes, with the rosettes of the Croix de Guerre and Legion of Honor in his lapel, Aly was whisked up to the thirty-eighth floor to see Hammarskjöld and then down to the second for the usual briefing by protocol officers. Secretaries and receptionists lingered in corridors to see him go by; Aly's face relaxed into a smile as he left the building. His biography, distributed to the press later than was customary, concentrated mostly on his war record.

His staff was lodged in a large and shabbily ornate building that had once been a social club on East Sixty-fifth Street off Fifth Avenue. Ross, an elegant, unflappable American with considerable charm of his own, quietly came in as "American counselor." "I was not a substitute for any of his Pakistan advisers," Ross says. "I think Aly thought of me as a clearing house—a man who could keep a lot of details in his mind and deal with them in a systematic and organized way. He was a hard man to get anywhere on time. He wasn't exactly the kind of guy who kept regular office hours but when he worked, he worked like hell." Aga Shahi, one of the Pakistan foreign service's top men, came up from the Washington embassy to be Aly's deputy. Shahi, short and scholarly, now Director-General of Pakistan's Ministry for External Affairs, recalls: "Aly acknowledged that he had much to learn. His strong points were his personal contacts with the most important people in the world. He was truly cosmopolitan. He could be at home in Pakistan or in any other country. He could walk with kings and still have the common touch. He could talk to a waitress with the same charm. He was completely natural."

One of Aly's duties as a diplomat of a country closely allied with the United States was to explain Pakistan's UN policies to American public opinion. But Aly was wary of the press. It was hard for the mission's press officer to get him to agree to interviews and public appearances. Even when he did, it was often difficult to pin him down long enough to brief him. But Aly had a quick and retentive mind. Once, just before he was to appear on NBC's *Today* television news program, the press officer caught up with him as he came out of a swimming pool. After Aly dried himself and dressed, they went over the questions the program's interviewer, Dave Garroway, might ask about Pakistan and the UN. Aly listened intently for half an hour and went through the interview as if he had been studying Pakistan all his life.

Three weeks after his arrival Aly gave his first official party in commemoration of Pakistan's Constitution Day. Eleven hundred guests were invited, and more than that appeared at Pakistan House, which was heavily guarded by New York and United Nations policemen because of rumors that some of the invitations had been sold on the black market. The guests ranged from Cabot Lodge, British Ambassador Sir Pierson Dixon, and Soviet Ambassador Arkady Sobolev, to Elsa Maxwell and Hedda Hopper and tactfully included the UN press corps. Aly, the experienced host, had a private word for each person who filed up the red-carpeted stairway to the receiving line. "The most magnificent party I've ever seen," he said afterward with an enthusiasm reminiscent of the Pré Catalan.

Arriving each weekday at about 9:30 A.M. at his large, barren office, with its heavy leather furniture, shelves of dusty reports, and a view of a synagogue across the street, he held meetings with Ross and Shahi, busied himself with reports and correspondence, then went out to lunch, usually an official one; afternoons there were the sessions at the UN, conferences, endless "corridor work" and buttonholing that spilled over into the innumerable cocktail parties and official dinners at which a good deal of the UN's work gets done.

The Assembly's regular sessions required him to be in New York only from September to December but he took to spending half the year there. He moved from Carlton House, a hotel on Madison Avenue, into an elegant duplex co-operative apartment which he bought and redecorated at One Beekman Place, overlooking the UN. He brought over a staff from Ireland: Mrs. Donellen, the efficient housekeeper, and Mary, a cheery red-cheeked cook celebrated for her soufflés. The luncheons she cooked for Aly's UN colleagues became famous; women's clubs even wrote to Aly asking for his favorite recipes. He ordered the Pakistan Mission redecorated. But he had not come to the UN to make his mark as a good host, or an attractive man about town. In those fields, he already was pre-eminent. He was looking for a commitment. And he found it. In a sense, while it lasted, it was the war all over again.

## 2

Aly's first speech in the United Nations came in August and then, fittingly enough, at a special emergency session of the General Assembly called to deal with a crisis in the Middle East, a part of the world which he knew well and to which he felt emotionally attached.

Lebanon had charged that its independence and integrity were menaced by the infiltration of guerrillas and arms from the neighboring United Arab Republic. Invoking the UN charter, the Lebanese government had asked the United States to send troops; American marines had swarmed ashore; the Jordanian government, similarly threatened, had asked the British to send troops. The UAR and the Soviet bloc were insisting that American and British "intervention" threatened Arab independence. In an atmosphere reminiscent of the Korean crisis, the UN met.

On the fifth day of the heated debate, Aly rose and spoke for Pakistan. His speech was a careful statement of Pakistani government policy, but it also reflected his own dislike of narrow nationalism. He reminded his listeners that not all the Moslem states were Arab—Pakistan, for one—and all had different points of view. He said that the Lebanese and Jordanian governments "acted fully within their rights, and in accordance with the spirit and letter of the United Nations Charter in requesting assistance from America and Britain."

There was nothing surprising about Aly's stand—Pakistan was, by treaty and alliance, a member of the Western bloc— but it was welcomed by the West as one more voice disputing the contention of the UAR, and the Soviet Union, that all small countries, and Moslem countries in particular, were opposed to the Anglo-American intervention. *The New York Times* headlined its story: "Aly Khan Backs West in Mid-East." *The Herald Tribune*'s headline said: "Pakistan Backs Troops in Mid-East." The newspaper articles went into Aly Khan's reputation as a playboy and his sudden emergence as a United Nations figure. The *Times* went on to say:

"The speech had been drafted by members of his staff, which recently retained John C. Ross, a former member of the United States delegation, as an adviser. But the Prince went over this speech with an editor's pencil, making extensive changes in the language."

Overly sensitive, Aly had one of his staff deny to the *Times* that Ross had had a hand in his speech; the *Times* refused a retraction, knowing full well that no delegate writes his own speeches—that's what his staff is for. Aly's embarrassment was unnecessary; he was making a success of the job.

Delegates and reporters who had been suspicious of him at first began warming to him. The Asians and Africans felt he was one of them; so did the Latins. The British knew he had grown up among them, the Americans that he had served with their army. The French considered him one of their own; after all, he lived in France. Aly spoke three languages well and a few words of half a dozen others. He had been nearly everywhere. He knew nearly everyone. Those whom he did not know, he sought out, like the Russian Ambassador Arkady Sobolev. "We've got different views," he explained to a friend, "but I believe in personal relations."

Aly was working at top speed to make good in this new milieu. "I find the pace very fast," the indefatigable Aly admitted to an interviewer. "It is nonstop and exhausting."

On September 17, at his first regular session, Aly was elected vice-president of the General Assembly.

When the explosive Kashmir issue came up in October Aly spoke forcefully, warning that it was a problem that could threaten the peace of the world. He knew that he was risking personal reprisals from the Indian government which was pressing tax claims against the Aga's estate at the time. He was in eloquent form later that month when he called for the suspension of nuclear tests. Five days later, on October 23, 1958, the Pakistan government which had appointed him was swept out of office, amidst charges of corruption and mismanagement, by a new regime headed by General (later Field Marshal) Mohammed Ayub Khan. It suspended the constitution, revamped government policies and made a wholesale sweep of old officials. Aly survived the coup. When debate on Algeria came up in December, he could handle himself with confidence—calling for French negotiations with the Algerian rebels "without delay," yet injecting his own personal regard for France and General de Gaulle. Aga Shahi, his deputy, understood Aly's emotional predicament over Algeria: "He was in deeply personal conflict —but to his credit he was convinced Algeria should be independent and had the right to be independent. He carried out the policy of Pakistan despite the fact that he lived in France and had so many friends there."

Aly had become a full-fledged diplomat, in his first session at the UN. Ross recalls: "I was quite surprised to see how rapidly they came to respect him for what he was—a gay, charming guy with serious intentions. This was not merely something to do. He was determined to make a good try. I think very rapidly the diplomatic corps sensed that in him. They were willing to accept him at face value."

Lodge remembers: "It worked out just about the way I

thought it would. He decided to do it and he was very successful. He was always quick to understand something, to understand people, and he was full of good will and good intentions." Sir Pierson Dixon, the British representative, found that "he had the stuff of diplomacy at his very fingertips. You always felt better able to face the humdrum problems of the daily round after spending a few minutes with Aly Khan."

As Marcelle Hitschmann, the *Pakistan Times* correspondent who had reported her colleagues' first skeptical reaction to Aly's appointment, later observed: "You wouldn't have thought they were talking about the same man."

### 3

Aly was too busy—or too prescient—to go to Aswan in February, 1959, for the ceremony of placing his father's remains in the mausoleum, which the Begum had had built of hand-hewn pink granite on a hill above the Villa Noor El Salaam.

The night before the ceremony, Karim met with the Begum to discuss the details. They were in Egypt, Karim pointed out, where orthodox Sunni custom decreed that women play a retiring role. Sunnis, Karim went on, were contemptuous of Shiahs, and especially of Ismailis, whom they claimed were not true Moslems at all. To forestall any criticism, he had arranged that the Begum, along with the Ranee of Hunza and other wives of Ismaili dignitaries, would stay in a tent along the route where they could see the cortege pass and yet not be too obvious. The Begum was outraged to be relegated to the sidelines.

As the procession started up the hillside the following day, it was joined by the unmistakable figure of the Begum, clad in a white sari and clasping prayer beads in her hands. Trailing her were her maid and a house guest, the wife of a Swiss banker, also draped in white saris. Karim told a friend later that he had feared an unpleasant incident would erupt on the spot since there were Sunnis watching the ceremony. None did, but there was no longer any pretense of co-operation between the young Imam and his grandfather's widow, the woman who, by the terms of the Aga's will, was supposed to counsel him during the first seven years of his Imamate. Karim stood alone—an Imam without a regent. The Begum returned to Yakimour, her citadel, to live among her memories and her wealth, sallying forth to enjoy whatever prestige was left to her.

It must have seemed like sweet revenge to Aly.

## Chapter XXXIV

*"The misery and greatness of this world:*
*it offers no truths, but only objects for love.*
*Absurdity is king, but love saves us from it."*
—ALBERT CAMUS

Aly was growing restless again. A lifetime's pattern does not change overnight—or in a few months. He still needed movement, people, excitement. Back in France during the summer of 1958, he had as his house guests at l'Horizon the young American Senator from Massachusetts, John F. Kennedy, and his wife, Jacqueline, and Jackie's sister, Lee, and her husband, Michael Canfield. (A year later, Lee had divorced Canfield and married Prince Stanislas Radziwill.) Aly and the Senator knew each other from the days in London when Kennedy's father had been the American ambassador, and they had met several times since. They had many mutual friends, including Gene Tierney. But Aly barely saw his house guests.

He spent the summer flitting about. Baroness Michèle de Posson remembers inviting him to a dinner party at her summer home at Le Zoute on the Channel coast of Belgium. The day of the party, Aly telephoned her from Paris.

"I want to stop in Brussels on the way and see the World's Fair," he said. "Meet me there."

The Baroness had her party well organized. A chef would barbecue steaks at an outdoor fireplace and later, in Aly's honor, a woman would arrive with a gaily-decorated wheelbarrow bearing all flavors of ice cream. There was nothing more for her to do.

"All right," she agreed. "I will meet you at my house in town at three o'clock."

Aly arrived at five with Alec Head, his trainer, whom he'd picked up in Chantilly. It was raining but he still was determined to see the Fair.

"My dinner is for nine thirty," protested Michèle. "I don't think there is time."

"Of course there is," assured Aly. "Come quickly."

They set off in Aly's little BMW coupe, taking a short cut that led through a tunnel. Just as they emerged, the engine of the car began to sputter. They were out of gas. Head set off and soon returned with a can of gas. But then they discovered they had no funnel.

"It was impossible to get the gas into the tank," recalls the Baroness. "Aly finally managed to spill in a bit so we decided to push and see if the car would start. Aly was at the wheel, Alec and I pushed; just then a big lorry passed and splashed muddy water all over us. I had on a white chiffon dress, a real summer dress, and now it was all wet and streaked with black. Aly started laughing, and Alec and I began laughing madly. You should have seen our faces. We just stood there, helpless, and laughed. Well, we pushed the car, got some gasoline and went to the Fair. Aly wanted to see the American Pavilion to be able to say something when he went back to America, but he was not very interested."

After a quick look around, Aly had turned to Michèle.

"I want to see the amusing things, the gay things."

They first tried a girlie show but it was "worse than terrible," recalls Michèle. Then they went to the amusement park, going from one concession to another. One place had a gust of air blowing up from the floor to raise the women's skirts. "You're not going in there with a skirt like that," Aly told Michèle. "Alec and I will take a look."

In fifteen minutes they came out of the amusement section, grimacing.

"Really," remarked Aly. "If you want to be put off women forever, just stay there a bit longer. They were terrible."

Aly next headed his little party toward the "Joyous Belgium" area of the Fair where there were night clubs and cafés and reproductions of the old houses of Belgium. They ate sausages, pancakes, and ice cream. When they had finished, Michèle looked at her watch. It was nine o'clock.

"Aly," she said, "we really must start."

"We can't get to Le Zoute tonight," he replied. "Can't we sleep in Brussels and go there tomorrow? This is much more amusing."

"I can't," replied Michèle. "I must turn up at my own dinner party."

At ten o'clock she managed to convince Aly to start the ninety-five-mile drive to Le Zoute. Aly set off at eighty miles an hour, not fast by his standards but a strain on the small German car.

"Aly, please," Michèle protested.

"Put the wireless on," suggested Head. "He's tired."

Michèle thought that Head should drive but Aly refused.

"No," he said. "I'll drive, but please will you rub the back of my neck. I don't want to fall asleep."

With radio blasting and Michèle massaging his neck, Aly covered the ninety-five miles in an hour and a half. As they approached the house in Le Zoute, they saw the woman with her wheelbarrow of ice cream leaving.

"We've got to have another ice cream," shouted Aly, and zoomed off in pursuit of the woman.

Finally the bedraggled trio arrived at the house eating ice cream, Michèle's dress streaked with mud, her hair windblown. The other guests were in dinner jackets and evening gowns. They had just finished dinner. Aly looked at them, smiled at one and all, and said: "Come on, let's go to the Casino."

When Bettina later that year flew to New York on a surprise visit Aly was preoccupied with UN debates on Cyprus, Algeria, and Hungary and with the new friends he'd made. Elsa Maxwell was planning a party. "Aly telephoned," Elsa recalled, "and said, 'The old girl's in town. Would you please invite her?' I did. He never went near her all evening. He never once danced with her."

One of Aly's friendships at the time was with a beautiful young brunette, the socially prominent Pamela Turnure, who was on the staff of Senator Kennedy in Washington. They often dined out in New York with the Gordon Grands—unnoticed, perhaps—because Miss Turnure was not yet well known. After Kennedy was elected President of the United States, she became Mrs. Kennedy's press secretary and a member of the official White House "family."

2

At the London Ismailis' second anniversary banquet for their young Imam, Aly popped in unexpectedly. Karim was greeting his followers near the door. "How are you, my darling boy?" Aly enthused, leaning forward and kissing his son on both cheeks. "Didn't expect to see me here, did you?"

Karim flushed, shook his head. "No, I didn't. But now that you're here, you can help me on the door." There was the same old joviality—and the same old reserve to overcome.

Only with Yasmin was there instant, unquestioning, kindred affection. Aly flew to California to see her, staying with his friends, the Ray Starks, picking up Yasmin when her school let out and rushing off to Wil Wright's for ice cream. But even those idylls were troubled. Rita had asked a Nevada court to force Aly to pay twenty-five thousand dollars in attorney fees. Aly claimed diplomatic immunity. He and Rita finally settled out-of-court at a meeting arranged by her fifth husband, James Hill.

His duties at the United Nations began to frustrate him. On those issues he cared deeply about, he could be impassioned, charming, and eloquent, but there was so little he could *do*. The issues simply lay there, immobile, moved only by powers greater than he. The Algerian question came up again in December, 1959, just the month when Pakistan's representative was chairman of the Afro-Asian bloc, so that it became Aly's unhappy assignment to sponsor a resolution chiding the French, demanding that they negotiate with the Algerian rebels on self-determination. In the bloc's preliminary meetings, he fought for and won some modifications to salve France's feelings. He even absented himself personally when the vote was taken (the resolution was defeated), but a storm of criticism broke around his head in France. His friend Jean Fayard, of *Le Figaro*, wrote a column explaining Aly's predicament, but Aly insisted it should not be published: "I have no excuses to make. I acted according to my beliefs, and I feel I have served both my country and the France I love so much."

Diplomacy did not move at his tempo. He was used to moving fast, to moving people—now he felt impotent.

In his private life, too, it was coming down to that. Only a few of his friends suspected it, and even some of them refused to accept that it could possibly happen to Aly. The same stories still circulated around him: Aly with this girl, Aly with that girl, Aly with two girls, a girl pregnant by Aly. Women still flocked to him, but his response was not the same. And some of the women who were mentioned in gossip columns never went out with him at all; their dates were press-agents' inventions. He sought, with guilty feelings, younger women who would be satisfied with less—with the shadow and not the substance. At his last Grand Prix ball, he had looked scornful when Errol Flynn brought a sixteen-year-old girl. Now the scornful looks were for him.

Gianni Agnelli was at a dinner party one evening: "I remember they expected Aly for dinner and they didn't know the girl he would be bringing. They left two chairs vacant and he came in late with this little girl, a model, who was very ordinary, much less attractive, much less interesting than any of the girls I'd ever seen him with. Seeing him that evening, I felt sad. An aging playboy is a very sad sight. He starts drifting down to girls who are less pretty and then instead of impressing them the first night, it takes three nights or they decide after three nights they don't like him after all."

Another perceptive friend, Gordon Grand, said: "Aly never

learned to grow old gracefully. It was a tragedy that he couldn't accept things that happen to a man when you approach fifty, and adjust his private life to the different standards which increased responsibilities demanded. At forty-seven he tried to do the things that he did at twenty-five."

## 3

On the evening of December 31, 1959, Aly and Bettina were walking out of the Monte Carlo Casino after a gala New Year's Eve ballet performance. In the foyer, Bettina spotted a tall figure moving regally through the throng. She turned to Aly: "Have you seen the Begum?" "No," he said. Bettina pointed her out. Aly strolled over, the crowd cleaving before him, until he stood before his old adversary. He smiled, took her hand, raised it as he bowed, and kissed it. Then, stretching on tiptoes, he kissed her on both cheeks.

The day after Albert Camus, the French author and Nobel laureate, was killed in a car crash, Count Charles de Breteuil, Aly's friend from Foreign Legion days, turned to Aly at lunch and said: "Why do you drive so fast? You've had several accidents. One day you too will get killed." Aly's face became uncommonly grave. "Well, I don't know. Life is very short. If I kill myself, it's not very important. All the things I had in life, I have had. Now I'm getting older and I can only get less out of life." (Count Charles died in 1962.)

Soon afterward, Aly flew to Pakistan for official consultations on the Kashmir issue. But President Ayub Khan and other government officials were too busy to see him right away. While waiting, he went to Lahore to see the Horse and Cattle Show; in an interview there he said he no longer rode in races: "I am too old and too fat now."

In Lahore, Aly got the usual tumultuous welcome from the Ismailis of the region—including an odd dissident group with whom he had been in touch for several years. This group, made up of a handful of families from upcountry towns, believed that Aly was the true Imam. They had never accepted Karim. They had broken with the main body of Ismailis and started their own *jamat-khana.* A few of them had seen Aly on his previous visits to Pakistan in 1958 and 1959. The fact that he had received them and had given an autographed photograph of himself to their leader, Dr. Aziz Ali, a homeopathic doctor in Chiniot, had convinced them that he had tacitly consented to be their Imam.

As soon as Aly arrived, Dr. Aziz and his group took up positions outside his bungalow. They were to spend most of the next three days there, patiently, hopefully waiting, enduring the taunts of "persons having faith in Karim's Imamate," encouraged by every sight of Aly. One morning they were rewarded by a brief audience as he left the house. Dr. Aziz recalls it ecstatically: "He patted with love and affection all of us one by one and took us in his arms, showering his prayers and blessings." Another evening, arriving to take up their vigil, they found that about a hundred other Ismailis had gathered outside the bungalow too. As Aly passed by to get into a waiting automobile, the large crowd sent up a shout of "Prince Aly Zindabad" (Long live Prince Aly); Dr. Aziz's group promptly countered with their own cheer: "Shah Aly Imam-e-Zaman Zindabad" (Long live the Imam, Shah Aly). Dr. Aziz noted significantly that Aly did not ask them to stop cheering him as Imam: "Rather he was pleased to hear all these slogans." Dr. Aziz and his friends finally followed Aly back to Karachi to get a private audience with him. There they again spent long hours waiting under the disapproving stares of Ismaili officials who tried to shoo them away. Finally, at 3 A.M. one morning, after a nine hour wait, they got to see Aly alone, and solemnly presented a formal report on their tiny *jamat-khana.* Aly read it carefully, advised them to start a trust fund with the sums they had collected, suggested the name of "Noor Allah" for the newborn son of one of their number and promised to visit their *jamat-khana* on his next trip to Pakistan.

### 4

After Pakistan, there was New York again and the United Nations. Friends had never seen him so distracted. One evening he took Sybilla Szczeniowska—now Sorondo—to a movie. "He couldn't sit still," she recalled later. "He kept changing his position, getting up, sitting down again. He had always wanted to go from one place to another, to change atmosphere, to change the people around him. But never like this."

When he left New York it was to make a speech before l'Académie Diplomatique Internationale in Paris. It was a successful speech, on Pakistan's role as a bridge between the West and East, delivered before a capacity audience that contained as many fashionable women as it did diplomats. Aly was due to leave for New York in a few days but he didn't seem to want to go. A young friend, Paolo Sanjust, a distant relative of the Rothschilds and Françoise Sagan's closest friend, invited him for cocktails. "He stayed only five minutes, said he didn't feel well. I asked him what it was, and he said an old injury was bothering him." He said he was seeing his doctor.

He flew over to London to see one of his oldest and dearest men friends. They had breakfast at the Ritz. Aly knew his friend recently had had a prostatectomy.

"I'll have to have the same operation that you did," he confided. "My doctor says this autumn."

The friend was not surprised; he had recognized one of the symptoms in the way Aly so often rubbed his abdomen.

They talked about the operation, what it did to a man's sexual activity.

"I only know my own case," said the friend. He made a sweeping downward motion with his hand.

## Chapter XXXV

> *"Aly was always late so we weren't surprised when he had not arrived for dinner by ten o'clock. We were already seated at the table; the telephone rang. My maid said it was Bettina and that she sounded very upset."*
>
> —LORRAINE BONNET

It was early evening, Thursday, May 12, 1960.

Aly stepped out of the tiny elevator and strode into the top-floor study of his Paris house. He was freshly showered and shaved and was wearing a maroon dinner jacket, matching bow tie, a soft white pleated shirt and black trousers. His secretary, Felix Bigio, waited for him beside the big mahogany desk which dominated the light and airy room looking out on the Bois de Boulogne.

"Good evening, Milord," said Bigio.

"Bigio," Aly acknowledged, and smiled.

He spotted a newspaper, *France Soir*, on the desk, picked it up and sank into a deep armchair. First he read the daily horoscope. He was a Gemini:

Business: Rather unproductive; your time will be spent re-
dressing your past errors.
Romance: Today you will undoubtedly prefer dreams to
reality.
Health: Bad.

Aly shrugged and glanced through the gossip column at
the bottom of the front page—no, his name was not mentioned.
Then he opened the paper to its sports pages, folded it lengthwise
twice, and sat back to read the racing news.

Bigio impatiently shuffled papers on the desk. He was an
Egyptian refugee of French nationality who had been an account-
ant and the secretary of a race track in Cairo before fleeing in the
wake of the Suez crisis. He was dignified, prompt, and methodical
and he lived on a different time scale from that of his employer.

Aly sat up, deposited the newspaper on the sofa, and sat
down at his desk. Bigio reached for a blue folder bulging with
papers. "One moment," said Aly. Bigio tucked the folder under
his arm and walked to the window, looking out on the Bois and
at the buildings in the children's amusement park, now empty and
quiet. The Prince dialed the phone. It was a game the two men
often played, a silent duel between work and pleasure, each
testing the other.

For a few moments, nothing but the clickings, buzzings,
yowlings of the French telephone system. Then a woman's voice
murmured in the receiver and Aly clamped it close to his ear.
His face creased into a broad smile, his eyebrows rose, his voice
fell.

Bigio stood by the window, lost in thoughts of his own.
He was privy to all his employer's secrets, but he lived apart
from them in mental suburbs of his own efficient design.

Aly was murmuring into the phone, one hand pressing the
receiver close to his ear, the other slowly massaging his abdomen.
He finished the call in a burst of laughter and hung up. As Bigio
started back toward the desk, Aly smiled mischievously. "Just
one moment more, Bigio." He made another call. On days like
this, Bigio despaired, silently, of getting anything done.

Aly went through the afternoon mail by himself; it was a

ritual he insisted upon. He looked at each letter's return address, shuffling out the obvious bills and adding them to a pile on the desk that, to Bigio's conscientious eye, looked mountainous already. A few letters were for Bettina; Aly put them aside. She was downstairs dressing for their dinner engagement.

He slit open the letters he had chosen to read, dropped the envelopes on the floor at his feet—Bigio would pick them up later for his stamp collection—and glanced at their contents. He outlined replies to some of them, switching back and forth from French to English, depending upon the language in which the reply would be written. Bigio stood at the side of the desk, jotting notes. When Aly paused, Bigio nudged forward the blue folder; but Aly ignored it and placed another call. Unfinished business marched through Bigio's mind: The Prince had just been named Pakistan's ambassador to Argentina. Would he go directly to New York Sunday? Or would he stop first in Buenos Aires to present his credentials? There were air tickets to confirm, invitations to send, papers to prepare, decisions to be made. But when?

Aly had spent the afternoon at Longchamps. As usual, he had darted in and out of the owners' enclosure, gossiping with Alec Head and with his jockeys, whispering tips to anyone he knew who approached him. To one man he had said: "Don't bet on my horses. It's not one of my lucky days." To Paul Lacroix, a theatrical producer, he had explained: "The ground is too dry."

Bettina had spent the day at home. She didn't like racing and went to the track only when there was nothing better to do; or when Aly insisted; or when there were particular friends there she wanted to see; or when she wanted to be seen—perhaps to scotch another rumor that she and Aly had broken up.

After the race, Aly had gone to the Travellers Club to play bridge. When he got back to the house on Boulevard Maurice-Barrès, Bettina reminded him of their dinner date that night with Gerard and Lorraine Bonnet. A number of good friends would be there: Baron and Baroness Guy de Rothschild, Baron Elie de Rothschild; Porfirio Rubirosa and his young wife; the Greek shipowner, Stavros Niarchos, and his wife. Aly quickly changed to evening clothes and came into his office to join Bigio, who had been stalking him all day.

After reading his mail, he placed a call to Jack Ross in New York, reaching him at his home on Long Island. It was a long call, almost half an hour. They discussed the trip to Argentina. As usual, Aly would be on a tight schedule. He decided to leave Paris the next night, spend Sunday in New York and then fly on to Buenos Aires; it was up to Ross to co-ordinate the plans. Aly wanted a list of his friends in Buenos Aires; he discussed the gift he would bring the President of Argentina from Pakistan President Ayub Khan, and the protocol of presenting his credentials—he was meticulous about such details.

"See you Sunday," he concluded.

Then he placed another call, to Cyril Hall, the manager of his racing stables in Ireland. Aly listened intently while Hall gave him a report on several horses. The big races were coming up soon: the Derby and the Oaks in England, the Grand Prix in Paris. As Hall talked, Aly fingered the invitation list for his annual Grand Prix dinner, only a month away. Before hanging up, Aly assured Hall:

"I'll see you soon."

Bettina came into the study to remind Aly that it was growing late and they still had a long drive ahead to the Bonnets' house, La Loge-Repose, in Ville-d'Avray, outside Paris. She wore a new Balenciaga wool suit. Her red hair was done in a soft pageboy; her face was composed and cool and yet, if one examined it in another light, rather sad.

Aly nodded and asked Bigio to call for the car.

"And then call Baroness de Posson at Champ de Blé," Aly instructed Bigio. Michèle was recuperating from a serious operation in Switzerland. Aly had invited her to use his new house there after leaving the hospital. But she was not at Champ de Blé, the operator reported after talking to the concierge—she was at the Hotel Beau Rivage in Geneva.

"Try there," Aly said. He and Bettina sat in silence while Bigio dickered with the operator. "The Baroness," Bigio said finally, handing the phone to Aly.

"Why aren't you at the Champ de Blé?" he demanded crossly. "You said you were going."

"Aly, I could not arrive at six o'clock or half past five. The concierge did not know we were coming; there was no time to prepare the food. You know, my mother is with me."

"It's stupid of you to stay in the hotel when I have a lovely house. The concierge would be glad to take care of everything. No problem. I think it is much wiser to go straight to the Champ de Blé right now. It's much too tiring for you at the hotel."

"I am tired now. Anyway we are settled here."

He suddenly relented. "How are you now?"

"Very well."

"Did you find a name for our baby?" He was grinning.

"How about *Sabre au Clair*?"

"What?" The connection was poor, or her voice was weak. "What was that?"

"*Sabre au Clair*, you know, in war, when soldiers on horseback are going to fight."

"Cavalry," he said.

"Cavalry," she acknowledged. "The commander shouts, '*Sabre au Clair*.' The perfect name for a horse."

Aly liked it. "*Sabre au Clair*," he said in a voice so exuberant that Bettina looked up from the newspaper and smiled at him. He smiled back. "Bettina wants to talk to you," he said, and handed over the telephone receiver.

Bettina asked Michèle how she was feeling and promised to come to Geneva to see her. Then Aly took the phone again.

"You must take care of yourself," he said. "I am going to Argentina, but when I come back, I want to see you. Come to Paris if you are well enough; stay with us at Neuilly."

Michèle recalls that it was five minutes past nine when she hung up. Bigio, too, noticed the time, and knew that it was now or never to get a fraction of the day's work done. He picked up his pen and pad. While Aly and Bettina went down in the tiny elevator, Bigio raced down the narrow winding staircase to the first floor and then down the main staircase to the ground-floor entrance hall. He hurriedly asked Aly about several letters that needed replies, and got rapid-fire answers. The butler held open the door and one of the Spanish maids helped Bettina on with a new green silk coat.

"Let's take the Lancia," Aly said and motioned Lucien,

the chauffeur, to get into the back of the low-slung coupe parked on the Boulevard Maurice-Barrès. Aly had bought it just four days before.

Aly took the wheel, Bettina beside him. Lucien sat in the middle of the rear seat so that he could get a clear view of the road and drive, mentally, with his employer. Aly loved to drive, but tonight he seemed more interested in a quiet intense conversation with Bettina.

They turned into the Bois, past the riding stables and then, close to the Longchamps race course, they crossed the Seine on the Pont de Suresnes. The Coty cosmetic plant was on their left. Now they started up the Boulevard Henri Sellier which curved through Suresnes in a series of sweeping turns, past new apartment houses beyond which they could glimpse the lights of Paris. Traffic was heavy for that time of night in the suburbs. They passed under a railroad bridge and began the sweeping turn that would take them into the Carrefour du Val d'Or, named after a famous race horse.

Aly knew the corner well. It was near the St. Cloud race course. Ahead were the lights of an Azur gas station. On the right was a bar, La Belle Etoile. The traffic lights were green.

As the Lancia came up into the Carrefour, a tiny Renault, containing two young men and a girl, was moving along slowly in front of them, blocking their way. Lucien wondered whether the light was going to change. Aly apparently was thinking of the same thing. He pulled to the left to pass the Renault. For an instant the road was clear and the Lancia leaped ahead. But a yellow car, a Simca Aronde, was coming toward them, in the same lane. If Aly saw it, he didn't react. He went on talking to Bettina. Lucien gasped and pressed his palms against the back of the front seat. The Simca was almost upon them. Bettina threw up her hands and braced herself against the dashboard. The brakes of the onrushing Simca squealed. But the Lancia went rushing forward to its own destruction. The two cars collided head-on. Bettina, Lucien, and the driver of the other car were only slightly injured.

Only Aly was killed.

# EPILOGUE

The Koran says that in Paradise a man will find:

"Two gardens of a dark green; in each two fountains of welling water; in each, fruit: dates and pomegranates; in them women, smooth, lovely, black-eyed damsels kept in pavilions, whom no man has yet enjoyed, nor even a spirit; the believers shall lie with them on green rugs and lovely soft carpets."

And Paradise is eternal.

*ABOUT THE AUTHOR*

This is Leonard Slater's first book, after twenty years in journalism. After graduating from the University of Michigan, he worked as writer, correspondent, and editor for NBC News, *Time, Newsweek* and *McCall's* in and about Washington, New York, Los Angeles, Paris, Prague, Tokyo, Hong Kong, and Frenchman's Flat, Nevada. He wrote this book while living in a drafty villa on the French Riviera between Nice and Monte Carlo, two of the cities Aly Khan called home. Mr. Slater considers California his home, probably because his wife Betty, a writer and editor too, and his two daughters, Amy, ten, and Lucy, eight, were born there. Eventually he plans to settle down, but meanwhile he is writing a novel on the Balearic island of Menorca, in the Mediterranean.